Part of the Trauels of Capt IOHN SMITH a mongst TVRKES,
TARTARS, and others, extracted out of the HISTORY by IOHN PAYN

How hee releeued OLVMPAGH by a stratagem of Lights Chap. 6.

His three single Combats Chap. 7.
His Encounter with TVRBASHAW Chap. 7.

The Coast of Tunis BARBARIE

Bugia

Algier

S.t Maries Ile

The Coast of SAVOY

NICE

Tullowne

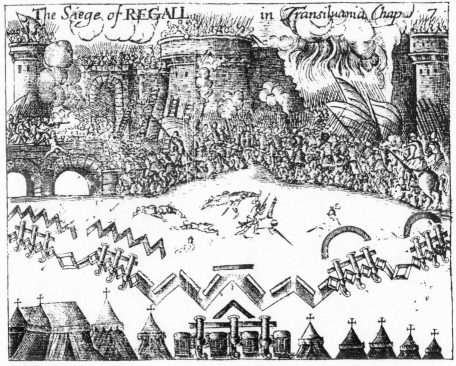

THE VIRGINIA PLUTARCH

PLATE I. *From the painting after the engraving by De Passe in Smith's* Generall Historie of Virginia. *Photo Cook.*
CAPTAIN JOHN SMITH

THE
VIRGINIA
PLUTARCH

BY PHILIP ALEXANDER BRUCE, LL.B., LL.D.

*Former Corresponding Secretary of the Virginia Historical
Society; Corresponding Member of the Massachusetts
Historical Society; Author of History of the University
of Virginia; Economic, Institutional and Social His-
tories of Virginia in the Seventeenth Century, etc.*

IN TWO VOLUMES

VOLUME I

THE COLONIAL AND REVOLUTIONARY ERAS

NEW YORK / RUSSELL & RUSSELL

PUBLISHED IN 1929 BY
THE UNIVERSITY OF NORTH CAROLINA PRESS
REISSUED, 1971, BY RUSSELL & RUSSELL
A DIVISION OF ATHENEUM PUBLISHERS, INC.
BY ARRANGEMENT WITH
THE UNIVERSITY OF NORTH CAROLINA PRESS
L. C. CATALOG CARD NO: 75-139474
PRINTED IN THE UNITED STATES OF AMERICA

TO

THE MEMORY OF MY MOTHER

A SOUTHERN MATRON OF THE OLD PLANTATION RÉGIME

BEAUTIFUL IN PERSON, CLEAR IN INTELLECT, VIGOROUS IN

CHARACTER AND IMMOVABLE IN PRINCIPLE

THIS BOOK

IS GRATEFULLY AND REVERENTLY

DEDICATED

PREFACE

THE MAIN purpose which I had in view in the composition of the present work was to produce, not a series of detached character studies, but rather a continuous narrative of deeds running from the beginning of the Colonial age to our own times. I have considered first, not so much what these eminent Virginians were in their personal qualities, as what they, one after another, achieved in the course of their respective careers. In short, what did they contribute in *action* to the greatness of America? Their individualities are sufficiently disclosed in the general current of their biographies.

It has been impossible, without too great a degree of voluminousness, to bring in all the figures that had at least a fair right to admission to this Plutarchian circle. In several instances the scales had to be used with minute discrimination before preference could be shown. For example, should Robert Carter or William Byrd be chosen to represent the plantation magnate of the eighteenth century? Byrd was selected because he was the more accomplished and versatile man of the two. Light Horse Harry Lee gave way to General Daniel Morgan because Morgan was victor in more important battles. John Tyler was inferior to Henry Clay in ability, but throughout his career he was a typical public servant of the Virginia of those times, while Clay remained Harry of the West to the end. Scott was preferred to Zachary Taylor because it was his campaign, and not Taylor's, which closed the Mexican War and added an empire to the domain of the United States. Maury was preferred to McCormick because the scientist was a more lasting benefactor to mankind as a whole than the inventor. Stuart was preferred to Joseph E. Johnston because he was the more brilliant and chivalrous soldier of the two. There were other parallel careers which could be successfully judged only by like comparative tests in seeking the points of superiority.

PREFACE

It was during the Reconstruction period alone that Virginia failed to produce even one character entitled to be considered Plutarchian in proportions. During that period she was simply a conquered province, with her people absorbed in a struggle for their local existence. During the other periods of her history she had ample continental room for the development of figures of the first magnitude. The procession from century to century is a splendid one as it passes before our mind's eye—Smith, Pocahontas, Dale, Yeardley, Berkeley, Bacon, Nicholson, Spotswood, Byrd, Henry, Jefferson, Washington, Mason, Richard Henry Lee, George Rogers Clark, Morgan, Sevier, Meriwether Lewis, Madison, Marshall, Monroe, Randolph, Houston, Tyler, Scott, Poe, Maury, Robert E. Lee, Jackson, Stuart, Woodrow Wilson, and Walter Reed. Nor should Mary Ball, Martha Washington, and Dolly Madison be forgotten, although their distinction was primarily derived from their connection with a celebrated son or husband.

The names which make up our roll belong not alone to Virginia. They belong even more to America. Indeed, they are all continental possessions and in some instances, world possessions. The permanence of their fame is demonstrated by the fact that the passage of time has served to brighten and not to dim its lustre.

PHILIP ALEXANDER BRUCE

University, Virginia
July 1, 1929

TABLE OF CONTENTS

VOLUME I

LIST OF ILLUSTRATIONS

VOLUME I

LIST OF ILLUSTRATIONS

THE COLONIAL

AND

REVOLUTIONARY ERAS

Chapter I

THE EMPEROR POWHATAN

Certain French philosophers of the eighteenth century confidently asserted that it was only man in a state of nature who was really happy. Whatever truth there was in this theory was reflected in the life of Powhatan, the grim forest despot of Virginia. The physical character of his realm was the first constituent of his good fortune. The poet Drayton summarized its beauty and charm when he pictured it so sententiously as "Earth's only Paradise." "Heaven and earth," said Smith, who had traversed the whole country from the shores of the Lynnhaven to the banks of the Potomac, "never agreed better to frame a place for man's habitation." "Virginia, the fortunate, the incomparable, the garden of the world!" exclaimed another contemporary explorer with unrestrained enthusiasm. "I have travelled over eighteen several kingdoms," said a third, "and yet all of them, in my mind, came far short of Virginia."

These delightful impressions of the land in its aboriginal aspects were, on the whole, not too much embroidered. How suggestive of primeval purity and beauty is the fact, recorded at the time, that as the voyagers drew near the Capes, and even before they sighted the looming pines on the horizon, their sense of smell was titillated by elusive wafts of perfume from the endless leagues of leaves and flowers that grew behind the sandy bulwark of the shore.

It was Powhatan's habit to visit in turn the wigwam villages of his vassal werowances; and in doing so he had to thread vast reaches of woods full of oak, walnut, hickory, poplar, cedar, and mulberry, and yet without undergrowth, if we omit the blossoming or fruit-laden masses of grape-vines which sprang up in the rich mold and encircled the boles of the trees. Every now and then he would cross a savanna carpeted with lush grass and matted weeds, or enter an abandoned cornfield speckled red with strawberries and shaded here and there with little groups of sassafras, sumac, or persimmon trees. As he tramped along, he would pass under the white clusters of the dogwood or the purple buds of the judas tree; and if he skirted the borders of a swamp, he would catch the pungent odor of the blooms of the bog magnolia. On either side of the path flowers would be growing in countless varieties and in gaudy profusion.

Each brook which he leaped over would so teem and sparkle with small fish that he and his attendants could with perfect ease kill them by striking them with sticks; and if his journey by chance brought him to the banks of a river, there sheepshead, trout, and other large varieties could be scooped up from the weirs that had been erected at every point of advantage in the stream; and with still fewer impediments, wherever the water was salt, oysters could be scraped from the bottom by the bushel. Wild turkeys, fat and of incredible weight, would be frequently flushed. Sometimes, too, the sky over his head would be darkened during several hours of the day by the careering flight of passenger pigeons in the course of their annual migrations from region to region.

As he gazed in winter at the waters of the Chesapeake or of the open sea, flocks of swimming ducks, geese, and swans were to be seen, in many places strung out in a line several miles long; and as he wandered about the forests around Werowocomoco and Orapaks, he had constantly in sight quail, bluebird, dove, robin, mockingbird, redbird, and the splendid blue jay. Whenever he took part in the hunting expeditions of his people, his quarry were deer, elk, bison, beaver, raccoon, panther, hare, fox, squirrel, and opossum. The swarthy population of his kingdom had always been so widely dispersed and had possessed weapons of destruction so imperfect, that in spite of the passage of centuries they had been unable to check the incalculable increase in the multitudes of birds and animals haunting those aboriginal woods and waters.

Powhatan was fortunate, too, in the overlordship of subjects who were skillful in cultivating the fertile soil which lay close to the banks of every stream. Wherever he rambled in spring and summer he came upon fields planted thickly in tobacco, maize, peas, beans, and pumpkins. At Kecoughtan, the modern Hampton, the area in tillage spread over three thousand acres; and the extent of cultivation elsewhere was almost equally impressive.

When the old woodland monarch squatted at his meals, he had always before him bread, made of maize or the roots of the tuckahoe plant; and he had also in reach of his hand a palatable liquor brewed from the juice of hickory nut kernels. His other victuals, like those of his people, changed with the season. In March and April he lived generously on the catch of the weirs and wicker-traps; and he also received, by the hourly excursions of his huntsmen, as many squirrels, hares, and wild turkeys, as he, his wives, and his immediate bodyguard could devour. In May, besides the fish, there was provided for his houshold a daily quantity of venison, oysters, tortoise, and strawberries. Until the end of summer he depended for sustenance mainly on fish, the tuckahoe root, the numerous varieties of nourishing berries, and the milky grain of the unripe maize. Between the first of September and the first of March he was limitlessly supplied with the flesh of animals trapped, snared, or shot with bow and arrow in the woods; with wild fowl captured in the streams or in the marshes; and with the tributes of maize delivered from the stores of the subordinate chiefs. The meal of this grain was cooked by itself in the form of cakes and hominy or mingled indiscriminately in a pot with peas, beans, and pumpkins.

But this bountifulness of food was not confined to the rude table of the monarch. The same plenty was enjoyed by all his people. During every season of the year they, too, subsisted so liberally and lavishly as to arouse the fierce envy of the starved English adventurers at Jamestown. Nuts and

3

berries in baskets; ducks, geese, turkeys, and venison on platters; fish on fire sticks; oysters on dry leaves; vegetables in pots—such were the principal viands which they spread out before themselves or before their guests. Smith, describing a Christmas that he had passed with the Indians at Kecoughtan, said that he was as unstintedly entertained by them as he would have been had he been seated at the table of the most hospitable host residing under the most generous and lavish roof in England.

The climate was so temperate, except in midwinter, that Powhatan and his people did not need the protection of a complete covering for their bodies. A shoe for the foot, known as the moccasin, a dressed deer hide for the shoulders, a bright feather for the hair, a leather pad or apron for the loins, with an immoderate amount of oil and vegetable paint for the skin, were the common garments to be seen. Powhatan himself possessed besides these a mantle composed of the gray fur of raccoons and squirrels. His wives were more elaborately and tastefully clothed. Their vestments next to their bodies were not only fringed and shagged, but also embroidered with figures of birds, fruits, and flowers; and in addition they wore beads and copper trinkets in profusion. Their mantles were made of the feathers of bluebirds, redbirds, herons, swans, and other birds of equally beautiful and equally conspicuous plumage.

In every large village of his kingdom Powhatan had ordered to be built for the use of himself and his wives a long low-pitched house constructed of saplings and overspread with mats. His principal residence at first was situated at Werowocomoco on the banks of the modern York River. This primitive palace was thirty feet in length and full of turnings and windings before the main apartment was reached. Here he lived until the nearness of the spot to Jamestown—which encouraged frequent visits from the Englishmen settled there—caused him to fear that his personal safety was in serious jeopardy, since the intervening ground could be traversed by the strangers within six or seven hours and without any warning of their approach.

4

Indeed, his distrust of these strangers was never really allayed, in spite of the alliance which followed the marriage of Pocahontas to John Rolfe. This feeling led him in 1609 to retire to a village which had been built in the dark woods lying between the two principal tributaries of the modern York. This place was known as Orapaks. In the beginning his dwelling house there had been designed for the single purpose of storing his various treasures. Here was kept a large quantity of bows and arrows, furs, copper, beads, and pearls—a collection of precious articles reserved for the decoration of his body after his death and for the adornment of his arboreal mausoleum during his life. This structure is said to have been sixty feet in length. At each corner of it had been erected an image of terrifying aspect—a dragon, or bear, or panther, or gigantic man. What he had heard of the commodiousness of the houses at Jamestown must have aroused in him a spirit of emulation, for at his request several Dutch carpenters were sent to him before he abandoned Werowocomoco, and there they put together a frame building for his occupation. The brick chimney of this building remained in its original shape until a date within the recollection of living men. It was remarkable for its size. The object of this magnitude was probably to allow space enough before the hearth to accommodate the presence of a large number of his wives and attendants. It is said that after the completion of the structure he found amusement in passing from room to room toying with the locks and keys.

Wherever Powhatan happened at any time to be dwelling, he was at night fully defended by sentinels stationed at the four corners of his house. At fixed intervals an officer of his corps on guard would call to them in a loud voice, and each was required to respond promptly to show that he was vigilantly performing the duty assigned to him. At all hours some forty or fifty of Powhatan's tallest and most robust warriors were expected to be near enough to his person to be summoned on the instant, should their services ever be needed. And this number could be increased to two or even three hundred if a large force were desired.

THE EMPEROR POWHATAN

On occasions of ceremony Powhatan made a throne of his bed, with one handsome young wife squatting at the head and another at the foot. A row of warriors crouched on either side of the open way that led up to the royal seat; and behind them sat his numerous concubines of various ages.

So far as the observation of the first English adventurers went, Powhatan's supremacy was not disputed within the well-defined limits of his woodland kingdom. His only cause for apprehension came from without. At any hour his frontiers towards the north and west were likely to be invaded by the Monacans and Mannahocks; but apparently these hostile tribesmen never pushed their incursions so far down as the lower reaches of the great rivers. No enemy of his own race, within the historical period, had been successful in driving him away from either Werowocomoco or Orapaks.

There was a belief among the Indians, when the Englishmen arrived, that Powhatan himself was not a native of Virginia, but a native of a region washed by the waters of the Gulf of Mexico; but whether this country was a part of the main coast or a large island was not known. Equally in the dark was the manner in which he had risen to power in the north. Had he come as a conqueror, with fierce warriors behind him? Or had he, as a single individual, gradually acquired dominance by the exercise of an extraordinary degree of bravery, resolution, and subtlety? However won, the kingdom over which he ruled was knit together in one strong central administration for the whole country, with a subordinate administration for each of its several parts. Apparently, these lesser districts were modeled on the kingdom at large in their form of government. As that kingdom, as a whole, had a supreme chief in Powhatan, so each district had a local chief in its own werowance. The only exception was the Chickahominies. They were under the control, not of a divisional chief, but of their priests and elders, who apparently were not subject to Powhatan to the same degree as the werowances, if at all.

The greater number of the separate Indian districts lay in the fertile valley of the James. On the north side of that

6

stream were situated Kecoughtan, Paspaheigh, Chickahominy, Wyanoke, Arrahattock, and Powhatan; and on the
south side, Appomattox, Warrosquoyacke, Nansemond, and
Chespiack. The principal districts on the modern York were
Cheskiack, Werowocomoco, and Pamunkey. There were
several in addition between the Rappahannock and the
Pyanketank, and one, known as Accomac, was situated on
the other side of the Bay. The size of the population of these
combined divisions was a figure for conjecture only. The
inhabitants were widely scattered. Not more than six or
seven hundred were seen by the English at any one time or
place.

The orders of Powhatan passed as laws with his subjects,
just as if they had been adopted and promulgated by a
general assembly representing every part of his kingdom.
There were doubtless few occasions on which he exerted his
authority over all his people simultaneously; but if he did
do so, his commands were promptly and strictly obeyed.

There are many indications that he was a man of strong
intellect and vigorous character. One of the conspicuous reflections of this fact was his stern aspect. In person he was
tall and well-proportioned, robust in health, and agile in
movement. It was thought that when Jamestown was founded
by the English he was about sixty years old; but his appearance, owing to his active outdoor life, probably created
an impression of his being less advanced in age than he
really was. He said to Smith in 1609 that he had seen the
death of all his people thrice and that the only individual
of those three generations who survived was himself. This
statement was probably colored by exaggeration.

The bearing of Powhatan was in harmony with the kingly
power which he wielded. In 1608, when visited by Newport
and Smith, he carried himself, according to the testimony
of these critical witnesses, "so proudly yet so discreetly, in
his savage manner, as made us all admire his natural gifts,
considering his education." His deportment, while sitting
on his throne-bed, was "so majesticall," as we learn from
Smith, who saw him for the first time in that situation, that

7

it was not surpassed in impressiveness "by the deportment of pagan or Christian." "He had such a grave majesticall countenance," Smith again records, "as drove me into admiration to see such state in a naked savage." And yet it was reported of him that he was both able and willing to make his own robes, shoes, bows, and arrows with his own hands, and that as a hunter he was as skillful and as enduring as the most hardy and experienced of his subjects.

His character was a bundle of contradictions. Although cruel, he was yet capable of leniency and magnanimity. This trait was manifested in several recorded instances, especially in the instance of Smith's release after Pocahontas' plea for mercy. Although stern in his bearing towards his people, he was affectionate in his relations with his two youthful daughters. He told Hamor that he loved the youngest of these "as his life." "If I cannot often behold her," he said, "I cannot possibly live." He complained with bitterness that Dale was seeking to withdraw this daughter from his sight in order to marry her himself, as Rolfe had married Pocahontas. "It was not a brotherly part," he exclaimed, with an air full of reproachful feeling.

He recognized and, on the surface at least, observed the laws of hospitality. When Smith visited him at Werowocomoco, as the herald of Newport, Powhatan with great courtesy of manner seated him at his side in the place of honor. Perceiving on another occasion that Hamor, who had just arrived from Jamestown, was acutely fatigued, he urged the visitor to retire to a couch, and the next morning the monarch called on his guest and saw that he was provided with a bounteous breakfast.

Whenever Powhatan received something of value from the English, he would promptly bestow in return valuable articles peculiar to his own country. For swords, beads, copper, and the like, he would give wild turkeys, brought in by his huntsmen, or well-cooked meals of other tempting foods, or skins of deer neatly dressed. Very frequently he would load Smith's followers down with such quantities of bread that they were unable to carry it all away. The

8

English captains, especially Newport and Dale, were very
liberal and even profuse in their presents to him. Dale once
heaped on him at a single offering a very dazzling mass of
copper, white beads, blue beads, knives, and fishhooks.
Powhatan was always eager to obtain guns and once sent
a squad of his warriors to Jamestown to procure them.
Smith pointed out several demiculverins to be taken away
by them, but they shook their heads in dismay; and when
the cannon were fired off, they fled in consternation to the
woods near by.

In spite of Powhatan's acts of hospitality and professions
of good will, Smith for one was never thrown off his guard.
The astute old foe asked him on several occasions, with a
plausible manner, to order his men to put up their weapons
on their arrival at Werowocomoco. Smith always refused to
comply. This caution had its origin, not only in his in-
stinctive sense of prudence, but also in a warning which had
once been given him by the werowance of Warrosquoyacke.
"Don't trust him," said this chief to Smith, who was about
to visit Werowocomoco. "He will receive you kindly, but
will use the first opportunity to cut your throat." This
truculence was not simply the impulse of a savage. Powhatan
very justly suspected that the ultimate purpose of the
English was to expel his subjects from their immemorial
homes. Where were they to go? Were the Monacans and the
Mannahocks not already lurking along the frontier ready
to tomahawk them? "You have come here," said Powhatan
bluntly to Smith in 1609, "not to trade, but to invade my
people, and possess my country." How was this to be prevented by him and his warriors? By destroying the Englishmen; and in the teeth of those terrible English firearms,
this could be accomplished only by slyness and treachery.
"Your guns are not needed here," he said insinuatingly to
Smith in the course of the same conversation. "We are now
all Powhatans."

He showed great shrewdness in a trade. On one occasion in
1608 he asked Newport to place on the ground all the
articles which he had brought to barter. "What I like, I

9

will take," he coolly said. Newport readily consented because
he hoped that the value of the several objects would be enhanced in the old king's eyes by such a profuse display of
them. But the effect was not what he had anticipated. Smith
always took the opposite tack. He refused to exhibit his
store for exchange openly in a mass, but picking from it
under cover some trifling article, he would flash it before
Powhatan's fixed gaze and pretend to consider it extraordinarily precious. On one occasion he succeeded in getting for
a pound of blue beads two or three hundred bushels of corn,
while Newport obtained only four bushels for the same
amount of similar ornaments. During one visit Smith received in return for one kettle ten quarters of maize.

But Powhatan did not rely on open trade alone to acquire
the various articles which he desired of the Englishmen. He
used the Dutchmen, sent to build his framed house, to
purloin, directly or indirectly, swords, pike-heads, and shot
and powder from the stores at Jamestown.

The distrustful old monarch resisted every seduction to
put himself in the power of the colonists. Newport dispatched
Smith to Werowocomoco to urge him to visit Jamestown
to be crowned; but he declined the invitation, and his reply
was not without dignity: "If your king," he said, "has sent
me presents, I also am a king, and this is my land. Your
father [Newport] must come to me, not I to him, nor yet to
your fort."

It was with emotions of fear and suspicion that he submitted to the ceremony of a formal coronation, even at
Werowocomoco. "There was fowle trouble," says Todkill, a
friend of Smith, who was present, "to make him kneel to
receive his crown. He neither knowing the majesty nor meaning of a crown, nor bending of the knee, endured so many
persuasions, examples, and instructions as tired them all. At
last, by leaning harde on his shoulders, he a little stooped,
and Newport put the crown on his head, when, by the warning of a pistoll, the boats were prepared with such a volley
of shot that the King started up in a horrible feare, till he
saw all was well. Then remembering himself to congratulate

10

PLATE II. *From the engraving by P. Hunshallwood after the painting by Chapman. Photo Cook.*
THE CROWNING OF POWHATAN

their kindness, he gave his old shoes and mantle to Captain Newport."

Powhatan was governed by all the religious convictions of his people. His worship, like theirs, assumed the logical form of propitiation of those evil spirits which manifested themselves in nature through the agency of fire, lightning, thunder, storm, famine, and epidemic. Annually, in the company of his wives and bodyguard, he took part in certain violent ceremonies which were thought to be necessary for their protection against the furtive designs of the principal devil. In the temple of Orapaks there was an image of this devil, which was most hideous in feature but adorned in body with beautiful chains of beads and pearls and copper.

Powhatan expected to be translated after death to a heaven where his associates would be limited to priests and werowances. In this aristocratic company he would remain forever, his body anointed with oil, painted with puccoon, and ornamented with gay feathers and strings of pearls and beads. His only occupation there would be to dance and sing. This paradise was supposed to lie beyond the mountains in the west. Entrance to its precincts could never be obtained by his subjects at large. These, when consigned to their graves, had no other destiny but to rot like carrion. Their plebeian spirits had been extinguished so soon as the breath had left their frames.

Chapter II

CAPTAIN JOHN SMITH

CAPTAIN JOHN SMITH was not a man of distinguished lineage. In this particular he was unlike the great majority of the foremost adventurers of the Elizabethan age. He was the son of a respectable tenant-farmer of Lincolnshire, who had some independent means. From his father he inherited a very small property; and this acquisition, combined with a bold and enterprising temper, caused him to chafe against his guardian's refusal to permit him to go to sea while still a mere lad. But a boy of such ardor and intrepidity was certain to break away early from the monotony and seclusion of a mercantile apprenticeship. From this spiritual thralldom to which he had been assigned, he was rescued by a son of Lord Willoughby, his landlord, who easily persuaded him, although not of age, to accompany him on a visit to France. With this brief tour he began that career of European adventure which was to equip him for the part he was destined to play in Virginia many years afterwards.

Long before Smith reached manhood he had undertaken to study the art of war as laid down in Machiavelli's famous treatise. At Havre, during a second journey into France, where he was robbed by his road companions and left penniless, he was enrolled in a free company of Englishmen organized by Captain Duxberry to take part in the campaigns of Henry IV against the Catholic League. When these ended, this jolly and reckless band of soldiers of fortune decided to join the army in the Low Countries, where, as usual, lively fighting was going on. Here, though often hotly engaged, Smith remained unpromoted in the ranks during a period of three or four years.

At the close of that interval he set out for Scotland, but his ship was dashed on the rocks and most of its passengers and crew were lost. At a later date, during a voyage in the Mediterranean, he was pitched overboard by his fanatical companions because they thought that he was a Huguenot heretic, and he escaped drowning only by swimming to the neighboring Isle of St. Mary's. The vessel which rescued him from this lonely situation turned into a privateer and shortly afterwards overhauled a Venetian merchantman loaded to the gunwale with corn, silks, and cloths of gold. His share of this booty was sold for two hundred and twenty-five pounds sterling. With his pockets thus bulging, he entered the corps of General Meldritch, who commanded a part of the army of the Austrian Emperor, then engaged in blocking the advance of the Turkish hordes up the valley of the Danube towards Vienna.

Many were the sieges and defenses in which Smith now participated. In one instance he was able to relieve the garrison of a fort by a method of signaling which he had ingeniously invented; and owing to his success in this case, he was promoted to the captaincy of a troop of horse. Marching with his superior officer into Transylvania, he soon distinguished himself in a siege in that country by hurling bombs of his own device into the crowded streets about the citadel, which set fire to the surrounding houses and caused a panic among the defenders. Smith was wounded in the battle which soon followed, but recovering before the operations ended, he aroused his comrades' enthusiasm by accepting the challenge of three separate Turkish champions and defeating them in rapid succession. The trophy of victory in each case was to be the head of the unsuccessful competitor. The first challenger came forward to a broad field situated between the two armies, accompanied by a flourish of hautboys. To his shoulders were attached wings made of eagle feathers, while his person was decorated with ornaments of silver and gold and with precious stones. Smith

13

pierced this Turk's head with a spear. He killed the second champion with a pistol and as victor took possession, not only of his antagonists's head, but also of his horse and armor. The third champion was run through with a sword, and his head was also cut off. Gathering up the three bleeding trophies and impaling them on a single pike, he marched back to his camp under the escort of an admiring guard of honor. This was the origin of his famous coat of arms of three Turks' heads, which was recorded in the Heralds' College in London and engraved on his tombstone in Saint Sepulchre's Church in the City.

After taking part in one successful battle, Smith and his comrades, Ensign Carleton and Sergeant Robinson, who afterwards went out to Virginia with him, were the only soldiers of the English company to survive. Wounded severely, captured, and sold into slavery, he won the love of Princess Tragbigzanda, the sister of his master, and having struck the latter a fatal blow with a flail, in resentment of inhuman treatment, he fled into Russia, with a prisoner's iron ring still encircling his neck. He subsequently made his way through many perils and hardships into Transylvania, where he was presented with three hundred ducats of gold by Prince Sigismond. Thence he traveled on in leisurely fashion through France to Spain, and crossing the Straits of Gibraltar, he landed in Morocco. The ship in which he was sailing was afterwards blown by a tempest as far south as the Canaries; and here he took part in a sea fight brought on by two Spanish men-of-war, which seem to have been worsted in the desperate engagement. Glutted with a life of danger and excitement, Smith returned to England, where he quietly remained, apparently without employment, until he left Blackwall with the expedition of 1606, bound out for Virginia.

This brief description of Smith's early adventures cannot be omitted from our narrative, since it reveals the preparation which he had received to enable him to become the chief bulwark of the colony at Jamestown. His encounters with the Indians seem, after all, small in real importance

PLATE III. *Statue by William Couper on Jamestown Island. Photo Cook.*

CAPTAIN JOHN SMITH

when compared with those sanguinary battles with the Turks and Spaniards in which he had won his spurs. He had been hardened against the dangers and privations which he had to pass through on the James River by his experience of even worse evils in remote Transylvania and Africa. Newport and Gosnold certainly surpassed him in the art of seamanship, but in the skillful use of purely military force they were to be ranked far below him. Not one of his higher associates in the expedition of 1606-7 had acquired courage, foresight, and power of endurance in so thorough and so harsh a school as he had known.

Smith, as we have seen, was born in a plain walk of life. Apart from the transmitted friendship of his father's landlord, Lord Willoughby, he possessed no influential personal connections to advance his fortunes; and yet, although he had not risen higher than a captaincy in the continental wars, he had won in this subordinate rank so much reputation for intrepidity and efficiency that, when the King came to appoint the members of the Virginia Council in 1606, he included Smith in this honorable and conspicuous company. He had inherited neither a great name nor a great fortune, but he had, nevertheless, made such good use of the courageous and enterprising spirit of his young manhood that he found himself in the noble expedition to Virginia on a footing of equality with veterans like its commander and the commander's grizzled assistants.

The personal distinction which Smith had won by this time was opposed to the probability of his proving himself, under any seduction, to be a man of a treacherous and disloyal nature; and yet, in the course of the voyage which began at Blackwall and ended at Jamestown he was charged, not only with secretly encouraging, but even with heading, a mutiny among the crews of the three vessels, and he was actually put under arrest. This arrest was afterwards shown to have been entirely unwarranted, and he was able to recover very heavy punitive damages in consequence.

What was the origin of the accusation? Perhaps it lay in the voyagers' discontented frame of mind resulting from

15

the fatigues and depressions following a long passage through unknown waters. Instead of ending in two months, as was confidently expected and predicted, the passage lasted through five. Factions, started among the adventurers soon after the Canaries were reached, came to a full head on arrival at the Isle of Nevis. A murky atmosphere of suspicion and distrust had by that time been created, and Newport, in supreme command of the fleet, and those in control immediately under him went to the point of erecting a gallows on which to hang Smith, who was supposed to be chiefly responsible for the disaffection. So firmly yet so uncomplainingly did he bear himself in the teeth of these charges, that the voyagers in the mass rejected the imputation of guilt as unjust and severely criticized the men who had made it. His enemies had gone so far as to assert that he had conspired to murder the principal officers of the expedition in order to assume the leadership of it himself. If there was anyone on board the three vessels who had the vigor, independently of the inclination, to carry out such a rough and sanguinary program, it was Smith; but if his opposition to the slowness of the voyage was ever openly expressed, which seems probable enough, it took the form of a frank and legitimate criticism, and not of underhanded rebellion. Such conduct was foreign to the whole spirit of his career both before and afterwards.

When Jamestown was founded, it became at once, not simply a settlement of peaceful colonists, but a fort in a state of siege. From the very first hour after the debarkation, the Indians plotted to destroy it, and in addition to this acute cause for anxiety, the shadow of an expected Spanish assault hovered over the spot during many years. Why did not the colonists plant a wide instead of a narrow area in wheat around the town? Because too many blades would furnish a lurking-place from which the invisible Indians could with bow and arrow shoot down every settler who came sufficiently near their lair. Why did the colonists choose a site so fetid with miasma? Because it was an island and therefore the better protected from surprise in case a Spanish man-of-war should enter the Capes and sail up the river to attack.

During these initial years, in which Smith took so energetic a part, other influences also helped to produce the unfortunate conditions that soon arose. These influences may be briefly summarized:

First, there were no women to be found among the colonists. This fact in itself was sufficient to give a character of impermanence to the enterprise. In subsequent periods of wider occupation of the American soil, the pioneers were accompanied by their wives and children, although an extraordinary variety of perils dogged their advance. These sturdy forerunners never looked backwards for the reason that they carried with them everything which they possessed. When a body of men without domestic ties plant themselves, they do not fight for a lasting foothold with the ardor, persistence, and confidence of men who have at their side the families that are dear to them and dependent upon them for protection and subsistence.

Then again, at the start, these colonists of Jamestown had no reason to expect that they would be granted a fee simple share in the soil, however limited the bounds. On the other hand, the most powerful stimulus at work in the breasts of the first explorers of the virgin plains of the West was the certainty of acquiring sites there on which to build dwelling houses and to lay off fields for tillage. It was rather this anticipation than a thirst for adventure which carried that mighty host of emigrants across the lofty peaks of the Allegheny Mountains and beyond the turbid waters of the Ohio and Mississippi rivers.

Finally, there was a novel climate to depress the Jamestown colonists, with its not infrequent frigidity in winter and extreme heat in summer; and during the early spring and the late autumn alike, the weather had an eccentric way of shifting suddenly from a high to a low degree of temperature or the reverse. In addition to this—and also aggravated by it—there were those disorders of the bowels, diarrhea and dysentery, that soon followed from the use of the brackish waters of the Powhatan, which, at Jamestown was in reality

17

an estuary of the sea, subject to the regular inward flow of the tide. Doubtless, too, a despondent frame of mind was caused among the colonists by the failure at first to discover gold or other precious commodities, an expectation which had had a powerful influence in increasing the number of recruits for the expedition before the ships had sailed away from England. There seemed to be nothing to look forward to except partial starvation—in the intervals between the supplies from home—constant manual labor, and the continuous imminence of Indian assault.

In the final analysis, the colony suffered also from the moral quality of the adventurers as a body, although in reality they represented very fairly the average character of the English people as a whole. Success would probably have been earlier won had a larger number of trained men like John Smith and his two Transylvanian comrades, Ensign Carleton and Sergeant Robinson, and a smaller number of untrained gentlemen been found in the ranks of the immigrants.

Smith lamented the absence in Virginia of those indigenous advantages which had made Peru and Mexico such storehouses of treasure for the Spanish conquerors. The region in which the colony was planted, he said, was precisely as it had been when it first left the hand of God. Its inhabitants were rude, improvident, and dispersed. No gold, no silver, and no precious metal slept in its bowels. It is true that its lands were fertile, its woods full of valuable timber, and its waters teeming with fish, but all these sources of wealth called imperatively for labor and money for their adequate utilization, and neither at the start was obtainable in the quantity required.

The services which Smith performed in Virginia were as diversified as they were valuable. The most outstanding of these were (1) his explorations, which brought to light the resources of the virgin country; (2) the procurement of grain from the Indians, which on several occasions saved the colonists from starvation; (3) the exemplification in his own conduct of the proper manner of treating the savages,

18

if attacks were to be warded off, namely, by exciting their fear or winning their good will; and (4) his enforcement of certain practical regulations, while president of the colony, which demonstrated that its welfare could only in that way be successfully advanced and its permanence assured.

In regard to the record of his explorations, there is no proof that he took part with the other adventurers in the short expedition which was made into the region immediately south of Cape Henry after the three vessels anchored there in Morton's Bay in the Spring of 1607. Nor did he accompany the little body of men who, a few days later, sailed up the Powhatan in a shallop ahead of the fleet, with the view of selecting the right site for the projected settlement. But in the first voyage of Newport from Jamestown to the falls in that river, Smith was a conspicuous figure, without apparently holding even a subordinate command. A short time after this event he was restored to his seat in the Council, which had been withdrawn from him ever since the reading of the orders at the mouth of the Bay.

His first independent exploration seems to have been of the Nansemond River, on the banks of which he discovered a site that he thought to be peculiarly well fitted for the foundation of a colony. An expedition which he, in association with Scrivener, a member of the Council, had planned to push westward beyond the falls in the Powhatan, and for which they had assiduously prepared by drilling their men for fighting in the forest, was interrupted before it could be carried out. Had this expedition been pushed through, we should have been indebted to Smith for the European eye's first impression of the modern Blue Ridge and quite probably also of the great valley of the Shenandoah itself. As it was, his attention was diverted to the Bay, which was known to the Indians by the name which it still bears—the Chesapeake.

This expedition up Chesapeake Bay took place in June, 1608. Smith was accompanied by six gentlemen, four soldiers, a blacksmith, a fishmonger, and a fisherman. A small barge propelled by oars as well as by sails, was their only

CAPTAIN JOHN SMITH

vessel. A little corn meal was the sole food in their possession, besides the diet of fish, always available in those waters that teemed with edible varieties of every size. It was said at the time that not more than three of the crew had any practical knowledge of seamanship at the beginning of the voyage, but the others soon acquired skill under the influence of the active example which Smith set them in learning.

The first new ground reached seems to have been the island lying off the coast of Accomac, which later on received the name of Smith's Isles. After leaving this place, the voyagers turned their prow up the Bay close to the line of the Eastern Shore, passed by Russell Isles, and visited the werowance on the mainland, who was found to be in such a chronic state of hilarity that he was dubbed by them "The Laughing King." While ploughing these waters, they encountered one of those terrific gusts of wind to which this inland sea was, and still is, constantly subject. Their mainmast went by the board under the sudden impact. In skirting the western shore, it was noticed that the adjacent forests were full of deer, bear, and other wild animals.

The crew soon became apprehensive lest the lengthening of the voyage should carry them such a distance as to jeopardize their return to Jamestown. But Smith quietly ridiculed this fear. "It is less perilous," he said, "to go forward than to go backward"; and he gave a peremptory order for an advance as far as the mouth of the Potomac River, the next great stream. A formidable band of hostile Indians menaced the voyagers at this point, and they were driven off only by a volley of shot, leveled so as to graze the surface of the water. The barge sailed slowly up the broad river, and here and there a landing was made in the hope of discovering traces of a reported silver mine and of bartering with the tribes for rare furs and other valuable commodities. So large were the schools of fish which played on the river's surface, that members of the crew endeavored to scoop them up with frying pans.

The return voyage was uneventful. As Smith drew near to Jamestown, he ordered his men to trim the barge with

20

bright streamers; and the boat was in this way so disguised in aspect that the people at Jamestown, noticing it at a distance, were thrown into a panic for fear that the little vessel was simply the forerunner of a Spanish fleet.

The second exploration of the Chesapeake by Smith was undertaken only a few weeks after the termination of the first. The voyagers did not stop until they had reached the mouth of the Susquehanna, in which vicinity they found a tribe of Indians remarkable for their size, strength, and height. In fact, these aborigines grew to the physical magnitude of giants, but they do not seem to have been notably warlike, although they had an alert and constant foe in the neighboring nation of Massawomacks. Warriors of this latter tribe had threatened to rush upon the Englishmen as they passed northward of the Potomac's mouth, but Smith had awed them into inactivity by creating the impression that his crew were treble their real number. They soon afterwards gave signs of a friendly spirit and came on board with gifts of venison, bread, fish, fruit, birds, and bows and arrows. While returning from the Susquehanna, Smith sailed into the estuary of the Rappahannock and explored its waters as far as the falls. It was at the mouth of this stream that he was struck by a stingray and for a time was thought to be in imminent danger of losing his life, from the poison which the stingray was supposed to have injected into his body. Shortly afterwards a great storm arose in the night, and the little vessel barely escaped being swallowed up by the mountainous waves in the darkness. So black, indeed, was the outlook that the shore was visible only when the lightning flashed.

The most famous of Smith's explorations was the voyage which he made up the Chickahominy River. This ended in his capture by the Indians. One of the objects of that voyage was to find out whether this stream formed a direct waterway to the South Sea. Smith had pushed up its current in a canoe ahead of the barge attended by a few companions. Landing with an Indian guide when the waters grew shallow, he quickly fell into an ambuscade and, after mortally wounding one of the Indians, sank into a bog and was seized and carried off to the hunting lodge of Opechancanough, the werowance of that region. Thence he was led across country to the Rappahannock to be identified as the stranger from the sea who, the year before, had shot a member of one of the tribes inhabiting those parts. Some time later on he arrived at Werowocomoco, Powhatan's principal seat, and here, after he had been generously feasted, he was dragged to a sacrificial stone and his head forcibly laid on it. As the tomahawks were about to descend, Pocahontas threw herself before the prisoner, clasped Smith's head in her arms, and begged her father, who was looking on, to spare the Englishman's life.

Pocahontas' act was in harmony with the impulses of her compassionate nature which afterwards led her to defy all personal danger to ward off from the English colony both assault and starvation. The act of Powhatan, in releasing Smith at his daughter's prayer, was equally in harmony with an immemorial custom of the Indians that prevailed from Canada to Florida, namely, releasing a prisoner at the request of a woman of the tribe. At the same time, one of the rules of the American savages was to inflict the punishment of both torture and death on anyone who had killed a member of their tribe. Smith had, as we have already mentioned, shot one of Powhatan's subjects. And he could hardly have escaped retaliation had not some such powerful influence as that exerted by Pocahontas intervened to save him. He returned unhurt to Jamestown under the protection of an escort furnished by Powhatan, only to find that Englishmen could be more cruel than Indians, for he was arrested, tried, and convicted, under the provisions of a trumped-up Israelitish law which held him responsible for the deaths of those of his companions who had been murdered by the savages in the voyage up the Chickahominy. He was rescued from an ignominious execution on the gallows only by the timely arrival of Captain Newport from England, who at once threw open the door of his prison.

Perhaps the most practical services performed by Smith

for the struggling colony's benefit were his purchases again and again of maize from the Indian tribes, with which to supply bread for the people at Jamestown. It was calculated that during the first three years the provisions imported from England were at any one time sufficient only to ward off starvation during the space of a few weeks. Smith very soon perceived that the most reliable means of removing this danger was to make use of the natural resources of the country itself. There were sound reasons why the colonists could not so soon trust to their own labor in new grounds to obtain a subsistence. They must look to barter with the Indians for the food which was indispensable.

Smith visited the valleys of the Chickahominy, the James, the York, the Mattapony, and the Rappahannock in turn, in order to procure a supply of maize, a food which had in it much of the solid substance of meat. In the winter of 1607 he loaded a barge in the Chickahominy River with a full cargo of this grain, while he purchased enough from the tribe seated at the falls to fill the hold of a small ship. At Paspaheigh, near Jamestown, he also obtained about twelve bushels, and at Kecoughtan, about thirty. In the course of the following year he was again able to buy one hundred bushels at Chickahominy alone.

So liberally did he supply the colonists from these places that in the interval between October, 1608, and July, 1609, only seven men died at Jamestown, and these from normal causes. If the need of food was urgent and the Indians were not disposed to barter, he did not scruple to use force to take the grain in their possession. Such was the course he felt compelled to pursue at Nansemond, where he seized enough maize to fill the holds of two barges. But for this, as always under the same circumstances, he offered ample payment. He constrained the ferocious Opechancanough at Mattapony to load his vessel by grasping him by the hair of his head and presenting a pistol at his forehead; and Smith was also successful, by a like display of fierce resolution, in frightening Powhatan into following this werowance's example on one occasion at least.

23

Smith never suffered himself to be assaulted first by the Indians. He always anticipated his adversaries' blows. When the savages at Paspaheigh in 1609 showed by their demeanor that they were about to attack him and his escort, he ordered his men to fire on them. Six or seven were killed and many taken prisoners. He set the torch to their wigwams, pulled up their weirs, and carried off their boats. When he moved forward to capture the Chickahominy village, its inhabitants dropped their tomahawks, bows, and arrows, and implored him to be merciful; and this example of submission on their part was followed by the members of other tribes.

Smith was always severe in punishing the thievery of the Indians who visited Jamestown. In 1609 he threw into the jail there a youthful warrior who had stolen a pistol. The frightened savage soon lost consciousness under the influence of the fumes of a charcoal fire, and his brother, thinking him dead, raised a wild lamentation. Smith promised that he would bring the supposed corpse back to life if thenceforward they would refrain from purloining further. By means of simple remedies, the limp brother in a few minutes evinced signs of recovering his senses, and the two were sent to their village to relate the story of this incident of miraculous restoration to health. Powhatan was made so apprehensive by the tale, that he gathered up all the stolen articles at Werowocomoco and, together with the thieves themselves, returned them to Jamestown.

The secret of Smith's success in managing the Indians and colonists alike, after he entered upon the duties of the presidency, was to be found in his practical common sense, sustained by an unswerving and indomitable temper. He protested against the expedition which Newport led beyond the falls, because, he said, one hundred and twenty men were withdrawn from profitable employments at Jamestown to carry out a purpose which two explorers could have more easily prosecuted. He protested against the infatuation which, under the same leadership and with the same consequences, concentrated the thoughts and energies of the colonists on hunting for the surface indications of gold, digging

PLATE IV. *Engraved by William Hole, 1612.*

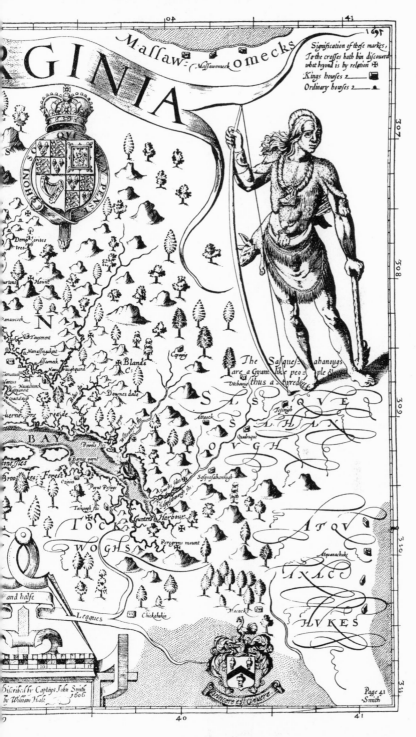

JOHN SMITH'S MAP OF VIRGINIA

in the earth for gold, and sifting the sands for gold. He protested against the dangerous inflation of Powhatan's conceit as to his own importance by giving him ceremoniously a crown and coronation robes. He protested against the policy which diverted the colonists from their own support by requiring them to collect from the forests supplies of articles which were obtainable at that time with far less expense from Russia, Sweden, and Denmark. He protested against the importation of food of all kinds from England at such frequent intervals, as reliance upon this constant source for subsistence had greatly weakened the settlers' determination to depend on the country for a livelihood.

As soon as Smith became president he put a stop to the further construction of the imposing house which Ratcliffe, his predecessor, had begun to build in order to accommodate the incumbents of that office; and he expressed the utmost contempt for Archer's scheme of drawing the colonists together into a parliament, as he knew that their first act would be to vote in favor of the desertion of Jamestown for England. He recognized the advisability of increasing the proportion of workingmen, carpenters, masons, blacksmiths, and other artisans, rather than gentlemen who had never been trained to labor with their own hands.

And yet he was not unfavorable in his judgment of the capacity of well-born men to show physical strength and endurance whenever imperatively called upon to do so. While Newport was exploring the region west of the falls, Smith employed a little company of gentlemen left behind at Jamestown in cutting down trees in the neighboring forest. As he observed them, he was amused by the delight reflected in their faces as they listened to the thunder of the great oaks and hickories toppling down. At every third stroke of their axes they would rip out a loud oath. This irritated Smith, and he gave orders that for every oath thus uttered a can of water was that night to be poured down the sleeve of each guilty person. The result was that in the course of a week hardly an oath was heard to escape from the lips of even the grossest of the former offenders.

CAPTAIN JOHN SMITH

Smith was an uncompromising believer in the beneficent moral influence of work. He divided the entire company at Jamestown into bands of tens and fifteens, according to the character of their respective tasks. Four hours of daylight were spent by all in manual jobs of one kind or another, while the rest of the interval was devoted to military exercises or to pleasant pastimes. "He that will not work," he announced, "should not eat. The labors of thirty or forty shall not be used to support one hundred and fifty idlers."

As opportunity offered, he employed the colonists in the manufacture of pitch, tar, and soap ashes. Under his supervision they also made glass, dug a well to assure the enjoyment of fresh water within the confines of the fort, constructed weirs in the river, wove fishing nets, restored the church and re-covered the roof of the storehouse. On the neck of land lying behind the town he ordered a blockhouse to be erected, where he posted a picked garrison to prevent the intrusion of prowling Indians. He saw to the building of a second blockhouse on Hog Island for watchmen who were to give warning of the appearance of strange vessels in the direction of the Capes; and he also raised a fort on a high bluff on the southern side of the James, to which the settlers could retreat in the last emergency.

Disabled by an explosion of gunpowder in his boat, Smith was left at the mercy of his enemies. His commission had not at that time been actually canceled, although he was aware that it would be on the arrival of Gates, the representative of Delaware, the new governor. A plot to murder him was formed and failed only through irresolution on the part of the would-be assassins. Ratcliffe and Archer quickly usurped the administration and took advantage of the power thus acquired and of Smith's helplessness, to draw up charges against him for submission to the Company oversea. But nothing further was heard of this indictment, and the very witnesses dispatched to London to testify against him ended by speaking emphatically in public in his favor.

Hardly had he reached England when, as the chronicler tells us, "all [in Virginia] found the want of Captain Smith.

Even his greatest maligners could then curse his loss; and for corn, provision, and contributions from the savages, we had nothing but mortal wounds with clubs and arms. As for our hogs, hens, goats, sheep, and horses—all were devoured. Then swords, arrows, pieces, or anything, we traded with the Indians, whose bloody fingers were so embued in our blood that, what by their cruelty, our Governor's indiscretion, and the loss of our ships, and five hundred [persons] within six months, there remained not more than sixty most miserable and poor creatures. It was too wild to say what we endured. The ocean was alone our own, for want of providence, industry, and government, and not the bareness and defect of the country. In those years, we lived off what the country afforded; but now, had we been in Paradise with those governors, it would not have been much better for us."

But the noblest tribute which Smith received after his departure was paid spontaneously by one of his faithful comrades: "What shall I say? But thus we lost him, that, in all his proceedings, made justice his first guide, and experience his second; ever hating baseness, sloth, pride, and injustice more than any dangers; that never allowed more for himself than for his soldiers with him; that upon no danger would send them where he would not lead them himself; that would never see us want what he either had or could by any means get for us; that would rather want than borrow, or starve than not pay; that loved action more than words, and hated falsehood and cosenage worse than death; whose adventures were our lives, and whose loss was our death."

Chapter III

THE PRINCESS POCAHONTAS

THE MOST exquisite idyll in the course of American history is woven, like a piece of embroidery, about the name of Pocahontas, the lovely maid of the forests and streams of aboriginal Virginia. We think of her as of some modest flower hiding its purity and beauty in the quiet shade of the woods or a frail and graceful fawn rising from its dewy bed of ferns to bound away into the leafy fastnesses of hill and dale. Indeed, she seemed to be akin to forms of nature that possessed a more sensitive and delicate quality than belongs to human beings. How was this to be explained? Perhaps by the fact that her early life had been spent in as constant association with birds and animals and trees as with her own people in their native wigwams and gardens.

The impression of guileless innocence which Pocahontas' personality leaves upon us is deepened by the recollection of her youthfulness. When first seen by Smith at Werowocomoco, she had barely, if at all, passed her tenth birthday. When lowered into her grave in the church at Gravesend, she was still under twenty-two years of age. Those who had known her as a maid as well as a matron have recorded their admiration of her regular features, expressive countenance, and agile figure. Mere physical charms were not the only ones which she possessed. At least one competent chronicler has described her as the "nonpareil" of her people in both "spirit and intelligence."

But the finest and most moving tribute which she ever received was paid by Smith when he said that she had a heart that was full of compassion and tenderness; and every known incident of her brief span of life proves the truth of this fervent yet impartial encomium.

Pocahontas' domestic surroundings in her childhood and girlhood were precisely those of every young Indian of the female sex. She was born in a dark and narrow lodge of saplings covered with mats; she bathed every morning as a child in the waters of the great river near by and played with her mates throughout the hours of day, with only the slight restraints required by Indian custom; she wandered where she pleased about the contiguous forests with all the freedom of a deer; she accompanied her father and his people in their hunting expeditions into the thick woods; she herself trapped, with ingenious wiles, hares, squirrels, and quail; watched with delight the dances of the elders; and listened eagerly to the shrill music of their reeds and rattles. All this time she was dressed with the scantiness which distinguished every Indian maid still too unripe to be chosen in marriage.

Very probably Pocahontas had as a child often looked on in innocent sympathy as Powhatan gazed from the threshold of his wigwam at his enemies' scalps suspended to strings between the trees in front of his door. This seemed to be a barren school for the cultivation of strong emotions of pity; but these scalps had belonged to men who had come down to tomahawk her own people and carry her and her playmates away into captivity. There was none of that romance of another world about them which in her eyes threw such glamor around the Englishmen at Jamestown, although these, too, were intruders of an ominous aspect and temper.

A rather unconventional glimpse of her when she was still a mere child or at least a very immature girl has been preserved by one of the contemporary historians. In this passing scene she is engaged in wheeling on her hands, with her feet dangling in the air, down the street at Jamestown, while the Englishmen look on with lively amusement at the innocent antics of herself and her imitating companions of her own age, sex, and race. She was as unconscious then of her own partial nudity as some little animal at large in the forest might be when leaping about in a similarly playful mood.

The first time that Smith saw the forest maid who was always to be so romantically associated with his own fame was at Werowocomoco, at the moment of his rescue from death by her rushing forward to ward off the stroke. She was the most conspicuous figure at that critical moment, while Smith, held down to the stone by the grip of his would-be executioners, was forced to remain impassive and silent. A few minutes earlier he had faced Powhatan seated high above the assemblage on his throne-bed. Pocahontas at that instant was certainly among the women squatting behind one or the other of the two parallel lines of warriors. Youthful as she was, some emotion of interest must have been aroused in her breast by the sight of the handsome and manly stranger of another color and different habiliments whose fate now hung apparently upon a word. When that word proved to be adverse, after the elders' solemn consultation, did pure compassion, sensibly deepened by the courageous bearing of the intended victim, prompt her to interfere? That seems to have been the chief feeling behind her impulsive act in saving him from the fatal weapons. But it is possible that there is another explanation.

However despotic Powhatan may have been in the government of his people, it is doubtful whether he would have ventured to ignore openly that rule of the Indian criminal law which ferociously required an eye for an eye and a tooth for a tooth. In other words, it would have been unwise for him, after the death of one of his subjects at Smith's hand, to release the prisoner when the sentiment of all his people demanded the culprit's execution. And yet he was shrewd enough to perceive that Smith could be made far more useful to him if kept alive to work than he would be if reduced to the inanimate state of a corpse. The old forest king keenly coveted the guns and hatchets which he knew were in the Englishmen's possession. Here was one of these very strangers in his power. What better use to turn him to than to compel him to become gun-maker and hatchet-maker at

30

Ætatis suæ 21. A. 1616.

Matoaks als Rebecka daughter to the mighty Prince Powhatan Emperour of Attanoughkomouck als Virginia converted and baptized in the Christian faith, and Wife to the worᵗ Mr Tho: Rolff.

PLATE V.   *From the Booton Hall Portrait.   Painted from life in England, 1616.*
Photo Cook.

POCAHONTAS

Werowocomoco? It would, without doubt, be a wise course.

But how was the prisoner's life to be preserved for these utilitarian purposes without violating one of the most cherished of all the immemorial customs of the Indians? The most certain and yet the most secret way of doing this was to give the cue to Pocahontas to throw her arms about the captive's head just as soon as the clubs were raised to strike. If such a part had beforehand been assigned her in the expected scene by the crafty monarch, her father, it was one that was perfectly congenial to her own tenderness of heart.

There was not a single aspect of Smith's reception which foreshadowed that it would end in his death. On the contrary, every preliminary incident in it indicated that he was held in the most extraordinary respect. The episode began in the largest apartment of Powhatan's wildwood mansion. As Smith entered, he was greeted with a shout from the assembled savages. The king himself, in his most imposing royal robes, looked down upon the concourse, surrounded by everything that could give distinction to his presence. The squaws were adorned with beads and pearls in profusion, while the warriors were decorated with their most brilliant plumes and reddest paint. The Queen of Appomattox at once brought water to the prisoner in which to bathe his hands; and another woman of rank offered a bunch of feathers to serve as a towel.

Were these the circumstances that marked the reception of Ratcliffe when he fell into the grasp of the same monarch? Was he led before the throne at once? Was he able, before sentence was passed on him, to gaze around upon a scene of Indian state comparable with the one which had met Smith's eyes a few years before? Far from it. The captive was dragged to the nearest tree; his limbs were securely tied to the trunk; and the women were permitted to scrape the flesh from his bones with sharp sea shells, until, in exquisite agony, he gave up the ghost. It was not his fate to return to Jamestown with an escort of honor, like the one in attendance upon Smith in the journey from Werowocomoco.

THE PRINCESS POCAHONTAS

It is known that Smith remained at least two days with Powhatan before he set out for Jamestown, but there is no record that Pocahontas saw him even once during this interval. Powhatan visited him in the wigwam in the woods which had been assigned for his shelter; and the old monarch showed how deeply he was impressed with his prisoner's manly quality by promising to make him werowance of Cappahoosic and to adopt him as his favorite son if he would deliver to his Indian escort, on arriving at the fort, two great guns, a grindstone, and other articles of value less cumbersome in weight.

The second time that Pocahontas was seen by Smith was in the course of May, 1608. This occurred several months after the rescue at Werowocomoco. Powhatan, it is plain, had not forgotten the incident and still bore in mind its possible impression on the memory of the settlers at Jamestown. He was crafty enough to recognize that the emissary who would be most likely to succeed in carrying out any mission of his to the authorities there was Pocahontas, because of the good will which she had won by her act in behalf of Smith. He was now anxious to recover several prisoners who were held by the Englishmen; and child-ambassadress though Pocahontas would be, he decided to send her to beg for their release. Not only her service in saving Smith's life, but her comeliness, her innocence, and her youth would, he justly expected, appeal to the colonists' partiality. This anticipation proved to be altogether correct, for when she arrived, the request which she submitted was at once favorably received, and the captives were told that they were free once more. Their bows and arrows were again put into their hands; and presents of great value in their eyes were offered them and accepted. To Pocahontas herself articles which she looked upon as precious were given; and she was asked to say to Powhatan that her mission had been successful simply because it had been confided to her. His "kindness" in sending her and not another on that mission was expressly acknowledged. Smith, as a member of the Council, was certainly one of the authorities who received her at Jamestown; and it is likely that her entertainment fell principally on him as the person present who had known her best and longest.

There was, undoubtedly, more freedom and less ceremony in the scene in which Smith met Pocahontas the third time. He had gone to Werowocomoco as the herald of a large body of Englishmen who were on their way to visit Powhatan. It is apparent that he and his small escort had halted at some spot in an open field, perhaps to bivouac or to rest. While thus engaged, thirty Indian girls suddenly issued in an ordered body from the woods near by. Their thighs were covered with a few green leaves, while their skins were painted, some in one color, some in another, so that no two of the maids presented the same aspect in this particular. Their leader was Pocahontas. She wore a pair of deer horns on her head, an otter skin around her waist, and another like skin on one of her arms. On her back a quiver was slung, and she held in her hand a bow and arrow. The first maid just behind her carried a sword; the second, a club; the third, a pot-stick; and the others, similar weapons. Each one of these attendants, like Pocahontas herself, wore a pair of deer horns on her head.

As the band rushed from the covert of trees, they raised a wild shout and, clasping hands, danced in a ring around the fire where the Englishmen were seated. This movement was accompanied by an Indian chorus, which at intervals, according to Smith, they broke "by falling into their infernal passions." But in a short time the song and dance were resumed. An hour had passed when they suddenly stopped, and then with the same wild shout as before they quickly vanished into the recesses of the dark woods.

The fourth sight which Smith had of Pocahontas was during the winter of 1608-9. Powhatan was now convinced that if he could obtain possession of Smith's person, he would be able to destroy the colony at Jamestown, for he supposed that its safety hung entirely upon that officer's vigilance and courage. During this winter Smith seems to have been exploring or hunting in the neighborhood of

Werowocomoco, and his exact position was known to Powhatan through the reports of his scouts. Here was an opportunity to capture him. To allay his distrust and lessen his watchfulness, Powhatan sent him daily supplies of venison, turkeys, and bread. Finally, he chose the hour of supper on a particular day as the best for the attack.

This selection came to Pocahontas' knowledge, and the night before the assault was to be made she stole through trackless woods, haunted by bears and panthers, to put Smith on his guard. She reached his camp unhurt and implored him to leave the spot at once with his companions. Offered a valuable reward for her kindness in risking her own safety to assure theirs, she refused to accept because she said her father would certainly kill her should he observe the gifts in her possession, as they would instantly arouse his suspicion. "So," records the admiring chronicler, "she ran away by herself as she came."

In his personal relations with Pocahontas, Smith is said to have acted with "honest reason and discretion." "He might have done with her what he listeth," remarks a contemporary writer, "for there were none who could have hindered his determination." But his attitude towards her throughout their association continued to be the attitude of a father towards a lovely and innocent child.

So great was the respect and admiration in which the Indians held Smith that he was suspected by his malicious enemies of a desire to make himself the sovereign of Virginia by taking to wife this daughter of the old forest monarch, but there was no ground whatever for attributing such an ambition to him. That he could have married her during his presidency if he had wished there can be no doubt at all; but with the exaggerated notions prevailing in that age about the sacredness of kingship, this would have been a dangerous step for him to have taken on his sole initiative, since information of it was certain to come in the end to the distrustful royal ear in England.

Smith, as one might have readily predicted from his handsome face, bold temper, and gallant bearing, was always a charming figure in the eyes of the women he knew. The Lady Tragbigzanda, the Lady Callamata, the Madame Shanoi, and lastly, the Princess Pocahontas, showed an equal sensibility to the fascinations of his personality; and yet he remained until the closing hour of his existence a bachelor, apparently without any reciprocation of the passion which he had excited in numerous susceptible female hearts in both the Old and the New World.

Pocahontas' benevolent services were not confined to Smith, although her partiality for him doubtless had much influence in prompting her to assist the colonists as a body. The correctness of this supposition would seem to be proved by her failure to visit Jamestown on a single occasion after his departure for England, until brought there as a captive by Argall. But whatever inspired or colored her action, whether it was love for Smith or pure compassion for suffering or a natural interest in the Englishmen, she was successful to a large degree in modifying the harsh conditions to which the strangers, huddled together behind the palisade on the great river, were exposed. During the trying first years, she was as often seen with her train of maids at Jamestown as within the precincts of her father's primitive village of wigwams at Werowocomoco. In no instance was she ever suspected of playing the part of a spy. On the contrary, she always appeared with her two friendly hands full of useful gifts. "Next under God," we learn from Smith, "she was the instrument to preserve the colony from death, famine, and utter confusion, which, if, in those times, it had once been deserted, Virginia might have lain as it was at our first arrival to this day."

It would not have been unnatural had Powhatan looked upon the favor with which Pocahontas was treated by the English settlers with some aversion, if not with positive misgiving, at the very time that he was disposed to make use of that partiality in carrying out some crafty purpose of his own for the injury of the detested strangers. It was certainly by the dictation of his masterful will that Pocahontas was sent to live with the family of Japazaws on the banks of the Potomac River. Here from October, 1609, when Smith went back to England—until April, 1613, when Argall sailed up the waters of that great stream, she remained, engaged in making such use of her time as was customary with an Indian maid of her rank.

Anchoring near the site of Japazaws' village, Argall, who had come to buy corn, heard of her presence, and it seemed to flash upon his mind at once that if she could be persuaded to return to Jamestown with him she might be made an instrument to establish a lasting peace between Powhatan and the English.

"Unless you deliver up Pocahontas to me," he said to his Indian host in private, "I will no longer call you my brother or even my friend."

"If I do as you wish," replied Japazaws, "I will arouse Powhatan's enmity, and he will make war on me."

"I will help you in the fight if he does so," Argall answered.

But this was not enough inducement. "I will give you a kettle," Argall then added, to clinch the agreement.

Though staggered by the prospect of receiving so precious a gift, Japazaws hesitated. Then he said that he would consult his brother, the King of Potomac. This he seems to have done, and in the end he promised to do what Argall had asked him; but he required it to be done in such a way as not to excite Powhatan's suspicion that the two had acted in collusion. His wife, who was in the conspiracy, pretended to be anxious to visit the ship, but he refused to permit her to gratify her feigned desire. With apparent spontaneity she burst into tears. Then he said that he would consent should she go in the company of some other woman. Pocahontas offered to accompany her. Argall received the three in his cabin and set before them an ample and tempting meal.

When the dinner was about to end, Japazaws trod on Argall's foot to remind him that he had performed his part of the bargain. Argall then asked Pocahontas to retire into the gun room; and when she was called out again, she was informed by the Englishman that she was to return to

Jamestown with him in order to help the colonists to make peace with her father. The deceitful Japazaws and his squaw at this announcement raised a loud howl, in which they were joined by Pocahontas, who alone was acting in a spirit of perfect sincerity. Japazaws and his wife, on the other hand, not being in earnest, were quickly pacified and assisted Argall in quieting Pocahontas. Soon afterwards they went on shore with the kettle, while Pocahontas sailed away with the ship, balking no more. But it was noticed that "she was exceedingly pensive and discontented" at first. Later on, however, the "extraordinary courteous usage" which she received is said to have brought "her little by little to patience."

Powhatan was soon informed by the English of his daughter's captivity, and he was sternly told to deliver up all the English prisoners in his possession if he wished to obtain her release; but he sent back only seven, with their entirely unserviceable muskets, all of which had been stolen by his people. He accompanied the liberation of the men and the restoration of these articles with a promise that he would give five hundred bushels of corn, should Pocahontas be set free, in which case, he added, he would also enter into a treaty of peace. To this the reply was returned that no peace would be consented to until he had delivered up every English weapon still in his possession. Not long afterwards, Dale, at the head of one hundred and fifty men, and with Pocahontas also in his train, went to Werowocomoco by water. When this force stepped on shore they were received with a shower of arrows, which so irritated Dale that he gave orders to burn the wigwams and destroy all the growing corn. Overawed by this prompt act of retaliation, the Indians made overtures for peace which were accepted, and two of Pocahontas' brothers at once came to visit her. She urged them to persuade Powhatan to cease his attacks on the English but positively declined to return to Werowocomoco.

By this time she was in love with John Rolfe, a member of an ancient English family who had set out for Virginia in 1609, only to be wrecked, with Gates and Somers, on the coral shoals of Bermuda. In this voyage he was accompanied by his first wife and his only child, who died on the island. After arrival in Virginia, where he lost his wife also, he foresaw the importance of the tobacco plant as a commodity that might be made to sustain the colony by its sale in England. He was the first to suggest its use for that purpose. Personally he was described as a man of upright spirit and correct behavior, of remarkable native intelligence, and of sound education. It was fortunate for the future happiness of the Indian Princess that he did not share the prejudices of his companions at Jamestown against the Indian race. "Pocahontas," said Dale, "is of a different and despised color; of different manners, and uneducated; of a hated nation, not one of whom has ever yet been looked on as above the meanest of the Colonists. His children and children's children will be regarded as of an inferior race." And yet the writer of these words really favored the marriage and used his influence to hasten it. The coming years proved him to be no prophet, since descent from Pocahontas has always been looked on as a patent of artistocracy in Virginia.

Among the most remarkable letters in American history is the one which Rolfe addressed to Dale in full confession of all the motives that governed him in making up his mind to espouse the Indian princess. These motives seem to have been a curious mixture of love for the woman, anxiety, through her, to convert the savages to Christianity, and also, through her, to establish a permanent peace between the two races. Dale informs us that Rolfe appeared "to be much concerned and troubled in mind" on the subject of his marriage. "He called God to witness the purity of his motive, and how deeply his conscience had been engaged in the decision; and that not until much suffering had been endured was that decision made." The future bride seems to have experienced no perplexity at all. Dale had already instructed the clergyman at Jamestown to teach her the principal doctrines of the Christian religion. The preliminary step to this was her public renunciation of her old pagan idolatry. She was soon prepared for the ordinance of baptism, in the celebration of which she received the name of the Lady

PLATE VI. *From the painting by Chapman. Photo Gramstorff.* THE BAPTISM OF POCAHONTAS

Rebecca; and there followed shortly afterwards the ceremony of the marriage under the roof of the parish church,
which was attended, no doubt, by all the population of the
little town. Powhatan sanctioned the union and sent one of
his brothers to give his daughter away. The marriage proved
to be a happy one. She is said to have "lived civilly and
lovingly with her husband," although she had learned the
English language sufficiently well to have quarreled with
him fluently, had she been so disposed.

Dale regarded the union with lively satisfaction from a
political point of view, saying openly that had he accomplished nothing more in Virginia than to bring it about, he
would not consider the time which he had spent there lost.
Powhatan, too, seems to have been pleased. When Hamor
visited him in 1614, the old monarch inquired about the
health and contentment of his daughter. "She is so well and
so happy," replied Hamor, "that she would not be willing
to live with you again." Instead of being offended by this
blunt speech, Powhatan laughed and turned the conversation.

Just as Pocahontas had shown that she was able to learn
and conform with ease to all the social usages of Jamestown,
so she proved herself to be equally receptive in her association
with the members of the most distinguished social circles of
London. What clearer evidence could we desire of her innate
refinement and of her acquired culture than the fact that
Rolfe, her husband, a well-born English gentleman, was
perfectly willing for her to visit England, where he was
aware she would be exposed to criticism and ridicule, if in
appearance, deportment, or conversation she should fail to
come up to the accepted social standards of those times. Nor
would Dale have consented to such a step had he not been
confident that she would make so good an impression as to
create a fruitful interest in the colony oversea among people
of the greatest political influence in England.

The ship conveying Dale, Rolfe, and Pocahontas anchored
in the harbor of Plymouth on the twelfth of June, 1616. In
anticipation of the Indian princess' arrival in London, Smith

39

addressed a letter to the Queen, in which he described the value of her services to the colony and also urged her claims as a woman to the respect and admiration of all. There were, besides Smith himself, at least three persons in England of the highest rank who were likely to show Pocahontas conspicuous attention. The first of these was the King, who was certain to exaggerate the importance of her royal descent; the second, the Bishop of London, to whose diocese all the outlying dominions belonged; and the third, Delaware, the governor-general of the colony, now residing in England.

After Pocahontas' reception at Court, she became the fashion of the hour, for the society of London was as mad in the pursuit of a lion or lioness in those times as it is in our own. It is said that at the fêtes and routs which she attended the guests crowded about her in their eagerness to gaze at her and converse with her. To such a degree was she honored as a royal princess that people leaving her presence backed and courtesied as if she were the daughter of James himself. She attended with her husband all the Court masks and a splendid entertainment given in her honor by the Bishop of London. Such were the dignity and refinement of her bearing on these distinguished occasions, that a contemporary observed there were many English ladies of the highest rank "who were worse favored, proportioned, and behaved, than she." And this seems to have been the general impression. A portrait of herself, dressed in the height of fashion, was also painted, in which she was represented in a large white ruff and scalloped cuffs, with a feather in her hand and a little round top hat set upon her head. She had now traveled far from the day when she amused the Englishmen at Jamestown by wheeling on her hands, in more than half-nakedness, down the street of that little village.

The most pathetic scene that occurred during her stay in England was the one in which she first met Smith, after many years of separation. At this time she was sojourning at Brentford, where Smith had gone with a party of friends to greet her and to talk with her again. "After a modest salutation, without any word," he says, "she turned about, obscured her face as not seeming well-contented, and in that humor, her husband, with divers others, we all left her two or three hours." But not long after, she began to talk, "and remembered me well what courtesies she had done, saying, 'you did promise Powhatan what was yours should be his, and he the like to you. You called him father, being in his land a stranger, and by the same reason, so must I do you.'"

"I durst not allow of that title," Smith hastily interrupted, "because you are a king's daughter."

"But," she continued, without noticing his protest, "were you not afraid to come into my father's country and cause fear in him and all his people (but me), and fear you here that I should call you father? I tell you then that I will, and you shall call me child, and so I will be forever and ever your countryman. They did tell us always you were dead, and I knew no other till I came to Plymouth, and yet Powhatan did command Ultamatomakkin to seek you and know the truth, because your countrymen lie much."

Her companion of her own race, known to history as Tomacomo, had been ordered by Powhatan to accompany her so as to assist her with his counsel. It seems as if the Indian monarch had thought that this old retainer would be more useful to her as an adviser in England than Rolfe, her husband, could be. But he had an additional mission. When he sailed from Virginia, he carried with him a long stick on which he had been instructed to notch the number of persons whom he should see when he reached the English shores. He began making the score as soon as he landed at Plymouth, but the people crowded before his eyes in such a continuous multitude that he finally threw away his tally stick in disgust. He had a very specific order to request Smith to point out to him the English God and the English King and Queen. After he had seen James, he said reproachfully to Smith, "You gave a white dog to Powhatan, which he fed as himself, but your King gave me nothing. Am I not better than your white dog?"

Pocahontas embarked with her husband and little son from

PRINCESS POCAHONTAS

London for Virginia in March, 1617. It was reported by a letter writer of that day that she set out for home "sorely against her will." When she arrived at Gravesend, she was too sick to continue the voyage. The following entry in the vestry book of the parish church in that little port tells the rest of the romantic story, "Rebecca Wrothe, Wyffe of Thomas Wrothe, Gentleman, a Virginia lady born, here was buried in the chancel." The chronicler informs us that "she made not more sorrow for her unexpected death than joy to the beholders to hear and see her make so religious and Godly an end." Thus she passed away far from her native forests. There is no record of the cause of her death. As smallpox was then an ubiquitous disease in the highest and lowest ranks of the kingdom, it is quite probable that she fell a victim to its contagion, to which she had, doubtless, been recently exposed in London. In our own times an unsuccessful attempt has been made to recover her bones with a view to their re-interment in Virginia as a fully deserved tribute to her public services and beauty of character.

There are today two monuments to Princess Pocahontas— the one, a stained glass window in the church at Gravesend; the other, a bronze statue at Jamestown. But these are frail and temporary memorials, indeed, as compared with the memorial to her that exists in the hearts of all living Virginians. To her compassionate spirit they pay an unstinted homage, and hold in the proudest recollection the association with their soil of the most romantic heroine who has appeared in American history.

Chapter IV

SIR THOMAS DALE

In THE early history of colonial Virginia, Sir Thomas
Dale stands out with some of the lowering features of a man
of blood and iron. This was not because he was by nature
harsh and inflexible, although of undoubted sternness of
temper, as because he had from the first years of manhood
been trained in the most rigid school of martial discipline
existing in that age—the military camps of the Low Countries. It was in these rough camps and on the bloody battlefields not far away that the foremost soldiers of the late
sixteenth century, and early seventeenth, learned how to
drill, march, and fight. Indeed, the Netherlands was then
the cockpit of Western Europe, where war's alarms rarely
ceased to be heard.

As we have already mentioned, Smith had during an
interval of several years served in the ranks of these northern scenes of perennial combat; so had Sir Thomas Gates,
who was afterwards to become the head of the Virginian
government in Delaware's absence; and so had Sir George
Yeardley, who was to call together the first English legislative assembly to convene on the North American continent.

The Low Countries offered not simply the most renowned
military school of that age; they were hardly second to
England as a seat of enlightened political principles and
reformed religious doctrines. This made it doubly congenial
to the gallant and adventurous Englishmen who crossed the
North Sea to acquire and practice there the art of war.
These soldiers soon found themselves quite as much at ease

under the Dutch skies as they had been under the British;
it was only physically that they had left their native shores
behind; and so strong became their partiality for their Dutch
military environment that most of them remained in that
service during a period of many years. Both Gates and Dale
were willing to accept the call to Virginia only because the
government of the Provinces had consented to re-admit them
to their old places when their mission beyond the Atlantic
should have been performed. The terms of their furloughs
allowed them to return to the military duties which they had
only temporarily dropped.

Dale's appointment to the office of high marshal in the
colony, which in the absence of both Gates and Delaware
empowered him to exercise the authority of governor, was
due primarily to the friendship of the youthful Prince
Henry, the heir to the British throne. The interval between
1595 and 1603 was passed by Dale in Scotland, whither he
had been summoned from Holland to become a member of
the Prince's personal retinue. Why this great honor was
conferred on him remains as yet unexplained, unless it was
due to his exceptionally high reputation as a soldier and a
disciplinarian. Thus began the association between the
veteran warrior and the youthful Prince which ended only
with the latter's premature and lamentable death. The story
of their mutual affection is one of the most beautiful in
English annals and convincingly refutes, if refutation is
necessary, the impression that Dale was a man who was not
susceptible to the more kindly impulses of the human heart.
On the contrary, it is a romantic fact in the personal history
of this stern soldier that the two most conspicuous episodes
of his life were episodes of extraordinary tenderness and
sweetness: he was, as we have mentioned, the friend of Prince
Henry throughout the latter's childhood and youth; and
he was also the friend of Pocahontas when that lovely
Princess had abjured the heathen creed, received the ordinance of baptism, and become the wife of John Rolfe.

Prince Henry died in his eighteenth year, but he had lived
long enough to reveal that he possessed very remarkable

moral qualities and equally remarkable mental powers. He exhibited a martial spirit at an early age and was an expert in horsemanship, in archery, in tossing the pike, and in playing tennis and golf. But he did not allow his love of these sports to interfere with a strict observance of his religious duties or with the pursuit of his studies. It was said of him that although he lived in the corrupt atmosphere of a court, he never suffered it to degrade his tastes or lower his morals; he neither told nor would listen to coarse jokes, and he was never known to violate the rules of honor and propriety.

The Prince acquired none of these superior qualities from his pusillanimous and undignified father. Rather he inherited them from his mother, a daughter of the gallant House of Denmark and a descendant of the brave Vikings who had plowed the northern seas. There can be no doubt, however, that his lofty and manly leanings were confirmed by his association with the upright and sturdy Dale at the most susceptible period of his life. He was also a friend of Raleigh, and it was perhaps chiefly through this friendship that his desire to forward colonization in the West by his patronage was keenly aroused. But when that interest had been once created, it was to Dale that his eyes were turned to carry out the noble plans which he had formed. By this time Dale had resumed his duties in the Low Countries, but he had not been forgotten by that high-minded young master whom he had left behind in Scotland. At Henry's earnest solicitation the King instructed his prime minister to urge the English ambassador at the Hague to use all influence to prevent Dale from being passed over "in the alterations and reversals of places among the companies"; and to show his favor even more graciously, he knighted Dale in 1606, when that officer happened to be visiting England.

One of Henry's first acts, after assuming the titular dignity of Prince of Wales, was to request the Dutch ambassador at the Court of St. James to obtain his government's permission for Dale's return to London, where he was to receive a formal order to set out for Virginia at once. Henry died during the ensuing year. So soon as the news of this national calamity reached Jamestown, Dale wrote to a friend in England, "My glorious master is gone that would have enameled with his favor the labors I undertake for God's cause, and his immortal honor. He was the great captain of our Israel, the hope to have builded up this heavenly new Jerusalem. He interred, I think the whole fabric of his business fell into his grave, for most men's forward (at least seemingly so) desires are quenched, and Virginia stands in desperate hazard."

Dale arrived at Point Comfort in May, 1611. He had sailed in command of a little fleet of three ships, which carried a general cargo and provisions sufficient to last the colonists during a period of twelve months. There were on board a large body of emigrants who intended to make their permanent home in Virginia. Sir Thomas Gates was expected to follow with six vessels spacious enough to transport three hundred men, one hundred head of kine, and a great quantity of diversified merchandise.

On leaving Jamestown to recover his health by a sea voyage, Delaware appointed George Percy to act as deputy governor until Dale, at the end of his long voyage, should make the land and disembark. The latter in turn was to yield to Gates, so soon as Gates should drop anchor in the river and come on shore. While Dale was stopping over at Point Comfort, he was at first depressed by the tales of poverty told him by the surviving settlers in that neighborhood, but afterwards, when he had had an opportunity to observe for himself, he concluded that the principal cause of this poverty was to be found in the colonists' disposition to shirk the planting of grain, in the hope that the supplies to come from oversea would in the long run afford them subsistence, however low the quantity in the magazine might sink from time to time. Perhaps the inefficiency of the upright Percy was the real secret of the prevailing want and discouragement. If so, this was not the first time that his infirm will and incapacity to govern men had brought the colony to the verge of starvation.

46

But a man of a very different temper had now stepped upon the ground. Dale's first act was to go over the lands lying close to Forts Henry and Charles at Kecoughtan, for the purpose of estimating their fertility; his next was to set the whole company then under his command to digging up the soil and planting it in maize. It is true that it was somewhat late in the season for seeding this invaluable crop, but a poor harvest was better than no harvest at all; and, moreover, the immature grain would furnish a nutritious and palatable supply of roasting ears. It is said that Dale did not withdraw his supervision until as wide an area had been put down in Indian corn by his men as had spread out before the colonists' hungry eyes the previous year when the savages had the same ground in similar tillage.

On disembarking at Jamestown, after his voyage up the river, Dale found the inhabitants of the forlorn village absorbed, not in cultivating their fields, but in playing a game of bowls in the street. He was told that this was the favorite and almost constant pastime of the settlers, for they, like the Englishmen at Point Comfort before his arrival, were trusting to supplies from England for their support, and not to the labor of their own hands. The new governor promptly broke up this idleness by assigning to each group of men a task which he thought particularly suitable for their physical strength. He set some to felling the heavy timber which grew in the environs of the town; some to repairing the houses which had fallen into decay; some to hewing posts and rails for the impalement of the new town which he had been ordered to build on the banks of the upper reaches of the river. The exact site had been left by the Council in England to his own independent choice, and thus it became necessary for him to enter upon a course of exploration and careful inspection.

Before Dale went aboard his vessel he received a message from Powhatan that was intended to frighten him, but which only served to excite his amusement: "Unless you release my people now in your hands," ran the message, "I will destroy every Englishman by making him drunk and then killing

47

him." Powhatan gave Dale an interval of five or six days within which to obey this arrogant command. Dale laughed when he received it and found diversion in returning an answer of an equally bombastic nature.

After a visit to Nansemond, which was marked by the double disadvantage of proximity to the Capes and a thick aboriginal population, Dale turned the prow of his vessel up the river towards the great falls. Like Newport a few years before, he was soon stopped in his westward progress by the presence of this long cataract in the stream. Although fertile, the lands in the vicinity offered few inducements for a permanent settlement, and Dale therefore dropped back down the river and anchored at Arrahattock. There was a wide sweep of land here which would have been surrounded on all sides by water but for a very narrow neck which united it with the east bank. Although pleased with the appearance of this half island and satisfied with its suitability for his purpose, Dale decided to wait until he had obtained Gates's approval of his choice.

While Dale and his men were engaged in hewing out a large quantity of pales, posts, and rails for the protection of the projected town, the information was brought by a messenger from Point Comfort that three large vessels, accompanied by what appeared to be three Spanish caravels, had been seen slowly making their way from Cape Henry to the mouth of James River. Knowing that his fortifications at Jamestown were too weak to resist a strong attack, Dale ordered his whole company to go at once on board his little fleet of two ships and a pinnace and to confront the foe on the water. His plan, as he afterwards revealed, was "rather to fire the Spanish ships with his own than either basely to yield or to be taken, assuring his men that, if, by these means, God had ordained to set a period to their lives, they could never be sacrificed in a more acceptable service." Such was the resolution of this gallant spirit! A reconnoitering shallop soon returned with the news that the fleet was not Spanish, but English, and that Gates was in command.

Gates arrived on the second day of August (1611) and

PLATE VII. *From the engraving by Brueckner. Photo Gramstorff.*

THE MARRIAGE OF POCAHONTAS;

SIR THOMAS DALE PRESIDING ON THE GOVERNOR'S THRONE

promptly gave his sanction to the site chosen for the proposed new town. Dale lingered until the first week in September before setting out for Arrahattock, but after he had begun to build there, he lost no time in pushing the construction of the town. By the order of the Council in England, he named it Henricopolis, in honor of the Prince of Wales. Before many days had passed, its site had been surrounded with a palisade. This site lay within a curve of the great river, which here flowed in the shape of a serpent's fold. In our own age the narrow neck has been severed by a deep canal, leaving the ground on which the town was founded a part of the western shore of the stream. The old bed of the river is now full only when the James is in flood. Dale was satisfied to raise a pale across this open neck to prevent hostile intrusion on that side, and at each corner of the palisade encircling the town further back he erected a tower to serve the purpose of a lookout. But his reliance for defense rested principally upon the occupants of five houses which had been built on the banks of the river. These men, however, did not confine their energies to the protection of the little community; they also worked in the ground in the character of tenants.

Dale's next step was closely in harmony with the nature of the man. He now built a church for public worship, an edifice that was a very simple framed structure at best, but a foundation was soon laid for a structure of brick. The parsonage was situated across the river on a glebe which had been surveyed for the Reverend Mr. Whitaker, the clergyman of the new parish. It was only after the erection of several storehouses that framed dwellings were built for the colonists. These were arranged in the form of three streets, and their convenience and comfortableness were attested by the satisfaction and contentment which they gave.

The site of Henricopolis was on ground higher and more open than the site of Jamestown. There were no extensive marshes in its neighborhood; the air, in consequence, was more salubrious; and yet, so soon as the settlement had spread to the other side of the river, Dale provided for

49

sickness by erecting there, at a place which he named Mt. Malado, the first hospital ever founded in English America; and he provided for the presence of regular nurses to administer to its patients' needs. The region in the vicinity of this public edifice was called by him Hope-in-Faith and Coxendale; and it was protected by five rude forts. On both sides of the river ample room was reserved, not only for the production of crops, but also for the pasturage of cattle and hogs.

Angered, no doubt, by this seizure of their immemorial lands, the Appomattox Indians furtively ambushed wandering parties of the intruders, and in retaliation Dale led a strongly armed force against their towns, destroyed these, and took possession of a large extent of their country. To this he gave the name of the New Bermudas. Widening this area by additions of both woodland and champaign, he divided the whole into five hundreds, the Upper, the Nether, Rochdale, West Shirley, and Digges. As his next step he built a palisade from one bank of the curving river to the other, about two miles in length, which enabled him to enclose an area large enough to be embraced within a boundary line of eight miles. Along this line many houses were soon erected, as the soil was highly suitable for the cultivation of maize. A cross pale, about four miles in length, shut out all hostile Indians from an area having a circuit of twenty miles; and here many hogs were turned loose to run wild.

It was apparently Dale's intention either to enlarge the size of Henricopolis as the permanent capital of Virginia, or to build a second town somewhere within the adjacent region which had been snatched from the Appomattox tribe. It is probable that he thought the site of Henricopolis, so near the banks of the river on three sides, too much exposed, for it is stated in the chronicle that his purpose in duplicating the town or substituting another for it was to "make a retreat against a foreign enemy." It is quite possible that in founding a town nearer to the falls than Jamestown, he had more than one object in view, namely, to acquire a more wholesome locality for a larger settlement, as well as to secure a site that could be more successfully defended in case of invasion from the sea. He had, it seems, no intention of abandoning Jamestown; but should it be attacked and captured, there would still be Henricopolis to reckon with at far more disadvantage to the enemy.

Apart from foreign assault there were two causes for uneasiness at work in Dale's mind. One had its origin in the constant prospect of Indian attack; the other, in a justifiable suspicion that disaffection was always smoldering in the hearts of a considerable section of the colonists themselves.

We have already related at length how Dale encouraged the union of Pocahontas and Rolfe in marriage, in the hope that it would bring about a lasting peace with the Indian tribes through Powhatan's more friendly attitude. Now there was one of these tribes which, as we have seen, occupied an independent position in the midst of that monarch's confederacy. This was the one seated on the Chickahominy. By treaty with Dale its members agreed to become King James's subjects, and they formally accepted Dale himself as their governor, without, however, giving up their own elders as their primary rulers or revoking their own code of domestic laws. They specifically bound themselves to carry off no cattle belonging to Jamestown nor to molest its people; and they consented to furnish three hundred warriors, should a conflict with the Spanish arise; they also agreed to contribute, at the end of each harvest, not less than two bushels of grain for every fighting man to be found in their towns. To show his appreciation of this promise of loyalty and service, Dale gave to each elder a red coat, a copper chain, and a picture of King James, and to the tribe as a whole a large quantity of hatchets and copper beads. He also bound himself to defend the tribe against any attack by Powhatan or the Monacans. It was really a burning fear of Powhatan which moved the Chickahominies to enter into this treaty at all. Whether they could have given substantial assistance in case of a Spanish invasion of the colony is highly debatable, as it was only in ambuscades that their coöperation would have been effective; and it was not likely that so shrewd a

107443 [51]

foe as the Spaniards would have pushed on into the forests after they had overcome the first resistance at Jamestown. Such a success as this would only have been accomplished, if at all, by broadsides from their ships anchored in the river. But an attack of this kind was always probable, and its shadow lowered without interruption over the little colony of Englishmen.

During Dale's administration a Spanish vessel actually hove to at Point Comfort and sent a boat and three emissaries to shore to ask the commander of the fort to furnish a pilot for the navigation of the neighboring waters. As soon as this pilot entered the boat, the crew plied their oars and left the wharf without even pretending to wait for the reappearance of the three messengers, who were still on land. The next day there was active but vain parleying between the captain of the fort and the captain of the ship for the mutual release of prisoners, and the vessel then sailed out to sea. The pilot was carried off and for a long time remained in custody in Spain.

Some days after the ship's departure, two of the strangers, now in jail, confessed themselves to be Spaniards; the other turned out to be an Englishman. This Englishman was afterwards convicted of having aided the Armada as a pilot in its descent on the English coast, and he was ultimately hanged for treason. All three from the beginning were suspected of playing the part of spies; and it was supposed that they had been dropped at Point Comfort to serve the Spanish King by observing and, later, reporting the conditions then prevailing in Virginia. Dale had promptly thrown them all into jail. The Spaniards endeavored to exculpate themselves by asserting that their commander had been groping hither and thither in ignorance of those seas and that he had had no intention whatever of attacking the colony. In fact, they said, he had expired early in the course of the voyage; but they acknowledged later that several Spanish vessels had been cruising together about those waters with the specific purpose of injuring, if not of destroying, the settlement at Jamestown. The impression created by this admission was

deepened by a conspiracy among some of the colonists themselves to seize a bark and sail away to the Atlantic under the
cover of darkness, but the plot was detected and frustrated,
and several of those who had taken part in it were executed.
One of the imprisoned Spaniards died, while the other, a
man of rank in his native country, continued to be held in
captivity until he was finally permitted to obtain passage
in an English ship, by which means he in the end was able
to reach Spain.

One of the most sagacious steps taken by Dale was to
create a system of tenantry, by which many carefully selected
persons acquired a definite interest in the soil. This system
was expected to stimulate industry in the colony and to encourage a feeling of contentment. It had been noticed that
when all the people were supported out of the common store,
there was a general disposition to shirk every one of the
tasks, however essential to the preservation of the people,
which were set them. And even when any work was done, it
was done in a spirit of languor and indifference. They could
look forward to no reward for their labors beyond a bare
subsistence. Why then should they put forth all their energies? After the tenant system had begun to operate fully,
three men, under the influence of the return which that system made certain, are said to have accomplished more with
their hands in one day than thirty men without such stimulus
did in the same length of time.

In carrying out the new policy, Dale assigned three acres
of cleared ground apiece to a large number of tenants, each
of whom was to deliver two and a half barrels of corn as
rent. This grain was to be contributed to the common store.
These tenants were to labor for the community as a whole
only one month in the course of the twelve, while all the
rest of the people were required to work eleven months of the
year for the community's benefit and were allowed only thirty
days in which to produce a subsistence for themselves, an impossible task had they not been granted a certain amount
of grain out of the public warehouse.

The Company believed that the time was not yet ripe for

a general subdivision of the soil in fee simple. This was to come a few years later when the colony's government had grown more firm in its organization and the population larger in size. There were cases of fee simple conveyance before Dale's departure. It is quite possible that, had the question of whether the soil should be universally apportioned to individual owners been left to him for decision, he would have adopted such a regulation from the beginning of his administration. But would it have been wise for him to do this? The Massacre of 1622 revealed the perils which surrounded the colonists so soon as they were dispersed over the surface of a large number of plantations.

Dale's reputation has suffered from his enforcement of the harsh and rigid laws which were introduced by Sir Thomas Gates in May, 1610, and approved by Delaware in June of the same year; but Dale's only part in connection with them was to broaden the scope of their application one year later. It seems that the military section of these laws had been used for the discipline of the English troops in the Low Countries. In reality, these laws were not severer in spirit than the laws for the punishment of crime in England, although they were perhaps less summarily executed there than in the beleaguered colony oversea, where prompter action would be needed if tranquillity was to be maintained at all. Gates and Delaware, two very enlightened rulers, had both thought that the remote situation of a new community like Virginia made necessary much sterner measures than an old community like England called for. Some of the regulations were known to be *in terrorem* only. Sir Thomas Smythe, the official head of the London Company, had not questioned their propriety; and this had also been the attitude of Parliament when these regulations were under discussion during one of the sessions of that body. Indeed, in after years it was admitted that the code of laws enforced by Dale had alone saved the colony, if not from actual dissolution, at least from temporary chaos. There were during his administration three small rebellions, led respectively by Webb, Price, and Abbott. Hamor, who was living in Virginia at the time, has recorded that these conspiracies were dangerous enough to disturb the equanimity of a "saint" by the "passionate impatience" which they would have excited in him. He asserted that Dale's course "was not so tyrannous, or severe by the halfe as there was occasion and just cause for it." These plots among the colonists themselves were really more threatening to the community's safety than the Indian assaults, as the latter could always be guarded against by the exercise of common prudence and foresight.

Dale's furlough, granted by the Government of the Netherlands, had by the spring of 1616 run out, and accompanied by Rolfe and Pocahontas, he sailed for England. One extension of his leave of absence had already been allowed by that Government at the personal solicitation of King James himself, who wrote that the colonists united in thinking that Dale's presence in Virginia was essential to the stability of the enterprise at that critical hour. In commenting on his stay at Jamestown, Dale afterwards said that it embraced "five years of the hardest labor that he ever undertook"; but he dwelt with satisfaction on the fact that he left the colony in a state of peace and prosperity far beyond the expectations of men. During his administration he had never allowed any detraction of Virginia in his presence to pass uncontradicted. In June, 1613, when despondency over the colony's prospects was widely prevalent in England, he wrote to friends there, "This one thing, and I pray remember it: if you give over this country and lose it, you with your wisdom will leap such a gudgeon as our state hath not done the like since we lost the kingdom of France. I protest now to you, by the faith of an honest man, the more I range this country, the more I admire it. I have seen the best countries in Europe. I protest unto you, before the living God, put them all together, this country will be equivalent unto them, if it be inhabited by good people."

The year after his return from Jamestown Dale applied for the command of the East India Company's fleet and was chosen to fill that responsible office. During the remainder of his life he displayed an unfailing interest in the colony and used every opportunity, whether arising in public or in private affairs, to advance its welfare by every means in his power.

He was a firm and gallant man, with a fund of kindness behind his stern exterior. This was shown by the fatherly attitude which he assumed towards Pocahontas. His whole conduct was colored by his religious convictions. While stationed at Henricopolis it was his habit to cross the river in a rowboat to visit the Reverend Mr. Whitaker in order to discuss with him the various dogmas of theology, as well as to devise plans for the moral improvement of the colonists. A tower of strength to all the people under his control, he was ceaselessly vigilant in their behalf and cheerfully granted them all the privileges which they could rightly claim, but he severely punished them when guilty of violations of the regulations which had been adopted for their safety.

Chapter V

SIR GEORGE YEARDLEY

Sɪʀ Gᴇᴏʀɢᴇ Yᴇᴀʀᴅʟᴇʏ resembled Captain John Smith in at least one fact of his life: his parentage was devoid of social distinction; but like Smith's also, it was entirely respectable. His father belonged to the trade of the London merchant tailors—one of the most important branches of business in the Kingdom—and therefore must have possessed sufficient means to bring his son up in an atmosphere of domestic refinement and to give him the advantages of at least a fair education. A certain plebeian shadow, nevertheless, fell on the junior Yeardley's career throughout its course, in consequence of his birth, and lingered about his memory after his death.

This is revealed by a scene which occurred as late as 1643 in the kitchen of Mr. Littleton, who resided on a plantation on the Eastern Shore. Thomas Parkes, probably an indentured laborer, and doubtless at the moment tipsy, had the impertinence, in the presence of the family servants, to sneer at Sir George's origin by remarking with a curled lip "that, in his youth, he did work upon a taylor's stall in Burchin Lane"; and this impudent fellow on another occasion repeated the same disparaging statement in a more picturesque form by asserting that Sir George "had leapt off a shop bench" in that part of the city of London.

To say that Sir George "leapt off" the tailor's seat at least proves that he was eager in his determination to abandon so uncongenial a trade. One of his nearest kinsmen followed the business of an apothecary, a most respectable calling but not one carrying much social repute in that age of rigid conventions as to the relative social importance of the pursuits in which men win a livelihood. In 1620, when the question of a successor to Yeardley in the governorship was under debate, a petition was sent to the Company in England praying that a "man of qualitye" should be chosen to be the next executive of the colony. This act would seem to indicate the existence of a certain restiveness among the principal citizens of Virginia under the administration of an official so lacking in ancestral distinction. But it is a fact of some humorous significance that the most conspicuous signer of this slightly querulous document was Francis West, who failed to extend to Yeardley's widow and Yeardley's estate that contempt which he apparently felt for Sir George himself in life, for West married the widow and enjoyed the estate as long as she lived.

Captain John Smith was almost to an equal degree the victim of the same preposterous stigma of caste on more than one occasion, in spite of his vigorous personality. The obstruction which he met with in asserting his authority over Captain West's company, stationed at the falls of the Powhatan, has been attributed to the difference in social rank between himself and that scion of a noble family in England; and during more than one interval Captain George Percy was appointed to high office in the colony seemingly on the strength of his great name alone; for although he possessed a fine character, he was also crippled by an infirm will. Captain Henry Spelman disparaged Yeardley to the treacherous Opechancanough by saying that it would not be long before "a greater man" than Sir George would arrive in the colony to serve as governor. This belittling remark was reported to the House of Burgesses, and Spelman was punished for it by being deprived of his office of interpreter.

Even as a young man Yeardley must have had a strong feeling of ambition, for although his father's lucrative trade was then open to him, he seems to have put aside its prospects without regret in order to follow the profession of

58

arms, the most honorable in that age, and the one offering the most numerous chances for personal advancement. How did he obtain the opportunity of joining the military forces in the Low Countries? Did he go there as a private in the ranks of an English troop or as a youthful officer whose commission had been purchased by his father or secured for him by some friend of influence enjoying a social position superior to his own? He must have revealed the possession of an unusual aptitude for his profession as well as high qualities as an individual, for in 1609 he received from Sir Thomas Gates, with whom he had been associated in military service, the very responsible office of captain of the company which was to go out with Gates to Virginia.

Pory, who was a cousin of Yeardley's future wife, tells us that Yeardley at this time had "besides a great deal of worth, only his sword to rely upon." But the two together were to carry him on to fortune. In the meanwhile, he was to pass through several vicissitudes which were to bring his life into serious jeopardy. On the voyage to Virginia, in the company of Gates and Somers, the vessel to which he had been assigned was blown out of its course and came to wreck on the coral shoals of the Bermudas. It was this disaster which is supposed to have suggested to Shakespeare the scenes of the *Tempest*. It was not long before the brave adventurers had built two frail vessels of the cedar trees abounding on the island, and by means of these little ships the company, which had been in such peril in reaching shore, made a very smooth and uneventful voyage to Virginia.

During the ensuing few years Yeardley filled several military posts in the colony that required unusual skill and vigilance. He seems to have been first raised to the command of the garrison occupying one of the forts at Kecough-tan; and at a later day, in association with Captain Brewster, he led the expedition which set out to explore the region west of the falls in the Powhatan, but which was prevented by conflicts with the Indians from pushing beyond that cataract. Six years afterwards he was in military charge of the settlement at Lower Bermuda Hundred, later to be known as

Charles Hundred, where there were seated about one hundred and nineteen persons, many of whom, under Dale's regulation, were employed in cultivating the ground as tenant-farmers.

The strength of the favorable impression which Yeardley had made on Dale's mind was revealed in his selection to serve as deputy-governor of the colony when the governor was about to return to England. Dale was a man of keen discernment and of an inflexible devotion to the public welfare, and in the mere act of choosing his lieutenant as his temporary successor, he paid a very exalted compliment to the ability and trustworthiness of that seasoned officer. In the interval of the one year during which Yeardley filled the position, he justified his appointment by the practical wisdom which he showed in every branch of his administration. This was particularly conspicuous in his constant encouragement of every form of agriculture, but still more in the unyielding firmness of his treatment of those Indians who failed to fulfill their agreements to make an annual contribution of maize to the public store at Jamestown. The Chicka-hominies, for instance, grew scornful in their refusal to carry out their contract. "You are only Dale's man," they sent him word contemptuously, when his messenger was about to return empty-handed to the deputy-governor. Yeardley's only reply was to start for their town with a band of one hundred picked soldiers. As this company approached the landing (for they went by boat), the savages on shore with insulting gestures defied them to disembark and fight hand-to-hand. Yeardley quietly ordered his men to get their guns ready, and at the word of command they fired a volley, bringing down twelve of their twenty opponents. Among the many prisoners who were taken on this occasion were two of the elders.

A long peace followed this decisive stroke, during which the Indians regularly and cheerfully supplied the people at Jamestown with all sorts of provisions and even served as hunters of wild game for numerous households.

Yeardley set out for England so soon as Argall arrived

to assume the duties of the governorship. But his absence from the colony was not to last very long. In November, 1618, hardly one year later, he was appointed by the Company to succeed the man who had so recently displaced him. This was even a greater tribute to his talents, fidelity, and experience than his elevation to the deputy-governorship by Dale, for his military rank was not high, and beyond the friendship and esteem of Dale and Delaware he could not have brought much influence to bear to raise his standing with his superiors in London. Indeed, he had been so long absent from England, whether in the Netherlands or Virginia, that there must have remained few partisans of his own to back his candidacy. As a matter of fact, Yeardley belonged to that type of manhood which wins its way in the active affairs of life, not by brilliant powers of mind or polished address, but by steadiness of purpose, unswerving integrity, the highest sense of duty, and absolute trustworthiness under all circumstances.

It is said that he disbursed as much as three thousand pounds sterling in England in preparation for the incumbency of the office of governor of Virginia. This was an enormous sum, a sum, indeed, equal to seventy-five thousand dollars in modern values. How did he acquire all that money, and if he did really possess it and spend it, how could such a sensible and prudent man indulge in this extravagance for the exploitation of a very small office in so remote a quarter of the world? On the day of his appointment to the governorship he received from the Company twenty shares of adventure for the transportation to Virginia of twenty-six persons, and six days later the King made him a knight.

At this time, James was at New Market. Philip Mainwaring, who was also present there, wrote to the Earl of Arundel that Mary Stuart's son "had a long discourse with Sir George about Virginia, in which he proved very understanding. He told the King that the people of that country [Indians] do believe in the resurrection of the body; and that when the body dies, the soul goes into pleasant fields [happy hunting grounds], there to solace itself until the

61

end of the world; and there the soul is to return to the body again; and they shall live together both happily and perpetually. Hereupon the King inferred that the gospel must have been, heretofore, known in that country, though it be lost and this fragment alone remain."

John Chamberlain, writing to Sir Dudley Carleton at the Hague, reported that the double honor of governorship and knighthood had set Yeardley so high that "he flaunted up and down the street in extraordinarily braverie, with fowerteen or fifteen fair liveries after him." But the object which he really had in view in this ostentatious display was not to exhibit his honors like a vain peacock, but to draw all Englishmen's attention to the increasing importance of the colony oversea.

Yeardley sailed for Virginia in January, 1619, and arrived at Jamestown about the end of the following April. His departure from the English shores was delayed by the appearance of a flaming comet in the heavens, for in the spirit of that superstitious age he thought that it would not be auspicious for his ship to face so sinister a portent when she sailed out into the wide ocean. On taking his seat of authority in Virginia he found the settlements there limited to the ones which had been established at Jamestown, Henricopolis, Charles City, Shirley Hundred, Arrahattock, Martin Brandon, Kecoughtan, Argall's Gift, Coxendale, and the Main. Only two church edifices were standing at this time—one of frame, situated at Jamestown, the other of brick, situated at Henricopolis. Only three ordained clergymen were present in the colony to perform the holy offices. The population did not embrace more than one thousand persons.

It was in this small, obscure, and remote community that Yeardley had been instructed to begin a series of radical political and industrial innovations which have survived in spirit to our own times, and which are destined in spirit also to last as long as free government itself shall last in the Western Hemisphere. First, he was empowered to release from public labor all those men still living in Virginia who had been living there previous to April, 1616. This was a step towards the complete emancipation of the people at large and their restoration to that individual liberty of action which they had inherited in reality as an English birthright. Before Dale's departure not even the tenant-farmers, in spite of the substantial privileges which had been granted to them, had been freemen altogether.

The second instruction to Yeardley was of even greater significance. He was to abrogate the harsh and rigid military regulations that had been adopted when dictatorial authority was necessary for the colony's preservation from domestic conspiracies and also from foreign perils. This was the second step required for the establishment of the spirit of English law in the community. The third instruction was of a still more impressive character. The proclamation which Yeardley issued soon after his arrival conferred upon the people of Virginia the right to be represented in a general assembly of their own, with authority to pass such acts as the public welfare, in their judgment, called for. Burgesses were to be chosen by ballot and apparently by unrestricted suffrage, from the several towns, hundreds, and plantations into which the colony was divided. These were to form a lower chamber, which was to complement an upper, composed of the governor and councilors.

This memorable Assembly embraced a membership of twenty in the lower house and about seven in the upper. It first convened on the ninth day of August, 1619. That touch of superstition in his nature which had held Yeardley back for several weeks before he would venture upon his voyage in the face of a comet did not prevent him from choosing so unlucky a day of the week as Friday for the inauguration of the Assembly's earliest session. The choir of the church at Jamestown was selected as the place of meeting. The initial proceeding was a prayer by the saintly Reverend Mr. Bucke, who had married John Rolfe to Pocahontas. The next was to elect John Pory to the speakership. Pory not only was a master of arts of Cambridge University, but had also been a member of Parliament, where he had had the opportunity to learn all the rules governing public bodies. The credentials of the burgesses were approved with two exceptions; the representatives of Ward's Plantation and Martin's Hundred were not permitted to take the oaths; the first only temporarily; the second, permanently, as he claimed that Martin's Hundred had been created with such privileges as gave it clearly the character of an independent community.

It may be stated in a broad way that the subjects which the Assembly debated related first to the charters, orders, and privileges embodied in the Company's formal grant; secondly, to the enactment into law of those instructions to the previous governors of the colony which were pertinent to present conditions; and thirdly, to the approval or disapproval of such proposals for the public welfare as the individual burgesses had submitted.

Among the important general regulations adopted was one which authorized the reservation of certain large areas of land in each of the four great corporations for the support of the several public offices, from the governorship down. Another granted one hundred acres in fee simple to every man who had come into Virginia at his own expense previous to April, 1616. If, however, he had entered at the Company's expense before that date, he was to receive one hundred acres, subject to an annual charge of two shillings. Every person who had been admitted to the colony after Dale's departure in 1616, having paid the costs of his own passage, was to be granted fifty acres conditional upon the same imposition. Ten thousand acres were set aside in the vicinity of Henricopolis for the support of a college and university. These projected seats of learning were in the first stage of permanent establishment when halted and broken up by the Massacre of 1622. One judicious regulation, in the light of this Massacre, was that no plantation should be separated from all other plantations by a distance wider than ten miles.

The numerous acts proposed by the different burgesses related to a remarkable variety of subjects, such as the

PLATE VIII. *Used by courtesy of Harper and Brothers. Photo Cook.*

THE FIRST VIRGINIA ASSEMBLY
SIR GEORGE YEARDLEY PRESIDING
JAMESTOWN, JULY 30, 1619 (old style)

treatment of the Indians; the rules that should govern trading with them; their education and religious conversion; the affairs of the church; the planting of corn and mulberry trees; the cultivation of English flax, aniseed, vines, and tobacco; the terms of land patents; the rights of landlords, artisans, tenants, and servants; the proper management of the magazine; and the suppression of idleness, gaming, drunkenness, and extravagance in apparel.

One of the most important laws adopted allowed the payment of rents and other obligations in the form of commodities, owing to the absolute dearth of coin. This simply meant that tobacco was to be from this time indefinitely the currency of the colony.

The land assigned for the support of the governor's office was situated at Paspaheigh, not far from Jamestown, the former seat of the subordinate tribe of that name. The Company had dispatched to Virginia, at its own expense, about one hundred laborers to till this land; and fifty of these had accompanied Yeardley in the voyage from London. In addition to this productive area of ground, he had been granted two hundred acres for two shares of adventure and two thousand for his personal services. This latter plantation was situated at Wyanoke on the Powhatan River. He had also acquired valuable land on the Eastern Shore, through the friendship of the Laughing King; and it was here that he probably spent some portion of his leisure in the interval between his first and second occupation of the office of governor.

Yeardley's proprietorship in the soil was perhaps further increased by his marriage to Temperance Flowerdew, whom he must have met for the first time during his sojourn in Virginia. She had reached the colony as a child in 1609. Her ancestor was John Flowerdew, so long and so actively associated with the concerted movement in the eastern counties of England in support of the cause of the Protestant Reformation, and whose family had during many generations been seated in the shire of Norfolk. A nephew of Temperance Flowerdew was Ensign Rossingham, who in 1619 sat in

65

the House of Burgesses as a representative of Flowerdew Hundred, which had acquired its name either from her or her father.

During his term of authority Yeardley and his family very probably passed most of their time on the land assigned to the governor's office, which was stocked with sixteen white servants and eight African slaves. The chief residence on this land was known as the Governor's Mansion. During Gates's administration, a dwelling house for the chief magistrate of the colony had been erected at Jamestown; and this building had been occupied by Gates himself and also by several of his successors. To make it more spacious and more convenient, it had from time to time been enlarged. It stood in a plat that contained an area of seven acres.

The Negro had been first imported into Virginia in 1619, the year in which patents to land in fee simple had become general in the colony. This right of absolute ownership increased the profits of tillage and therefore caused laborers to be more eagerly sought by persons engaged in extending the cultivation of the soil. It was only a question of a few years when the slave, so freely imported at that time into the Spanish West Indian settlements, would also be brought into Virginia, as the climate of that region was equally agreeable to the African frame. According to the *History of Captain John Smith*, the first slaves, twenty in number, were landed in the colony by a Dutch privateer which had been preying on the cargoes of Spanish vessels navigating the Gulf of Mexico and the adjacent seas. The *Treasurer*, a ship belonging in part to the Earl of Warwick, had arrived at an earlier date in the waters of Virginia with numerous Africans on board captured in Spanish bottoms; but her master had had such a cold reception from the authorities at Jamestown, in consequence of the fear of complications with the Spanish King, that he soon sailed away without disposing of his living booty.

The Africans landed by the Dutch man-of-war were regarded so askant, it was decided that the safest course to pursue with them—because they might turn out to be

Spanish property after all—was to place them on the plantation of Governor Yeardley.

A more interesting addition to the population made at this time consisted of the first batches of maids sent over, at the Company's expense, to become the wives of the farmers attached to the public lands. So soon as these young women disembarked, they were assigned to the protection of respectable families, until each should choose a husband without the slightest compulsion to direct her action. These maids had been picked out with scrupulous care from among those living in the several English parishes who were willing to emigrate to Virginia. Perhaps a larger degree of romance has been woven about the figures of these adventurous young women than they are entitled to. Beyond the brave spirit which they showed in committing themselves to the ocean— although this, too, was done in congenial companies—there was little to make their situation different from that of hundreds of other single women who went out at the expense of their friends in England, only to find in a short time after their arrival in the colony that they could not resist the pleadings of unanticipated suitors. An unmarried woman in that community, where unmarried men predominated in number, was more quickly snapped up than even a laborer seeking employment.

There was thoughtful provision during Yeardley's administration for the protection of persons who had just arrived in Virginia. An order was issued from Jamestown that a guest house should be erected within the limits of each of the four great corporations. These structures were to be, respectively, sixteen feet broad and one hundred and eighty feet long, and to possess twenty-five beds. Two milch cows were to be attached to each guest house. It was expected that the newcomer would remain long enough in some one of these inns to pass successfully through the period of seasoning, for it was during this period that the mortality among the new colonists was always so appalling. In 1621 about one thousand persons in a total of nineteen hundred who had sailed from England had died before the coast of

67

Virginia was even sighted; and of those who actually set foot on shore there during that year, eighty of every ninety soon perished in consequence of diseases contracted at sea or resulting from a change in climate and diet in Virginia.

It was during Yeardley's administration that the Pilgrim Fathers disembarked on the famous rock. Before sailing, they had obtained a patent to lands from the London Company, as it was their intention to make settlement, not in north, but in south, Virginia; but when they found themselves either purposely or accidentally in the waters of New England, they perceived that their charter, with its special powers and privileges, was unsuitable to the jurisdiction of the Plymouth Company. This led them to draft the Mayflower Compact, which has been held up as an original contribution to constitutional government, but which was simply a rehash of the charters and the like documents of the Jamestown colony, under which alone they had been empowered to set up a community in the Western Hemisphere.

In consequence of Yeardley's personal knowledge of the needs of the Virginia colonists, especially on the side of their industrial and political interests, and in consequence also of his firm way of carrying out his plans for the public welfare, every section of the inhabitants was by the end of his term in the enjoyment of great prosperity. There were now about two thousand people in Virginia; and so plentiful in their homes were all kinds of food, it was said at the time "that every man gave free entertainment to both friends and strangers." The food consisted of vegetables—peas, beans, turnips, radishes, parsley, onions, potatoes, thyme, hyssop, savory, lettuce, cabbages, cauliflower, pumpkins, and carrots; of grain in the form of either maize meal or wheat flour; of meat—deer, bear, pig, and ox; of poultry—chickens, tame or wild ducks, geese, and turkeys. Yeardley himself was the owner of twenty-four head of cattle, each valued, it was said, at fifteen pounds sterling. He provided the people with a cheap means of grinding their grain by erecting a mill which was driven by force of the wind. This was the first one of that character built on our continent. He was also assiduous in increasing the supply of salt by its manufacture from sea water.

Yeardley's term as governor expired on the eighteenth of November, 1621, and during the long interval ending in May, 1626, he served as a member of the Council at Jamestown. During Governor Wyatt's absence from the colony in 1624, he filled by appointment the post of deputy executive; and two years afterwards he received his formal credentials as Governor of Virginia for the second time. In the meanwhile, he had carried out successfully several important military and political missions. For instance, in retaliation for their part in the terrible Massacre of 1622, he attacked the Indians in several places, killed many of them, burnt their towns, and destroyed their growing crops. In 1625 he was authorized by the colony to visit England to enter a protest against the adoption of the proposed royal tobacco contract; and he accomplished this purpose, as well as procured for the people of Virginia a needed supply of shot, powder, clothes, and wine.

It is plain that Yeardley was a shrewd man of business who let no legitimate chance pass without increasing his fortune, a large one for that day and community. His estate was reported at his death to amount to six thousand pounds sterling, which was equivalent to one hundred and fifty thousand dollars in modern value. It was asserted by Pory that this figure was exaggerated, but even at a smaller computation the estate was of very respectable proportions. It had been built up by planting and trading. To his wife he bequeathed all his plate, linen, and household articles, while the remainder of his property was divided into three parts, which were devised: one to his wife, one to his son Argall, and one in equal shares to his son Francis and his daughter Elizabeth. Argall and Francis became useful citizens.

Yeardley was buried at Jamestown. Some years ago the site of the church edifice there, which had been erected early in the seventeenth century, was cleared away and among the relics brought to light was a tomb bearing traces of inlaid brasses, such as are still to be seen in some of the oldest parish houses of worship in England. The figure disclosed represented a knight wearing a pointed helmet and having a scroll flowing from the mouth. Under the tomb was found a skeleton of a man, with spurs lying in the dust near the heels, and with fragments of gold lace still clinging to the shoulder bones. It has been supposed that this was the grave and these the remains of the celebrated Governor, who was the instrument under God for the calling together of the first English legislative assembly to convene in the Western Hemisphere, an event of lasting importance in the history of the Anglo-Saxon race.

Chapter VI

SIR WILLIAM BERKELEY

SIR WILLIAM BERKELEY was sprung from one of the oldest and most celebrated families in the English peerage. Its seat, Berkeley Castle, was among the noblest models of feudal architecture to be found in the Kingdom. The political influence of the Berkeleys, derived from the enjoyment of a famous lineage and great wealth through a long period, had descended undiminished far into the seventeenth century. Sir William's brother was a member of the Privy Council, a position of supreme importance in the age of royal domination; and Sir William himself was, before he went out to Virginia, a member of the Royal Privy Chamber, an office that required him to spend most of his hours under the roof of Whitehall in close attendance upon the King. It was this intimacy with the Court at a very susceptible period of his life which perhaps first imbued him with such extravagant reverence for the occupant of the throne and inspired him with such preposterous notions of his duties as a subject, both of which, as we shall perceive, governed his action in all the critical political events he was afterwards to experience oversea.

But Berkeley was not simply an aristocrat and a courtier who was fully capable of assuming at will all the conciliatory graces of one long accustomed to the most polite society of his age. He was also a scholar of elegant attainments. In 1629 he had won the diploma of master of arts at Merton College, Oxford; and ten years afterwards—having in the interval gained political reputation as a commissioner for

Canadian affairs—he burst upon the town as the author of a successful tragedy. Handsome in person and polished in manner, he was in temper often impulsive and headstrong; in spirit, always masterful, and sometimes domineering, should his passions be aroused; courageous to recklessness; and on the smallest provocation ready to uphold his honor with the sword at his side.

Why did an accomplished man of the world like Berkeley seek the office of governor of Virginia? That colony was situated in one of the remotest parts of the globe in that age. In 1642, the date of his appointment, it was simply a vast primeval forest, only here and there broken by groups of plantations. The members of the educated class were too few in number for the social and intellectual advantages of the region as a whole to have any importance. Jamestown, the center of such refinement as existed, was merely a straggling hamlet. How was Berkeley able to make up his mind to abandon the excitements of Whitehall and the diversions of London at large, for which he was fitted by sprightly wit and charming culture, and to cross a tumultuous ocean in order to assume the reins of government over a small obscure population occupying a few widely dispersed communities? It is true that at least two of his successors, Culpeper and Howard, were in full possession of as high a social position as his own. Culpeper was also a man about town, with a taste as whetted as Berkeley's for all its pleasures and amusements.

But it was clearly known to all that both Culpeper and Howard had sought the office of governor simply to feather their nests by the unscrupulous use of the opportunities for acquiring money which it offered and which would enable them after their return to England to live in ease, if not in luxury. Apparently, Berkeley was entirely free from such sordid motives. He reached Jamestown a man of modest resources; he left it with a fortune only moderately increased. His stay in Virginia lasted nearly thirty-five years, and he was absent from it on but two occasions, and then only because the colony's affairs required him to visit England. No doubt the civil commotions in his native country had some influence in keeping him so continuously in Virginia; but after the Restoration, when he could have given up his post and retired to London to receive the reward of his inflexible loyalty during those years of the monarchy's eclipse, his devotion to the colony, however perverted in spirit during Bacon's rebellion, remained as strong as during any part of his career.

Throughout the early years of his residence in Virginia his conduct was marked by sagacity and discretion. It was only during his second incumbency of his high office, which followed the fall of the Commonwealth in England, that the native infirmities of his character and the bad effects of his training in an arrogant and bigoted school, revealed themselves. His course then was often not only indefensible from a political point of view, but also unpardonable from a personal.

Berkeley's conduct in 1642, when he assumed the reins of government at Jamestown, was wisely conciliatory. He appointed to seats in his Council several influential men who had been instrumental in deposing Harvey a few years before; he combatted, in harmony with public sentiment, the vigorous attempt of the Old London Company to recover its former overlordship of the colony; and he made no objection to the grant to the General Assembly of a right of appeal from the decisions of the general court, over which he himself presided.

The burgesses showed their appreciation of this tactful spirit by several valuable gifts. One of these was a tax for his benefit placed on every tithable in Virginia, to be paid, not in the normal form of tobacco, but in provisions of different kinds, such as geese, turkeys, hens, capons, beeves, goats, and pigs. The surroundings of the popular Governor's official mansion must have resembled the stalls of a modern livestock fair. There were so many heads of poultry, so many hooves of animals. Where could they have been penned or housed? At a later period he was the beneficiary of seven hundred pounds sterling appropriated by the Assembly from the fund annually accumulated from the tax of two shillings imposed by law on each exported hogshead of tobacco. He also received the castle duties by the vote of the same body.

At every stage of his official career Berkeley was always active in increasing the prosperity of agriculture, not only by advocating and ensuring the passage of laws that would diversify the products of the soil, but by setting on his own lands the right example in methods of tillage and in variation of crops. He expended not less than one thousand pounds sterling, a very large sum in those times, on experiments in flax culture. He planted cotton and sowed rice, and he was so successful with the latter grain that from every bushel of seed scattered by hand over his fields he harvested fifteen bushels. His orchard at Green Spring near Jamestown contained fifteen hundred apple, peach, apricot, quince, and other fruit trees. During one year he laid aside from the large quantity of silk which his worms produced three hundred pounds of the best quality as a present for the King; but he was prevented from shipping it by fear of its capture by a hostile fleet which appeared suddenly just then off the coast. At one time he supplied the members of his own household and his slaves with all the woolen clothes which they needed, from the shuttles of his own looms.

Berkeley's residence at Green Spring was one of the most solid and comfortable in Virginia. It was erected on part of the ground which had formerly been assigned for the support of the office of governor, but which in 1643 had been granted to him in fee simple by the General Assembly. It was partitioned into six spacious rooms, with a central hall ten feet in width running from the main entrance of the house to the back. The structure was built of brick, with two extensive wings and a general frontage of forty-eight feet. Each fireplace was four feet in width and three feet eight inches in depth. It was in this commodious mansion that Berkeley entertained his personal friends and the public men of the colony; and there is no reason to doubt that under his own roof, in this remote and still almost primeval spot, he displayed all the grace of bearing and all the urbanity of speech which distinguished him so preëminently when his object was to conciliate and to please.

Highly accomplished socially and deeply cultured intellectually as Berkeley was, he either felt or pretended to feel an aversion to general education which carried him far beyond the restraints of common sense. "Learning," he asserted in a memorable report, which, if sincere, reflected little credit on his liberality of opinion or discernment of view, "has brought disobedience and heresy and sects into the world." And then he added, in an outburst wholly unworthy of a native of that island which had established so many noble free foundations, "I thank God that there are no free schools in Virginia." This foolish sentiment was all the more preposterous as coming from a man who, at the moment he penned it, stood in less than a day's journey of at least one county in which two free schools, the Symmes and the Eaton, were in active and beneficent operation through their possession and expenditure of highly profitable endowment funds. Berkeley's object in making such a groundless statement was perhaps simply to impress the English authorities with his extreme loyalty to the Church and the Throne. It seems the more remarkable when it is recalled that only a few years before he had been deeply interested in the proposal to establish a seat of learning in the colony which was to partake of the united character of a free school and a college.

It would be unjust to Berkeley to condemn him as exceptional in the harshness of his treatment of the Quakers and Puritans, for this was the spirit of everyone in office in that age. There can be no question, however, that he pushed the laws then in force against these two sects to the verge of inhumanity. One of these laws, which was only a shade more heartless than the rest, condemned every female Quaker preacher to the whipping post, and a second suppressed all Quaker conventicles. There is at least no record of any Quaker's having been executed in Virginia for his faith. The only excuse that could be offered for this policy of oppression was that these peculiar people boldly refused to take up arms in the colony's defense and that they were in the habit of meeting secretly, which seemed to wink at conspiracy.

Berkeley perhaps detested the Puritans as acutely as he did the Quakers, but they do not appear to have suffered so conspicuously by his persecutions. A large body of persons of this sect were able to escape his clutches by emigrating to Maryland.

With all this incredible bigotry, Berkeley was at bottom a man of an uncommonly enterprising public spirit; nor could his zeal under that influence be cooled by personal danger. Sixty years after Newport's march toward the springs of James River west of the falls, Berkeley persuaded two hundred gentlemen of the colony to promise to accompany him in an expedition towards the wild region lying back of the mountains, where it was supposed the waters of the South Sea were plainly visible in the distance. The scheme came to nothing that year because continuous heavy rains set in which flooded the streams and made them impassable for man or horse. In the following year a party which had pushed its way through the forests in the same direction reported on its return that the intervening country offered almost insurmountable obstructions to successful exploration. This threw a damper upon the revival of the project which Berkeley had had in mind. It seemed to confirm the impression which prevailed in those times that it would be unsafe to press westward for a period longer than thirty days.

But the barriers of a boundless wilderness and the possible presence in every copse of an implacable foe with deadly weapons in his hands did not discourage Berkeley from taking command of the inflamed troops who had run together on the south side of the James in 1644, determined to avenge the slaughter of the settlers on this remote frontier which had occurred in the course of that year. This massacre, like that of 1622, had been chiefly instigated by Opechancanough, now very old in years, but animated by the same spirit of ferocity as had nerved his breast while he was lead-

76

ing his warriors against the Englishmen twenty-two years before. Berkeley pursued the murderous savages into the dark swamps and pine forests and succeeded in capturing Opechancanough himself, who was soon killed by a shot in the back from the musket of his exasperated guard. His successor, wisely accepting the verdict of defeat, made peace with the English and agreed to give them a full title to all the lands lying between the York and James rivers, as far as the falls in the latter stream. He also bound himself to pay an annual tribute of beaver skins as a proof of his fidelity to his promise. This promise he kept during the whole of the thirty years which followed.

But it was the Dutch War of 1665 that brought out in the most conspicuous way Berkeley's qualities of courage and energy. So soon as the first news of hostilities arrived at Jamestown from England, he ordered every man of military age to fly to arms in order to reinforce on land the large band of sailors who were then holding the merchant vessels in the rivers in readiness to resist an attack by the enemy. Altogether about fifteen hundred dragoons and twenty-five hundred footmen were called to the colors in this crisis. But it turned out that their services were not needed at that time. In the spring of the ensuing year the danger of invasion by the same foe was so menacing that Berkeley concentrated into a single fleet the twenty-six merchant ships which were then anchored in alarm in Virginian waters; and he appointed an admiral, vice admiral, and a river admiral to direct the movements of their captains.

Apparently twelve months more passed before the Dutchmen really sailed into the Bay. Their first act was to prepare fireships and their second to advance with these up the James River to where the fleet of merchantmen was lying under the shelter of the guns of an English man-of-war. This vessel was quickly set on fire by a broadside from the Dutch cannon. Pursuit then began of the retreating merchantmen, and in a short time six of them were wrapt in flames and were a complete loss.

Berkeley had not been informed of the urgent need of

assistance for these vessels, but when news of the disaster to them reached his ears, he dispatched Thomas Ludwell to York River to marshal all the English vessels there into one fleet. He quickly followed. On joining Ludwell he found that the captains of the vessels had objected to taking an aggressive step in defense of their crews and cargoes. Berkeley vigorously and angrily remonstrated with them, but it was not until he had promised to indemnify every commander whose ship should be captured or destroyed that he succeeded in persuading them to unite in resistance. Every sailor who should lose a limb, in case of a battle, was to be handsomely compensated therefor; and the booty to to be seized from the Dutch was to be divided among the men of the vessels which should take part in the fighting. Four regiments of foot had been summoned from the ranks of the militia to support the sailors. Nine merchantmen were picked out as those best equipped for a naval battle.

When Berkeley went on board the flag ship, he was accompanied by several members of the Council as well as by a band of forty planters drawn from among the foremost gentlemen in the colony. But the officers of the merchantmen, unlike Berkeley, had no stomach for battle, and one captain after another gave a thin excuse for his dilatoriness in moving forward to attack the enemy. In his uncontrollable impatience, Berkeley stormed at them for their pusillanimity; but before they could be shamed into activity, the Dutch men-of-war withdrew to sea, carrying thirteen prizes in tow, after destroying about seven which they were compelled to leave behind.

The course of the great civil war in England was anxiously followed by Berkeley and the loyal population of Virginia; nor did the repeated defeats of the royal armies weaken the passionate strength of their devotion to the Throne. By an act passed as early as 1642, no one who spoke in disparaging language of the King and the Queen was to be permitted to remain in the colony. Jealous as the General Assembly was of its rights, no exception was taken by that body to Berkeley's impressment of soldiers by his own warrant, be-

78

PLATE IX. *From the copy of the portrait by Lely originally at Greenspring, and later at Stratford, having been transmitted by inheritance from the Ludwells to the Lees. Photo Cook.*

SIR WILLIAM BERKELEY

cause they knew that his only object was to put the country in a posture of defense in case of Parliamentary invasion. When Charles was executed, the councilors and burgesses alike stigmatized the act as "murder"; and whoever defended it was arrested as an accessory to the "crime." All persons questioning Charles the Second's right to the throne after his father's death were denounced as "traitors."

Berkeley's influence was unweariedly used to confirm this popular feeling of indignation and horror. He expressed with characteristic violence his detestation of the Roundheads and his devotion to the person of the new sovereign.

In hearty sympathy with this attitude was the large body of Cavalier officers who had sought refuge in the colony after the collapse of their cause in England. Their social refinement, their elegant accomplishments, their training to arms by actual experience in the field, and their loyalty to the King, however disastrous the consequence to themselves, had very naturally given unusual weight to their convictions in the plantation homes. Some of these officers were persons of rank in English society, and all were sprung from the English gentle classes. They brought with them to the colony the tastes, the habits, and the spirit of the high sphere in which they had moved in their native country. Lunsford, Honeyman, Skipwith, Norwood, Stevens, Mason, Molesworth, Brodnax, Fowke, and others of the same Cavalier origin must have found in Virginia a very attractive substitute, from many alluring points of view, for the land in which they were born and on the soil of which they had been so recently fighting for King and Church. "There was the same disposition to enjoy to the utmost all the means of pleasure and happiness which life afforded; the same appetite for good cheer; the same taste for dancing, card playing, and other amusements around the hearth; the same interest in horse, dog, and gun, and in racing, coursing, and shooting. These gentlemen of high social position in England, these soldiers who bore in their persons the scars which proved the firmness of their courage and the strength of their sovereign, must, under the roofs of the principal planters,

SIR WILLIAM BERKELEY

have possessed an extraordinary distinction on account both of what they had suffered and of what they had represented socially and politically in the beloved motherland oversea."[1]

The numerical weakness of the Puritans in the colony and the overpowering influence of Berkeley and the Cavaliers, as the representatives of the loyal element in its population, were revealed in the fact that even after all opposition to Parliament had been overcome in England, there was no uprising in Virginia in sympathy with the successful party which Cromwell led at home. As a body, the small planters appear to have felt and acted politically as the great planters had done.

Parliament did not accept at once the gage which Berkeley and the General Assembly had so boldly thrown at its feet. The policy of blockade adopted by it was expected to be more effective than an army of seasoned soldiers. If no vessel should be able either to enter or to leave the mouth of the Chesapeake, how could the Virginians either sell their tobacco or purchase their supplies? But the proposed screw turned out to be unworkable, just as Berkeley had anticipated. Dutch ships passed in and out without hindrance from any English man-of-war, for vessels of that character at this time were too busy with patrolling and safeguarding the English coasts to turn their attention to putting a padlock on the waters of Virginia. The English merchants in time had to admit this fact. They then clamored for the dispatch to Jamestown of commissioners and an armed force to compel the surrender of the colony, and to this demand the English Government ultimately acceded.

In the meanwhile, Berkeley had been feverishly engaged in drilling the militia, and when the English fleet sailed within the Capes, the whole community of plantations was in a formidable state of defense. Whatever sympathy existed there with the commissioners' instructions did not dare to show itself in open acts. Berkeley promptly summoned the organized troops to his assistance, and he was not satisfied

[1] P. A. Bruce, *Social Life of Virginia in the Seventeenth Century* (Richmond, 1907), p. 80.

80

simply with erecting batteries on the banks of the James and loading the cannon, but he also impressed several Dutch ships anchored in the stream and ordered their heavy guns to be turned in the direction from which the fleet of the Commonwealth was approaching. No doubt he was fully aware in his own breast that resistance would in the end fail completely, but he was shrewd enough to perceive that it might secure more favorable terms of surrender than prompt submission would do; and in this conviction he proved to be right, for the agreement into which he entered with the commissioners was more like a treaty between two belligerents of equal power than between a great kingdom and a more or less feeble colony.

Virginia was to be granted all the privileges of free trade. The General Assembly alone was to possess the right to tax the people; and without its consent no fortifications were to be erected. Punishment was not to be inflicted upon those who had opposed Parliament, and everyone who wished it was to be at liberty to leave Virginia before the end of twelve months. Berkeley came within the scope of this provision, and he so far took advantage of it that he remained quietly and discreetly at Green Spring throughout the period of the Commonwealth. It was probably a small sop to his Anglican ardor that the churches of the colony were permitted to continue the use of the prayer book for at least one year.

Twelve months after Richard Cromwell's resignation as Protector, Berkeley was by a vote of the House of Burgesses reinstated in the governorship of the colony, an indication that they were anticipating the restoration of the monarchy without, however, declaring openly for it. Indeed, Berkeley was discreetly instructed to give in his allegiance to whatever power should finally obtain control in England. In 1650 Richard Lee, who had visited Holland, had brought back commissions for Berkeley and the members of Council to continue in their offices—Charles had recently succeeded his beheaded father—and these commissions were renewed the second time and with a better prospect of permanence in

1660, when the new king arrived in London to take possession of the throne.

In consequence of this act of royal favor, Berkeley now indulged to a very extravagant degree the preposterous spirit of loyalty which had governed all his actions both personal and political. "I throw myself," he wrote, "at the feet of my sovereign, in my thankfulness that I am still considered to be worthy of the honor of occupying a seat at the royal board. Did his majesty think that his servant had been guilty of weakness in taking office from the assembly? It could only be called a weakness. It was no more than a leap over the fold to save his majesty's flock when his majesty's enemies in that fold had barred up the lawful entrance in order to shut in the wolves of rebellion, who were ready to devour all within it."

It is easy to imagine the grim sense of amusement with which Charles, surrounded by so many courtiers who had formerly fawned on Cromwell, read these words of abject loyalty; but Berkeley at least was sincere in offering them, as had been demonstrated by his previous career.

Hardly had he been restored to his former office when there began to sprout in the Virginians' minds seeds of discontent which continued to grow in strength and number down to the explosion in 1676. In 1660 the second Act of Navigation, the more drastic and exclusive of the two, was adopted. The English Government had always resented the sale of Virginian tobacco to the Dutch, as it was unwilling that the English merchants should divide the trade even to a moderate degree with the merchants of that nation. The exportation of so much of this commodity in Dutch bottoms was also a cause of loss in freight to English shipowners; and the importation of Dutch goods in the same bottoms further reduced the English merchants' profits from the trade with the colony.

The welfare of Virginia called for a competitive market for the sale of its exports and also for a competitive market for the purchase of its imports. It was impossible for England to absorb the whole of the annual tobacco crops of the two colonies on the Chesapeake. The inferior grades had hitherto been disposed of in Holland, where they could be sold at a much greater price than they could be in London, because the Dutch freight rates and also the Dutch customs were lower than the English. The Navigation Acts threw back on the hands of the Virginian planter a large surplus of this kind, which, without the existence of those Acts, could readily have been marketed in the Low Countries, while for the best grades a rate of three pence the pound could be obtained in those provinces, as compared with half a penny in England.

During his visit to London after the Restoration, Berkeley boldly condemned the Acts as destructive of Virginia's prosperity. "If this was for his majesty's service," he said, "we should not repine, whatever our sufferings. But, on my soul, it is contrary to both."

There was really but one remedy for the unhappy condition of the colony. This was the general cessation of tobacco culture by royal order, to last until the price of the commodity should rise. A petition of the planters for a royal proclamation to that effect was at first rejected on the ground that the English Government could not give up the customs on tobacco without increasing the heavy taxation already prevailing in the Kingdom. The people of Virginia were so disappointed by the failure of the negotiations with Maryland for a cessation—which had finally been reluctantly allowed by the English authorities, should the people of that colony be willing to coöperate—that Berkeley was very apprehensive lest they should rise in rebellion. "Should a foreign war break out," he wrote to the Privy Council, "I am convinced that the great body of the Virginians, made desperate by the galling burden of debt, which has been heaped on their backs by the low prices of tobacco, could not be relied on to remain loyal to their English allegiance."

A second cause of popular discontent was the royal gift of the Northern Neck to Lord Hopton and his associates, and of the entire colony of Virginia for thirty-one years to Lords Culpeper and Arlington, two favorites at Court. The

Hopton grant diminished the patent revenues of the colonial treasury and clouded the titles of all the existing landowners in that region of country. The second grant, being broader in the rights and privileges which it bestowed, was still more obnoxious. So great was the bitterness which it aroused that the people consented to a special tax toward the fund needed for sending commissioners to England to petition for its revocation, which in the end was allowed.

The discontent excited by these two callous royal gifts was increased by a royal order to the General Assembly to build towns and establish ports in all the divisions of the colony. Every economic influence at work in every part was antagonistic to the success of such a measure. The economic system of Virginia derived its character from the fact that its inhabitants were widely dispersed. There was no disposition among them to reside even in villages. Each planter spent his life on his own estate. The only town which had flourished at all had done so because it was the capital of the colony; and even this was simply a straggling hamlet chiefly of inns and public buildings. The brick houses which were ordered to be erected there under instructions from England gradually fell into decay without having been sufficiently completed for occupancy by either owners or tenants.

The effort to lay off ports on the banks of the principal rivers was in the end equally abortive. The navigable streams were so numerous that every landowner was able to ship his annual crop of tobacco from his own wharf without having to incur the expense and the inconvenience of sending it by shallop—for ultimate transshipment to England—to some port which perhaps might be situated a day's voyage away.

A royal order for the erection of fortifications on the banks of the large streams was equally unpopular, not on account of the inconveniences which they would cause, but on account of the expense of building them. Five forts were actually constructed—one, respectively, on the James, Nansemond, York, Rappahannock, and the Potomac; but by 1672 all were said to have lost any power of resisting the enemy which they might have possessed when they were new.

SPROUTING SEEDS OF DISCONTENT

But perhaps the most serious cause of popular discontent as time went on was the reactionary course which Berkeley adopted after the Restoration. This was not simply a more relentless prosecution of the Puritans and Quakers, for whom, in reality, the bulk of the Virginians had as little toleration as their Governor. The main reason for the dissatisfaction was political. Between 1660 and 1676 there were apparently only two elections for the House of Burgesses—probably only one, and this in 1661. Had not the popular uprising occurred in 1676, there is reason to think that no dissolution of the Assembly, except for vacations, would have taken place until Berkeley had returned to England or died in the colony.

Vestrymen, justices of the county courts, sheriffs, and all other public functionaries were under his thumb. And as there was no longer any elections for burgesses, he had no cause to anticipate an expression of opposition by an adverse vote. His will controlled the members of his Council, since they had been appointed to office by him, and only through his good will could they expect further honors and profits; and this good will was won only by a spirit of obedience to his wishes. The people at large had little, if any, share in their local government, and none at all in the central government at Jamestown; nor had they any voice in making up either the local or the central tax levies.

In 1674 there was a small mutiny which was suppressed without loss of life; and there was also a lurking fear of an uprising when the Dutch invaded the waters of Virginia. It was the existence of these various reasons for discontent which prepared the fuel for the great conflagration of Bacon's rebellion; but it was an Indian incursion that set the match to these materials lying so ready for combustion. Almost from the hour of the first outburst, the career of Berkeley merged in the career of Bacon, and the two can from this time on be presented as a unity.

Chapter VII

NATHANIEL BACON, THE REBEL

THE REBELLION of 1676 began, not in the bosom of the colony, but at one of its extremities. It had its original impulse in an Indian incursion from the north and afterwards spread from the falls of the Powhatan, on the border of the Wilderness, all the way down to the sea. The Eastern Shore, protected by the barrier of the Chesapeake from Indian raids, alone escaped the contagion of the tumult. A party of Susquehannocks and Doegs, having stealthily crossed the Potomac in their canoes, waylaid and drove off the hogs of a planter whose home was situated on the south bank. They were quickly pursued and dispersed.

Retaliation soon followed. A band of warriors from the same tribes paddled over the river at night, tomahawked two men who were working on the plantation where the hogs had been stolen, and then fled into the coverts of the surrounding woods. A hue and cry was at once raised in the nearest settlements, and a company of seasoned frontiersmen, under Colonels Mason and Brent, hastened on the trail of the marauders, soon overtook them, and whilst one squadron of the rangers assaulted the rendezvous of the Doegs, shooting the chief and ten of his warriors, and scattering the rest like a covey of partridges, the other squadron rushed upon the camp of the Susquehannocks and slew fourteen of its defenders.

But the Indians were not intimidated by these defeats. Expecting an assault in force, they erected a fort on the north side of the Potomac in the midst of a densely wooded swamp. Here they were besieged by a large body of militia, supported by Indian scouts, who were burning with hatred of their hereditary foes. Seven weeks passed before the savages in the fort could be driven out. After killing fifty of the besiegers and most of their horses, the defenders, seeing that their situation was now desperate, stole away with their wives and children and all their portable articles under the blanket of night. They, too, had suffered very heavy losses, but their spirit had not been at all broken. In January, 1676, during a very icy spell of weather, the Susquehannocks again crossed the Potomac near the English frontier, scalped many persons on the plantations there, and continued to tomahawk as they crept through the woods southward to the banks of the Rappahannock; nor did they retreat until at least thirty people had been murdered by their weapons.

News of these outrages spread like a prairie fire over the colony. Sir Henry Chicheley, with a strong force of horsemen and footmen, was commissioned by Berkeley to go in pursuit; but before the troops could finish their preparations, they were peremptorily ordered by the Governor to disband and return to their homes. The excuse which he gave for this vacillating action was that the General Assembly alone was authorized to declare so formidable a war. Until this body should convene—which would not be until after a considerable interval of time had passed—the outlying plantations were to be left entirely unprotected. Soon a flight of the inhabitants towards the interior settlements began, but before they could reach a point of safety three hundred are said to have perished from physical hardships and Indian strokes combined.

When the Assembly met in the spring, the only remedy for these bloody conditions which they were willing to adopt was the construction of a rude fort in the wilderness at the head of each of the large rivers. This was looked upon by the frightened people of the frontiers as a useless measure, since the stealthy Indians could easily find their way between the forts, either to attack the planters living east of these defenses or to retreat westward after an incursion. The inhabitants in the older parts of the colony objected to the forts because their erection was certain to increase the burden of their taxes. The futility of the sylvan garrisons was increased by the fact that the Assembly refused to permit them to pursue the enemy in sufficient force without a specific command from Jamestown.

The killing, burning, and robberies by the diabolical Indians grew more numerous. The dismay and exasperation which these outrages caused were naturally more poignant among the people of the northern frontier because they were directly exposed, and they therefore frantically begged Berkeley to appoint a commander to lead a strong force recruited from their own circle against the barbarians. This he not only roughly declined to do, but even threatened to punish any person who should dare to repeat the prayer. His proclamation to this effect fell on desperate ears. The suspicion now spread that he and his councilors were finding the Indian trade too profitable for them to consent to its destruction by a declaration of open war. It is true that a suspension of this trade had been ordered, but was it not notorious that some of Berkeley's friends, presumably with his secret permission, were selling to the Indians the very guns which the savages were using to shoot down the unfortunate people in the outlying settlements? A report arose suddenly that a large band of warriors had actually started out to invade the lower valley of the James River itself. Berkeley was implored to take at once steps required to halt this incursion into the heart of the colony, but he paid no heed to the prayer and turned an equally deaf ear to the bitter remonstrances which his refusal aroused.

Why did he exhibit this spirit of unpardonable folly? Did he look upon a cry for protection as an act of insubordination? Did he really believe that the people had no right whatever to take any independent step at all for their own defense? Berkeley was now far advanced in years, he had been receiving for so long a period such perfect obedience from the members of all classes, and he had become

88

so insensible to the wishes of the lower orders, that antagonism to his will by them now stirred up his vehement anger
and wholly blunted him to every suggestion of common
fairness.

The inhabitants of the northern frontier soon saw that
they must look to themselves alone for a shield. They started
in to form volunteer companies and waited only for the
appearance of a competent and trusted leader to begin
their march against the savages. A leader was quickly
found who was worthy to command them. This was Nathaniel Bacon, a kinsman of Chancellor Bacon, a graduate
of Cambridge, and a nephew of the president of the Virginia
Council of the same name. A young man of fortune, he had
only recently settled in the colony and had almost at once
been appointed to high office by Berkeley. He was now
only twenty-nine years of age, tall and slender, with hair
of raven blackness and an expression of countenance at
once resolute and thoughtful. His ominous and melancholy
look, so suggestive of the great Napoleon at the same age,
was long remembered; and so were his imperious temper and
his capacity for moving public speech.

Bacon himself was full of bitterness towards the Indians,
for they had butchered the overseer in charge of his plantation at the falls. "If the redskins meddle with me," he exclaimed, "damn them, I will harry them, commission or no
commission." One of the Susquehannocks' bivouacs was
situated in that vicinity, and from this point the savages
were overrunning all the surrounding settlements. On the
south side of the James a tumultuous body of the impatient
people had come together with arms in their hands and
were crying aloud for some one to lead them. Bacon was
persuaded by their emissaries to visit their camp, where he
was received with a prolonged shout of welcome, "A Bacon,
a Bacon." He spoke to them in a strain of powerful eloquence upon the subject of their wrongs, whether inflicted
by the callous Berkeley, the oppressive General Assembly,
or the murderous Indians; and he ended the address with a
promise to take immediate command in order to protect

their political rights and punish their barbarous foes.

His first step seems to have been to head an expedition against the Pamunkey Indians seated in the modern county of New Kent. Berkeley passionately refused him a commission for this excursion, and on Bacon's arrival in that county, ordered him and his troops to return to their homes. Ultimately he issued a proclamation pardoning all Bacon's armed partisans, but Bacon himself he suspended from the office of councilor. The only effect of the proclamation was to confirm Bacon and his followers in their determination to destroy the Indians and reform the laws; and Berkeley was finally compelled to yield so far as to promise to call the General Assembly into session to carry out this latter purpose.

Before this could be done, Bacon led his troops against a temporary stronghold of the wandering Susquehannocks situated near the confluence of the modern Dan and Staunton rivers. This region belonged to the Occaneechees, who had built their principal town on a large island lying between the two streams not far from the encampment of the aliens. With Bacon's connivance the Occaneechees made a sudden assault on the Susquehannocks, drove them out of their entrenchments, and killed all who failed to find shelter in the woods. Elated by this sweeping triumph, they soon began to show a menacing attitude towards the English force, which they had come to regard with contempt on account of its perceptible numerical weakness. Finally they drew back into the log fortifications which they had erected on the outskirts of their town and revealed their hostile spirit by shooting down one of Bacon's soldiers who happened to be in range. A general battle then began. A rush was made for the forts in spite of the flight of arrows and fusillade of bullets from behind the logs; the inflammable material composing them was soon on fire, and the Indian defenders were compelled to withdraw into the adjacent coverts, from which they continued to shoot at the English. The conflict did not end until night had fallen. Then the Indians silently crossed the river and retreated into the dark inner fastnesses of the wild forest.

Bacon and his men did not pursue them but promptly began the march homeward. On their arrival at the first settlement they were told that the election for the proposed reform assembly was about to take place, and that all free-men were to be permitted to cast a ballot. Bacon was chosen a member by a great majority, and accompanied by a strong bodyguard, he set out in a sloop for Jamestown. When he arrived in sight of that place he sent to Berkeley for a guarantee of his personal safety, but the only reply that he received was a shot from the fort. Early the ensuing morning—he during the night having visited the town in secrecy—an armed vessel under Captain Gardiner's com-mand moved up to his sloop and compelled him and his entire escort to surrender. "Behold the greatest rebel that ever was in Virginia," exclaimed Berkeley when Bacon was brought before him. Bacon did not answer but cast his eyes down to the ground in great dejection. "Are you still a gentleman?" asked Berkeley. "May I take your word? If so, you are at liberty on your own parole." Having promised to submit without reserve, Bacon withdrew, but was soon recalled to resume his seat in the Council.

Unhappily, there were many influential persons who did not wish for the two men to be reconciled, since this would have put all chance of reform in jeopardy. They therefore whispered to Bacon that there was a conspiracy on foot to murder him, and they begged him to fly under the cover of night. This he did, and when he reached home and told his neighbors that no commission had been given to him, they blurted out with oaths and curses: "We *shall* have a com-mission for Bacon. Let them refuse us, and we will pull down the town or do worse."

Under Bacon's leadership a large company set out in a tumult for Jamestown. So soon as it was reached, Bacon drew up a file of soldiers in front of the state house, now occupied by the Assembly in session. Seeing them, Berkeley stalked out of the building in a fury, and boldly facing Bacon, denounced him as a traitor and a rebel and rudely

91

refused to give the commission requested. Throwing open his coat with a dramatic gesture, he shouted out, "Fore God, shoot, Sir," but as no gun was lifted, he hastily drew his sword from its scabbard and offered to settle the antagonisms between them by a clash of steel. Bacon replied at first quietly and respectfully, "I come for a commission against the heathen," he said. "They inhumanly murder us and spill our brethren's blood, and no steps are taken to prevent it." Then the bitter memory of these outrages suddenly inflamed him to a passion. "I come for a commission," he exclaimed in a loud voice, "and a commission I *will* have before I go." He turned abruptly to his soldiers, "Prime your guns," he sternly ordered. And this was instantly done. "For God's sake," called the burgesses in alarm from the capitol porch, "hold your hands and forbear a little, and you shall have whatever you please." Slowly and reluctantly Berkeley gave way. The document was signed. But Bacon was not yet satisfied. He insisted that at least thirty additional commissions should be drafted. "If you wish for more," replied Berkeley sullenly, "sign the rest yourself."

The Assembly now showed a very compliant mood. It authorized a levy of one thousand men to accompany Bacon in his expedition against the Indians and ordered that a large quantity of ammunition and food should be provided for this force. Moreover, the Assembly enacted that thereafter the councilors should be taxed like the rest of the citizens; that the property test for all voters should be abolished; that the people at large should elect their own representatives to sit in the county courts; and that the number of officeholders should be greatly reduced.

Bacon sent out a proclamation that the rendezvous for the first expedition should be at the falls in the James. A small army soon collected there; the oaths of allegiance and supremacy were administered to all the troops; and afterwards each soldier was also required to take a third oath that he would obey his commander. In the meanwhile, Berkeley was riding hither and thither seeking to enroll the militia to aid him in overawing Bacon and his men. So soon as news of this menace reached Bacon's ears, he ordered the drums to be beaten and the trumpets to be blown, and when his soldiers ran together in front of him, he addressed them in a spirit of passionate resentment. "Was ever such treachery heard of, such inhumanity?" he exclaimed. "They would rather that we should be murdered, and our ghosts sent to our slaughtered countrymen by their acts, than that we should live to hinder them their interest with the heathen. They have forced us to turn our swords to our own defense. If we do not do so, then we shall be either exposed to their mercies, or compelled to find refuge in the unexplored woods. They are damned cowards, and you will see that they dare not meet us in the field, to try the justice of our cause, and so we will march down on them."

Berkeley, who had been so energetic in his exertions to raise troops that on one occasion he had fainted in the saddle, gradually became sufficiently alarmed by the threatening words and menacing looks which met him on all sides to take refuge on the Eastern Shore, where the loyalty to his person had not been shaken. The perfect peace of that part of the colony, while the storm was raging on the opposite side of the Bay, is the best proof that without the provocation of the recent scalpings and burnings by the savages, the people of Virginia at large would have patiently endured all the other causes of dissatisfaction. In other words, the immediate origin of the rebellion was Berkeley's obstinate refusal to adopt or approve a vigorous policy for the punishment of the Indian marauders.

Not long after Berkeley withdrew, Bacon marched triumphantly into Jamestown and a short time subsequently advanced into Gloucester County, where he was received with popular ovations. From Middle Plantation he issued a proclamation asking the "Gentlemen of Virginia" to coöperate with him in reëstablishing peace, driving off the savages, and reorganizing the government. Not more than sixty-nine accepted the invitation, and these only in the hope that they could bring about a reconciliation between

93

Bacon and Berkeley; but after they assembled, they soon found that they had been locked into their hall, while they faced a peremptory order to sign a document that put them in sharp antagonism to Berkeley.

Bacon was not content to wrest a pledge of allegiance to himself from these leading men, which most of them were reluctant to give. He dispatched a copy of the oath to all the magistrates in the nearest parts of the colony, with an injunction to administer it to the people at large. The oath seems to have been taken by the majority of the citizens because they approved of the purposes which Bacon had in view; and by the minority, because they were afraid to draw down upon themselves his displeasure. Bacon's next step was to seize the guard ship, by means of which he expected to land a large force in the counties of the Eastern Shore, both to capture Berkeley and to reduce the inhabitants to subjection. But the two men to whom he turned the vessel over, Carver and Bland, were so indiscreet as to retain on board its hostile English commander and sailors.

Before this vessel could sail for Accomac, Bacon—after issuing a summons for a new assembly in the ensuing September—started upon an expedition against the tribe of Pamunkeys. At the falls he was joined by Colonel Brent and a large band of volunteers. Heavy rains stopped the troops as soon as they had begun to advance, and continued so long that a spirit of disaffection sprang up among them. "If there is any one among you," warned Bacon in a speech to his little army, "who subordinates the suppression of the heathen, and revenge for the murder of our friends, to a particular regard and care for his belly, then let him depart for home." "Begone," he cried out scornfully to three soldiers who had dropped out of the ranks, "begone." And then turned to those who stayed, he said, "Yonder deserters are the worst cowards, serving for plunder, and, by sharing the food, starving my best men, who would bear the brunt of it, and disheartening the others of half-metal from freely engaging."

The march was then resumed, with the Indian scouts

in front. In a few days they came upon an Indian fort. They found that the garrison had first taken flight to the recesses of a neighboring swamp, but afterwards emerging, had made an encampment in the deep woods some distance beyond. When this was discovered after a long search, an assault was launched against it, and many of the savages were killed or captured. An old squaw, who, as a guide faithful to her own people, had endeavored to divert the soldiers from the right trail, was brutally knocked on the head. The provisions soon began to run short, and Bacon, knowing that they could not be replenished, consented that the footmen, who had been fatigued by the long marches through the woods, should return to their homes. Most of the horsemen remained behind, although all who wished to leave with the footmen were permitted to go. After a few days' advance, the food got so low, it was feared that supplies would not hold out until the troops could again direct their faces towards the settlements. "All that abide with me," Bacon declared in a speech to his discouraged followers, "must be ready to endure all the hardships this wilderness can cause, dangers, and successes, and if need to be, to eat chinquapins and horse flesh before they return. I only want those who will freely adventure."

Some of the soldiers refused to go further; the remainder, obedient to their captain, resumed the advance through the silent woods and, after several hours had gone by, stumbled on an Indian camp which had been erected by the savages in a swamp made almost impenetrable by a matted mass of small oaks, chinquapin bushes, and wild grapevines. The foe, taken by surprise, frantically endeavored to escape, but many were shot down before they could hide themselves in the fastnesses of the great thickets. This terminated the expedition.

While Bacon and his horsemen were painfully treading the forest in pursuit of the Pamunkeys, Carver and Bland had set sail for the Eastern Shore in the guard ship, accompanied by its former commander and his seamen. On arriving there, Carver, intending to interview Berkeley,

disembarked with an escort composed of most of his loyal
followers, while Bland remained behind with only a handful
of men to overawe the English captain and his sailors. This
officer, perceiving his opportunity, sent an underhanded
message to Berkeley that if he would dispatch by boat a
force to the vessel, it would be admitted by the port holes,
and that Bland and his supporters could in this way be
overpowered. This was done with complete success. When
Carver and his escort, not suspecting danger, drew up to
the vessel sometime afterwards, they were confronted with
the muzzles of numerous muskets and compelled to deliver
up their arms to the enemy. In vain Carver fell on Bland
with bitter reproaches. Irons were placed on the limbs of
both, and subsequently both forfeited the lives which they
had been so incautious in protecting. By means of the
captured ship, Berkeley, with a large band of exultant followers, was able to reach Jamestown in triumph, where he
issued a proclamation stigmatizing Bacon and his lieutenants as "rebels to the Governor, and traitors to the
King."

When Bacon heard of this proclamation, he and his troops
joined in an oath that they would neither ask nor give
quarter; and in this stern and resentful mood, they shouldered their arms and started upon the road to the capital.
As the little army tramped along through the intervening
counties, many volunteers fell into its ranks, while the people
at large showered their gratitude on Bacon as their savior
in the past and as their shield in the future from the Indian
arrows. They crowded by the way offering quantities of
food to the soldiers, while the women exclaimed that should
their fathers, husbands, and sons shrink from flying to arms,
they themselves would rush to Bacon's support.

Berkeley had collected around him one thousand men. It
was reported that these had been carefully drilled and
equipped. When told of this, Bacon simply smiled as he said,
"I fear them not." Near Green Spring, when the enemy
were almost in sight, he cried out to his troops, who were
keeping step behind him, "Come on, my hearts of gold. He

96

GOVERNOR BERKELEY AND BACON THE REBEL

that dies on this field, lies on the field of honor." Although the soldiers had that day already traversed forty miles on foot, they eagerly took up the march again. At Paspaheigh, where the town could be descried in the distance, they halted, and with but one spade and two axes constructed by dawn a strong fortification of earth and logs. When the sun had dispersed the darkness, six of the soldiers, defiant of the peril of the act, quickly leapt forward and emptied their guns at the enemy's sentinels and then drew back unwounded to the protection of the breastworks. "This talk of unwillingness to shed blood first!" exclaimed Bacon bitterly when informed that Berkeley had so spoken of himself, "Did he not send his boat to places where the public provisions were stored for the maintenance of the war against the Indians, and carry them off by force in order to support a war against the people themselves? Cannot our men show the scars which his bullets have inflicted?"

The earliest advance was made by Bacon, but the simultaneous fire from the ships in the river and from the palisades of the town halted his troops, and they retreated to their defenses which they now proceeded to enlarge and strengthen. A scout had been posted on a tall chimney in the neighborhood to call down the movements of the hostile soldiers. These now started to make a sally, but after debouching a short distance from the town, they hastily retired to cover. A second sortie then began, with a narrow and unsteady front; but when the participants had almost reached the position of their opponents and had delivered their first fire, they seemed to be swept by a panic, and throwing to the ground all their accouterments and even the corpses of their comrades who had been killed in the first impact, they fled for safety behind their own bulwarks.

Discouraged by this pusillanimous spirit, Berkeley hastily decided to go on board of the guard ship and retire to the Eastern Shore. Twelve hours later Bacon marched into the town and at once made up his mind to give it over to the torch. With an army approaching from the Rappahannock, under Colonel Brent, to attack him in the rear, and with many hostile vessels lying in the lower reaches of the James ready to sail up and pour broadsides into the ranks of his troops, he concluded that it would be unwise to try to hold the place. As long as the town should stand it would be liable to assault. His friends, Lawrence and Drummond, are said to have hurled firebrands into their own halls. Every house soon went up in flames. Not even the church and capitol were spared.

Bacon now sat down at Green Spring. In a short time he had drafted an oath of fidelity to himself designed to be taken by the Virginians in the mass. In the documents accompanying this oath it was declared that should the English Government send troops to the colony to suppress the popular uprising, the people would have the right to resist with arms in their hands; and that in preference to submitting in case of failure, they would retreat from the colony to some place of refuge in the remote back country. The fate which overtook Braddock in the following century might reasonably have been anticipated in the seventeenth, had an English army ventured to pursue the retiring planters through the somber forests of the Alleghenies. There would have been a lost colony far more numerous than the little company which had vanished like ghosts from Roanoke Island a hundred years before. The fugitives would perhaps have found a new seat in the "dark and bloody ground" of Kentucky or in the green valleys of the Watauga and Tennessee.

Bacon now exhibited a spirit of great moderation. He struck the irons from many prisoners captured during the war, and he forebore to execute others who had been guilty of capital offenses. Observing that his soldiers were inclined to be aggressive in their bearing towards the planters about their camps, he resumed the strict discipline of actual warfare, with severe penalties in every case of contempt for the ordinances. He was especially stern in punishing the men arrested for plundering.

All opposition to Bacon's supremacy had been crushed in the entire region west of the Bay; and he was now able for

98

the first time to start upon an unhampered policy that would quickly pacify the unhappy country. One of the most important measures which he adopted was that a committee of citizens whose plantations were situated near the frontiers should regulate there the intercourse between the white people and the Indians in time of peace and should take command of the troops in time of war. An equally important measure was that no provision should be seized by the army without the authority of a committee of officers appointed to decide upon the propriety of the action.

Before these statesmanlike measures could be put in practice, Bacon died in the course of a journey of inspection through Gloucester County. Exposure during his marches up and down had filled his overstrained body with the germs of malaria, which in time took the form of chronic dysentery. His corpse was committed at night to the waters of one of the inlets, and to this day the exact spot where his bones repose is unknown. The privacy of his burial preserved his body from the disgrace which befell the remains of Cromwell after the King's return. Thus perished a hero who, although at times headstrong and ruthless, was a determined upholder of the inherent rights of the people when those rights were treated by the local government with arrogant contempt. With his eyes fixed resolutely on that purpose, he sacrificed his ease, his fortune, his very life itself, for the sake of his country.

It is not necessary to give in detail the events which followed the passing of the supreme leader. By sudden excursions from the Eastern Shore Berkeley was able to make several successful attacks upon the counties on the mainland. Encouraged by that fact, he crossed over the Bay with a large fleet of vessels of different sizes, which had been collected from far and near to transport his army, but his various marches against the rebel troops, now commanded by Colonel Ingram, ended in defeat. He was able, however, to take complete possession of all the country situated south of the James. An emotion of weariness of the war had penetrated the breasts of the people there, and this state of mind soon spread to the inhabitants of the region lying on the north side of the river.

Overtures were now made to Ingram by Berkeley to surrender; and this he and his principal lieutenant, Walklett, agreed to do on an offer of very favorable terms for themselves and their followers. The troops under Lawrence and Drummond alone continued to resist for some time, but they, too, finally dispersed.

With the entire colony now at his feet, Berkeley started upon a course of vengeance which is only paralleled in the history of the English race by the bloody assizes of Jeffreys. Colonel Hansford had already been hanged in spite of his pleading for a more honorable manner of death. On the scaffold this first martyr in the cause of popular freedom on the American continent exclaimed, "I die a loyal subject, and a lover of my country." Captain Cheesman, too, met with the same fate through hard usage in jail. When his wife prostrated herself at Berkeley's feet and implored him to grant her her husband's life, he spurned her from him with a coarse word that will blacken his memory as long as it survives in history. When Drummond was brought into his presence he cried out with the glee of a fiend, "You are more welcome than any other man in Virginia." As Drummond was ordered to stand up before his judges for his foreordained sentence, his coat was rudely torn from his back and his ring from his finger. The travesty of a trial had ended in a few minutes, and in a few more he was led away to the gallows. Prominent men like Thomas Hill, Henry Pope, and Thomas Young had already met with the same ruthless fate, after trials equally devoid of dignity and fairness. The wives, widows, and children of men who had served in Bacon's army were treated as brutally as if they, too, had grasped the sword to resist the wretched tyrant.

The imminent prospect of the arrival of the English commissioners, accompanied by an army, seemed only to spur on the half-insane Governor to recoup himself and his councilors for their losses, by confiscating the estates of all who had taken a prominent part on the opposite side.

100

When the commissioners landed, their sympathies were soon aroused in behalf of the unhappy people. Although in their instructions Berkeley was ordered to return to England, he positively refused to do so, because a clause in that document stated that he was to be permitted to consult his own convenience in embarking; and he asserted vehemently that as long as he lingered in Virginia he could not be deprived of the office of governor. He had the boldness to modify the royal proclamation, which granted a pardon to all except Bacon, by condemning to the gallows Giles Bland, William Scarborough, and four others of Bacon's followers of equal prominence, through a subservient court-martial. Anthony Arnold was hanged in chains, in spite of his having shown by speech and conduct that he was mad; and Robert Jones, a veteran of the civil wars, missed the same fate only by the resolute interference of Lady Berkeley. Even the General Assembly, so loyal to Berkeley, was revolted and begged him to desist. The stern presence of one thousand regulars at Jamestown alone put a damper on the revival of the former commotions.

The puerility to which Berkeley could descend in the midst of his ruthless violence was illustrated in the insult which he offered the dignified commissioners by sending them away from his house, after a polite call, in his coach driven by the common hangman.

Jeffreys, who had been appointed Berkeley's successor, now took a firmer stand, and the old Governor, both hated and discredited, was constrained to leave the colony, although he refused to acknowledge the right of the new Governor to occupy his place. He was a sick man when he departed from Jamestown, and his health was desperate by the time he sighted the English shores. After his arrival there, he died before he could take advantage of the King's consent to receive him in a private audience. His death would probably have occurred earlier had a report of Charles' indignant comment on his recent career in Virginia reached his ears, "That old fool has taken more lives in that naked country than I have done for the murder of my father."

Chapter VIII

SIR FRANCIS NICHOLSON

O<small>F</small> ALL the men who occupied the post of governor or lieutenant-governor of Virginia between the years 1624 and 1754, a fruitful and eventful period, the most liberal in political spirit and the most uniformly successful in administration was Francis Nicholson. Alexander Spotswood, who was of a higher stature from a merely personal point of view, was alone comparable with him in the disinterestedness of his public policies, in the energy of his devotion to the public welfare, and in his constructive political ability. The foundation of the College of William and Mary, so largely due to Nicholson's original suggestion, personal encouragement, and official assistance, would be sufficient by itself to shed remarkable distinction on his incumbency of the governorship.

But this was only one of his practical services for the colony's benefit. He had scarcely taken his seat at Jamestown, when, in his impatience to inform himself fully about the people's condition in every part of the country, he started upon a tour of inspection from county to county, in the course of which he invited men of every social rank, from the proudest to the humblest, to join him in his meals and there, in the privacy of his own table, to state both the needs of their several communities and how best to satisfy them. This tour he repeated from year to year for the same purpose. In this way he made the acquaintance of a representative body of experienced and observant planters, both large and small, whose sentiments would otherwise have remained unknown to him; and in this way, too, he broadened his personal influence and increased his ability to be useful to the inhabitants under his rule. There was no aspect of their lives in which he was not interested, and not one which he was not eager to brighten.

He warmly favored the stimulation among the people at large of a taste for the old English sports, both indoor and outdoor; and as the most powerful means of fostering this taste, he contributed out of his own purse the money for the purchase of prizes for distribution among the victors in the exercises of jumping, running, shooting, wrestling, and fencing.

He also kept a watchful eye upon the military establishment, with a view to invigorating and increasing its efficiency. With unbroken regularity he attended the musters in the different groups of counties; and he required the officers who superintended the military maneuvers to refer to him for adjustment every controversy that should arise to divide them. He periodically traveled far through trackless forests, in all sorts of trying weather, to review the companies of rangers stationed at the heads of the rivers. He also recommended that the indentured servants should be armed and drilled; but this proposal was received by the General Assembly with coldness because that body was afraid lest a military training and the possession of guns should encourage these men to rise in rebellion. Moreover, it would certainly draw them away from the fields just at the season when the crops would call for most attention. Annually he visited the different fortifications which had been erected on the banks of the large streams; and he made provision for their being kept in a state of thorough repair.

Nicholson was equally determined upon a firm enforcement of the law, although it was said that he sometimes exhibited a reckless temper while presiding in the general courts. He was very much in favor of the introduction of the system of pleading which had been always in use in England, but apparently his advocacy of that system made no impression, since the looseness of the one followed in

103

Virginia never ceased to be a subject of criticism. In 1690 he issued a proclamation that all persons heard to speak with contempt of the laws of the colony would be sternly punished; and so keen was his interest in the legal administration of the community that even after he left it he contributed to the erection of a courthouse at Yorktown.

Nicholson was indefatigable in urging the adoption of more successful methods for conserving the soil of the plantations and making it more productive. At this time—and the same condition continued to exist throughout the Colonial period—the manner of tillage was destructive of the lands under cultivation. There was but one crop designed for sale. This was tobacco. So soon as a field gave indications of exhaustion, owing to the failure to employ rotation or apply domestic manures, it was turned out to grow up in broomstraw and dwarf pines. A substitute for the old field was found in a new field created by the removal of the original forest from the surface of the ground. Nicholson endeavored to modify the bad effect of this system of tillage by recommending a different crop for each year of a definite period. To carry out this program, cottonseed was to be planted in its turn by the cultivators of the soil.

But the concern for the welfare of agriculture which he displayed, keen and constant as it was, was not quite so keen or so constant as his zeal for the promotion of the best interests of religion. He seemed to act with the customary intolerance towards the Quakers, but simply because that sect refused to do its duty in the defense of the community from Indian or foreign attack. His breadth of religious sympathy was very faithfully indicated in his liberal attitude towards Mackenzie, the founder of Presbyterianism in Virginia. He informed that indefatigable dissenter that not a single right which his sect could properly claim should be abridged. To his own church, the Anglican establishment, he was always loyal and generous. By law he was entitled to certain fees for tavern and marriage licenses issued in some of the border counties. Instead of reserving these fees for his own use, he set them apart for the support of lay readers in parishes too impoverished or too scantily populated to afford a clergyman. He contributed from his own purse to the building of new church edifices in the more remote corners of the colony and to covering the expense of providing shelter and food for newly arrived ministers of the gospel, until they could be appointed to benefices rich enough to assure them the possession of a rectory and glebe and the enjoyment of a stipend.

Nicholson was an uncompromising advocate of the clergyman's right to permanent induction. The rule which had sprung up in Virginia allowed every vestry to enter into a limited contract with the incumbent of the parish pulpit. His occupation of this pulpit was dependent absolutely upon the terms of that contract. If the vestrymen thought it advisable for any reason, they could at the end of the agreement decline to renew it, and the clergyman in consequence was thrown back on his own individual resources. In England, on the other hand, a clergyman once inducted, after receiving his appointment from the patron of the living, could not be compelled by his vestry to resign. His tenure was independent of the vestry and therefore permanent.

Commissary Blair, although a devoted churchman, upheld the colonial view. He sided with the vestries, and not with the clergymen who were so persistently complaining that their right to induction was trampled under foot. Blair came almost at once into collision with Nicholson by his approval of this irregularity; and the conflict was intensified by the Governor's claim that he, and not Blair, was the real head of ecclesiastical affairs in Virginia. Under the influence of this antagonistic attitude, the Commissary censured the Governor, on the ground that he was neglectful of the welfare of religion. The clergy of the colony had from the first bristled up in defense of the Governor in this contention. "With the exception of the King," they said in a public announcement, "he is the greatest support of the church in America." They indignantly disputed the correctness of Blair's assertion that "there was not a clergyman on the continent who would not swear in favor of

105

Nicholson for five pounds stirling"; and they boldly referred to the Commissary as "lying under the scandal of being a perjured person."

An impression prevailed everywhere in Virginia that all attempts to Christianize the newly imported African slaves was a useless expenditure of time and effort. "The gross bestiality and rudeness of their manners," it was stated by the General Assembly, "the variety and strangeness of their language, and the weakness and shallowness of their minds, make it practically impossible to teach them even the rudiments of the Christian religion. It is only those born in the country, and brought in contact with the family life of the plantations, who could be reached; and every thing was done by their owners to improve their disposition and manners." Although there was good reason to think that this view taken by the burgesses was correct, the sanguine Nicholson was not satisfied to accept their pessimistic attitude as entirely justifiable. By every means open to him in the course of his official duties he endeavored to improve the moral condition of these unhappy bondsmen, snatched from their distant homes without their consent.

His interest in education was quite as keen as his interest in the established church and religion in general. His principal reason for approving the act for building towns at the public expense was that each of these towns would be able to support a schoolmaster thoroughly competent to teach the art of writing and reading; and even after he had vacated the post of governor, he assigned a lot in Yorktown for the use of Robert Leightenhouse, the parish schoolmaster, which was to pass to his successor should he die or move away. No one was permitted during his tenure of office to teach without being able to show that he had been properly trained for that profession. How disinterested he was in encouraging education was revealed by his willingness to contribute from his private purse to the emolument of any lay reader in the parishes of Norfolk County who would be willing to add to his regular duties on the sabbath the duties of a schoolmaster during the week. And he went so far as

to offer to buy the old courthouse still standing at Jamestown and to convert it into a schoolhouse for the instruction
of the children residing within or near the town.

But a scheme of far greater dignity and usefulness was
the one which led to the foundation of the College of William
and Mary. The first person to suggest it was apparently
Nicholson himself. During July, 1690, he was in Howard's
absence filling the office of deputy governor; and this fact
prompted him to revive the proposal to set up a free school
and college which had so often been brought forward in a
general way, but never with any tangible result until
Nicholson took hold of the project in his characteristically
earnest and practical spirit, by issuing an order to all the
county courts to retain a list of citizens residing in their
respective jurisdictions who would be likely to subscribe to
a fund for the establishment of the suggested seat of learning. There was now a keen desire among the planters in
all parts of the colony to found such a seat, and the reasons
for this feeling were, first, that the number of persons there
who had been educated in England had rapidly increased
in the course of recent years, and naturally these persons
favored the duplication in Virginia of the academies of the
mother country, so far as it should be practicable. And,
secondly, the remoteness of England and the necessity of
crossing a wild ocean to reach it discouraged the great majority of even the wealthiest parents from sending their sons to
English schools. A college in their own community would
alone supply facilities to all.

The House of Burgesses, in an address drafted in May,
1699, declared that after the King, Nicholson had been
the most zealous patron of the new seat of learning. It was
Commissary Blair, however, who had been most directly
instrumental in procuring the charter. In 1691 he had received from the Assembly a grant of two hundred pounds
sterling to pay the charges to be incurred in the double
voyage and during his residence in London. He was authorized, not only to engage a headmaster, usher, and writing
master, but also to canvass among the English people for

donations and subscriptions. The Virginians had already raised a fund of at least two thousand pounds sterling, and this sum had been increased by the English Government's gift of the moneys which were then lying in the auditor-general's hands, amounting to nineteen hundred and eighty-six pounds sterling. That Government also generously assigned for the college's support the annual return from the quitrents and the tax of one penny on intercolonial shipments of tobacco. It also granted for the same use twenty thousand acres situated on the Blackwater River and in Pamunkey Neck, and also all escheated lands not otherwise disposed of.

Blair returned to Virginia in 1693 with the charter in his possession. In carrying out his mission in England, he had exhibited sturdiness, energy, and sagacity, and at times a wise indifference to snubs. Having begun a discourse in Lord Seymour's presence on the pressing need of erecting a nursery of learning and piety in the New World, that nobleman expressed his dissent.

"But, my Lord," remonstrated Blair, "the Colonists have souls to save."

"Souls!" brusquely exclaimed the choleric peer, "Damn their souls! Make tobacco."

It was not until August, 1695, that the foundation stone of the college was laid. Two years later, the buildings had been so far completed that the door of the grammar school had been thrown open. The institution had reached such a solid footing by the beginning of Nicholson's second administration that bequests were made to it by persons of prominence in Virginia and England. Henry Hartwell left it by his last testament one hundred and forty pounds sterling, while Robert Boyle, also by will, presented it with Brafferton Manor in Yorkshire, which, valued at fifty-four hundred pounds sterling, brought in an annual revenue of two hundred and fifty. The charter provided for the establishment of five chairs, two of which related to theology. The fact that all these professorships were not created simultaneously did not seriously detract from the prestige of the college in the long run, for even a limited operation was an assurance that a higher education—to that degree, at least—could for the first time be obtained in the colony.

The pride which the authorities felt in the new seat of learning was revealed in the unanimous adjournment of the House of Burgesses in April, 1699, in order that its members might be present at the final exercises of that year. Nicholson seems to have attended at their head. On their returning to their own chamber, he congratulated them on their participation in so significant a ceremony. "The most proper place for you at that time," he exclaimed, "was to be at his Majesty's College of William and Mary, where you might not only be eye witnesses of one of his Royal Majesty's bounties and royal favors to Virginia, but also judge of the improvement of your youth in learning and education; and I hope in God you are satisfied as to both."

The burgesses in turn felicitated the Governor on the college's prosperity; and they declared that "they considered it an unspeakable blessing to have their children brought up in so fair a way of being rescued from barbarous ignorance."

The commencements had by this date become occasions of extraordinary distinction in the life of the colony. In 1700 an unusual multitude of people attended, and these visitors counted among themselves many persons residing in communities as remote from Williamsburg as New York and Pennsylvania. The planters whose homes were situated in the surrounding counties made the journey in their coaches or on the backs of horses, while the strangers from distant regions had sailed up or down the coast in sloops on their way thither.

It was through Nicholson's influence that the seat of government was removed from Jamestown to the place first known as the Middle Plantation and afterwards as Williamsburg. It was here, as we have seen, that the site for the college had been chosen. The Governor perceived clearly the advantage which would accrue to that institution by its proximity to the transposed capital, necessarily the heart of

109

the colony wherever it might be situated. To make the college's site also the site of the capital, he said, would be "as great a kindness to the college as if some one had presented it with two thousand pounds sterling." He proposed that the new town should be laid off in the shape of the initial letters of the names of the reigning King and Queen, which happened to be exactly the same in form if one or the other were turned upside down.

With the capital in addition to the college established at Middle Plantation, the town which sprang up there in a short time took the place of Jamestown as the center of the social as well as of the political life of the colony; and from this center radiated to the remotest corners of Virginia the influence of the literary and intellectual interests which were born and fostered there by the college, year after year.

Although the building of a mansion for the Governor in his official capacity would be a draft on Nicholson's small salary of one thousand pounds sterling by constraining him to entertain more lavishly, nevertheless, with characteristic disinterestedness he threw all the weight of his approval in favor of the proposal, because such a building and the style of living which it would make necessary would increase the dignity of the Governor's position and bring the people into closer social affiliation with it by the opportunity of attending official receptions under the new roof. The General Assembly, however, refused to consent to the assumption of the greater burden of taxation which the construction of the mansion would have unavoidably entailed.

The breadth of Nicholson's statesmanship was not displayed merely in his determination to advance the cause of religion, increase the facilities for public and private education, strengthen the colony's defenses, and promote the welfare of agriculture by encouraging the diversification of crops. He advocated the policy of joining all the colonies under the administration of a viceroy appointed by the King. This was a novel suggestion for that age; and it could only have had its origin in the mind of a man who looked

110

PLATE XI. "*Respectfully inscribed to the President and Faculty, the Visitors, Alumni and Students of that Venerable Institution by their very obed't serv't, Tho. Ch. Millington.*" *Signed E. J. P., 1840. Photo Cook.*

WILLIAM AND MARY COLLEGE

far beyond the present into the future, when the continent should have expanded into a series of great communities, remarkable for the wealth as well as for the size of their population. He actually drafted this scheme of confederation; but, unfortunately, it made no appeal to the English Government. Had it been adopted by that Government, and a vice-royalty established in accord with it, the unity of the colonies would have been gradually brought about. In the end they would have become a group of communities converted practically into one by sharing the administration of the same ruler, who, by his residence on this side of the water, could have understood clearly their antagonistic and their mutual interests and who could have reconciled those interests, should they at any time seem to be drifting towards open collision. Through his leadership the colonies would have had the power to act promptly and sympathetically together in case of an emergency; and through his interpreting voice, their wishes would have carried more weight with the Government in England.

A disturbing influence in Virginia during these times was the probability of a descent upon the coast at any hour by bands of pirates scouring the outlying sea for richly laden merchantmen. They always arrived suddenly. Sometimes they attacked the plantations and carried off plate and other valuable articles, but more frequently they anchored in a remote, secluded inlet, and, like a spider waiting for its prey, remained quietly there until a vessel from England hove in sight between the Capes and fell into their trap. Quite often their stay on the coast was limited to the short interval necessary for them to procure a new supply of water and fuel or to make a raid for beef on the cattle which had been turned loose on the islands in the Bay.

So great was the quantity of plate, coin, precious stones, silks, and costly cloths captured by these outlaws in their excursions in the open seas, ʽhat there was always reason to dread lest the mere reports of such success should tend to demoralize the more restless individuals in the colony's population and prompt them to run away and follow the

111

same occupation. In 1691 a sensation was caused in Virginia by the news that a vessel, pretending to be a privateer, a common dodge in those times, but in reality a pirate ship, had recently arrived in Charleston and that its sailors, on going ashore, had received enormous sums in the division of the booty. "I fear," wrote Nicholson when he heard of this fact, "that, if such people are encouraged, it may prejudice his majesty's service by debauching the inhabitants to make them leave planting and follow ye same trade. These kinds of privateers, or rather pirates, when they have spent lavishly what they have got, then they are ready, if not before, to make disturbance in the governments." And there was substantial ground for these apprehensions. It was notorious that when they showed a peaceful disposition on coming ashore, the buccaneers had a hospitable reception from many of the planters who seized this opportunity to exchange food and tobacco for the tempting articles which the outlaws offered in abundance. There was a popular saying that they must not be driven off too relentlessly because "they brought good money into the country."

Captain Kidd very often hovered on the coast. In 1699 a vessel commanded by this notorious pirate came to anchor in the waters of Accomac. It carried a large complement of men and was armed with forty-two cannon. A sloop, armed with eighteen, accompanied her. This vessel is said—probably with some exaggeration—to have had stored in her coffers £52,000 in coin. The precious metals in her possession were reported to be equal in weight to thirty tons. When the division of all this booty should take place, it was calculated that each sailor's share, in the shape of gold and silver alone, would reach the sum of four thousand pounds sterling, a large fortune in itself at that time.

In the course of the same year Captain Aldred, of the guard ship *Essex Prize*, while patrolling, observed a large pirate ship, the *Alexander*, at anchor in Lynnhaven Bay. She was more formidably armed and manned than his own vessel, and he therefore, after delivering a broadside, drew off for support. The buccaneers now began to plunder the

112

contents of every boat and sloop that passed over the neighboring waters, and having in this way procured the supplies immediately needed by them, they turned the prow of their vessel towards the Capes. There they met the *Roanoke*, a large merchantman, and ordered her to lower her flag. They were satisfied with robbing her of her stores of pork, tallow, beans, muskets, tools, rope, and water. They also forced several of her officers to go aboard of their ship and remain there when she weighed anchor and sailed out to sea. As it was confidently expected that those pirates would reappear in the Bay within a few days, Nicholson gave orders that the coast should be patrolled in order to warn the people against their possible return.

Either the same outlaws or their fellows disembarked on Smith's Island in the course of October, 1699, and slew many hogs and cattle, skinned and cut up the carcasses, and carried off the meat to their vessel.

During the ensuing year the depredations of the sinister strangers increased in number and in boldness. A staunch guard ship named the *Shoreham* was now constantly on the watch for these outlaws' entrance between the Capes. Captain Passenger, the officer in command, was skillful and intrepid, and he found in Nicholson a backer who was ready to risk his life in his support when the occasion for it should arise. In April a message was brought to Passenger that several piratical vessels had come in in the night and anchored in Lynnhaven Bay. Before three days had gone by, every community on the west and east shores of the Chesapeake within Virginia had been warned to assume at once a posture of defense both on water and on land. Nicholson in the interval had hastened to Kikotan, where he impatiently waited for the replenishment of the *Shoreham's* water casks.

The first pirate ships had now stolen away to sea, but their place had been taken by a large vessel, afterwards found out to be the *La Paix*. She carried twenty guns on her main deck and eight in her hold, with a supply of powder amounting to thirty-two barrels. The pilot was the

113

only Englishman aboard. Originally she had been engaged
in the Dutch trade with Surinam; but after her capture
by the buccaneers, who thereupon abandoned their own vessel, she had pursued a career of successful depredation along
the Atlantic coasts and in the adjacent seas. Only the day
before her arrival in Lynnhaven Bay, her crew had seized
a large merchantman and, after rifling her, had given her
over to the flames.

So soon as Captain Passenger had filled his casks, he
directed the prow of the *Shoreham* straight for the piratical
craft quietly riding in the harbor on the further side. On
arriving within three leagues of the outlaw ship, it was
too late to attack, and he stopped for the night. Nicholson,
who in his impatience had left Kikotan the day before and
passed over to the south side of the Bay to reconnoiter, now
came on board under cover of darkness, in order to take part
in the battle to be fought on the morrow. Before day had
fairly broken, the *Shoreham* was under sail and by the end
of an hour had approached within half a mile of the *La
Paix*.

Weighing anchor, the pirates endeavored to maneuver to
the windward, but in vain. Skillfully balking their purpose,
Captain Passenger fired a shot at their vessel as it passed
and then, down to three o'clock in the afternoon, continued
his broadsides, until the masts, rigging, yards, and canvas
of the enemy had been thoroughly riddled and shattered by
the balls. In order to escape with their lives, the outlaws
took refuge in the hold, and the ship, being left to float
without a pilot, drifted helplessly on shore. The ensign at
its peak was then run down and a boat put off with a messenger to inform Captain Passenger that there were thirty
barrels of powder on board and that, if quarter and immunity from punishment were not granted, the magazine
would be touched off and the ship blown up. Nicholson sent
word in reply that if the outlaws should surrender quietly,
he would recommend them to the royal mercy.

The prisoners were afterwards taken to Kikotan. Three
of them died there; the three who had been most deeply

114

implicated in outlawry were hanged; and the remainder were sent in shackles to England.

It was in the course of Nicholson's administration that a large band of French Huguenots arrived in the colony, and they were followed in succession by three other bands under the guidance of trustworthy leaders. At least one thousand persons of both sexes and all ages were embraced in this interesting company. About one-half of this number, divided into families, received patents to lands situated in the region above the falls of the James occupied by the Monacan tribe of Indians at the time of the first colonization. A tract of one hundred and thirty-two acres was assigned to the head of each family; but in harmony with the French custom, the immigrants did not disperse to their several plantations. They settled together in a single village, which contained, in addition to the dwelling houses, a church, a parsonage, and a school building.

It was not until all peril of Indian irruptions had passed from that region that the inhabitants gradually withdrew to their original separate assignments of land and established their permanent homes there, after the manner of their English neighbors. But they earned a livelihood by more varied methods than the natives, for, in addition to planting maize, they found a substitute for planting tobacco in breeding cattle, expressing wine from their own grapes, and manufacturing cloth by means of their own looms. The French language continued to be used by them during more than a generation after their arrival.

With all his high and useful qualities as a public administrator, Nicholson sometimes exhibited in his private life strange infirmities of temper that tended to weaken his personal influence. He became a suitor for the hand of one of Lewis Burwell's daughters, for instance, and although persistently repulsed by her and her parents, he angrily refused to give up the pursuit. The extravagance of his conduct and language, while he was under the influence of this hopeless passion, was unworthy of his own personal dignity and of the conspicuous office which he held.

115

SIR FRANCIS NICHOLSON

It was asserted by certain members of his Council that his behaviour to them was unpardonable whenever they ventured to differ with him at the board; that he denounced them for that reason as "dogs," "rascals," "cowards," and "rogues"; that he abused the lawyers practising before him in the general court on the smallest provocation; that he turned a credulous ear to slanderous reports; that he showed no restraint in his rudeness to his inferiors; that he had been known to strike some of the first gentlemen in the country in a spirit of mere wantonness; and that he did not scruple to throw into prison citizens who had offended him. In short, according to these councilors, Nicholson had been guilty of every social outrage and of every moral impropriety.

But this extreme condemnation of his character and conduct did not pass unchallenged. The clergy came to his defense by emphatically denying the accuracy of these adverse reflections. The House of Burgesses also refused to give their countenance to such accusations and significantly pointed out that at least four other members of the Council had positively declined to join in them. The commanders of the vessels trading in Virginian waters were equally emphatic in combatting the pertinency of the charges. "By his prudent and careful management in continuing the embargo from time to time," they said, "and by the pains, trouble, and expense he has been at to aid us in loading and getting ready to sail, and further by his judicious use of the guard ship for our protection, he has benefited the interests of the King, the people, and the merchants alike."

But above all, no complaint was raised against him by the great body of planters. On the contrary, they very gratefully acknowledged the constant zeal which he showed towards the advancement of agriculture; his ceaseless care in watching over the colony's religious welfare; his personal sacrifices to increase the educational facilities of local communities; and his success in reforming the court procedure, in strengthening the military arm, and in encouraging the

116

athletic amusements of the people at large. All these facts to his credit as a man and an official very naturally tended to lift him to a height in their respect and affection which could not be seriously lowered by his vagaries as a lover or by the occasional intemperance of his hasty tongue in personal intercourse.

Chapter IX

GOVERNOR ALEXANDER SPOTSWOOD

ALEXANDER SPOTSWOOD enjoys an almost unrivaled distinction among Virginia's colonial governors. Why has this been always so? It was not because he possessed a greater degree of social prestige as an accomplished man of the world and also as the descendant of an archbishop and a chief justice of Scotland—a fact which in that age conferred on him more dignity than if he were living in our more democratic era. It was not because he had served as an officer of rank in Marlborough's army and assisted in winning the greatest victory of the age. Nor was it because he had gallantly spilled his blood on the soil of that renowned battlefield.

Virginia had already been under the rule of governors who, like Percy, Berkeley, Culpeper, and Howard, could claim an ancestry even more exalted in birth than Spotswood's, and perhaps not less famous for actual achievement in the different walks of life. Smith, for instance, had run a far more adventurous career than he. Dale, the warrior, had been longer familiar with the shock of contending armies, and that, too, in the very region in which his successor in the next century won his spurs as a soldier. Not the veteran of Blenheim himself had taken part in a more dangerous enterprise than some of those raids which Yeardley made through the unknown forests of the Pamunkey in pursuit of the cunning and pitiless savages. Berkeley had been just as resolute and courageous in spirit when he went aboard of the merchantman in York River to move down on the Dutch men-of-war hovering on the horizon, like a flock of birds of prey poised to dart straight at their quarry. Nicholson, too, had shown his stout heart, when instead of loitering quietly out of the zone of danger, he posted down to Kikotan to join the *Shoreham* guard ship in its now imminent attack upon the strongly armed and fully equipped pirate vessel then riding in Lynnhaven Bay.

It was not the celebrity of his ancestry, therefore, which has cast over Spotswood's memory such a remarkable veil of distinction. It was not his firmness and intrepidity in battle; it was not his sacrifice of his blood for his country's cause, when that cause was at stake on the plains of Continental Europe; nor was it the practical wisdom which he exhibited throughout the whole course of his government. What then was it?

Deep down in all men's hearts there is a lurking sense of romance which responds at once to the appeal made to it by an heroic episode. There are few incidents in American history touching this sense so acutely as Spotswood's passage of the Blue Ridge, which, without being the greatest, is one of the most thrilling explorations that ever took place on our continent. Other men may have crept silently through those same wooded fastnesses before he did, but he was the first to do so with the flare of a Spanish conquistador; and he was also the first to concentrate upon himself the gaze of a whole people as he opened the door which gave entrance to the boundless region of the West, destined in time to become the principal seat of empire on this side of the globe. In the mind's eye his figure will always stand on the lofty pinnacle of the Blue Ridge, with a guiding, uplifted finger pointed straight towards the Pacific Ocean and the land of infinite fertility between.

But before we describe this sylvan excursion, which has bestowed such romantic renown on Spotswood's name, let us offer in some detail the most salient features of his official career in Virginia. Although the Governor's reputation is based chiefly on a single event remarkable for its poetical character, he was at bottom an administrator of a peculiarly

119

utilitarian bent. So soon as he arrived at Jamestown, he began bringing his powers of persuasion to bear on the General Assembly to pass certain measures that would either facilitate the enforcement of the existing laws or sensibly increase the community's prosperity.

During many years the Act of Navigation, which required that all shipments of tobacco from Virginian wharfs should be made either to England or to its colonies, had been persistently violated by shipmasters' smuggling on board great quantities of this commodity, designed, not for London or English colonial ports, but for the alien dominions in the West Indies, where it could be promptly placed in foreign bottoms and transported to the marts of Continental Europe. The first procedure in the voyage was to transfer this tobacco at the Capes to the hold of some waiting vessel. This practice which, according to modern view, had nothing in it but what was promotive of the true welfare of the Virginian people by broadening their market, was scotched by Spotswood's success in obtaining a special guard ship to patrol the waters at the entrance to the Chesapeake. As there was really a sharp antagonism between the colony's interests and the interests of the mother country, this act of the Governor did not tend to increase his popularity in the community under his rule.

His next act was one which, from its benevolent character, won the good will of the officers and crews of the merchantmen trading in those waters—he urgently recommended that a hospital, with every convenience attainable in those times, should be built as a part of the fort at Point Comfort, for the use of sailors needing medical or surgical attention; and what was of equal importance to men of this calling, that a commodious dockyard should be constructed there for the repair of all vessels requiring renovation. In our own day, within convenient reach of the site of this proposed dockyard, there stands the greatest shipyard in the Western Hemisphere, where vessels are launched of such a size as to make the colonial merchantman appear a cockle boat in comparison.

Whether Spotswood was successful or not in bringing about these important public improvements, he seems at least to have persuaded the General Assembly to appropriate the sum that was necessary for the completion of the state house. No building in Virginia during the Colonial period had been so often swept by fire as this. Only once, however, had it perished by the torch of the incendiary. This was on the occasion of Jamestown's capture by Nathaniel Bacon. At other times it had fallen a victim to mere accident, so hard to anticipate and to circumvent in an era when no real provision could be made for the suppression of flames once started on their destructive course.

In 1705 the College of William and Mary had suffered the same fate as the state house, and Spotswood, immediately after his arrival, being an enlightened friend of learning, began to coöperate most energetically with Commissary Blair in restoring this structure also to its former proportions. He did this with all the more personal interest because he was told that the original had been put together in harmony with the model supplied by Sir Christopher Wren. The Reverend Hugh Jones, who examined the building after it was finished, praised its beauty and commodiousness; and he attributed to Spotswood the principal credit for "its nice contrivance, skilful alteration, and tasteful adornment." This English visitor, a man who had seen all the finest examples of architecture in England, was reminded of Chelsea Hospital as he gazed at the walls of the restored edifice.

In 1712, through the clergyman of Bruton Church, Spotswood submitted a plan for a new building to serve its parishioners, and he offered to pay out of his own purse for the construction of twenty-two feet of one of the walls. The cost of two wings was defrayed by the General Assembly. The Governor reserved a pew for himself, which was raised above the level of the floor and shaded by a canopy, on the interior side of which his name was woven in letters of gilt.

He also finished the construction of the governor's palace, which was in progress at the time of his arrival. Complaint was made that he spent over six thousand pounds sterling on this building, but the imposing appearance of the edifice amply compensated for the outlay. "It is a magnificent structure," said the Reverend Hugh Jones, "furnished, and with beautiful gates, fine gardens, offices, walks, a fine canal and orchard." It possessed also the novel feature of a lantern, which illuminated the town on the occasion of the public celebrations.

Another building which the town obtained through Spotswood was the Powder Horn, constructed in the shape of a hexagon. It was this building, still standing, which was associated with one of the most interesting incidents in the early history of the great Revolutionary movement.

Spotswood's practical spirit was further revealed in the sobriquet, the Tubal-Cain of Virginia, which he won as the first permanently successful promoter of the iron industry in the colony. It is true that the pioneers of Falling Creek, who were slain in the Indian Massacre of 1622, had gone before him, but their primitive furnace had been destroyed before it could be made really productive, and it was never restored. He was the owner of a large tract of land at Germanna, on the Rapidan River, which had been found to contain iron ore of a decided richness. The expense of extracting the metal was thought by him at first to be too heavy for one purse to defray, and he sought, but in vain, the assistance of the General Assembly's public resources. Ultimately he was able to secure the labor of numerous German workingmen, who had been induced by him to make their homes on the Rapidan, after finding it impossible in consequence of an Indian invasion to settle at the place in North Carolina originally chosen for them. In the beginning Spotswood very generously undertook the burden of supporting these foreigners and later aided them to earn their own livelihood. Perhaps their presence on his lands and his knowledge of their intelligence, industry, and skill in manual trades suggested that they might be the very instruments which he needed for the erection and the successful management of an iron furnace. The ore was to be obtained for the digging, and here were the laborers both to dig the ore and run the furnace so soon as constructed. In time, three furnaces were added to the first one built, and for all four the required workingmen were found at his threshold, first in these Germans, and afterwards in his own slaves.

There was at this time, as there had been and was to continue to be throughout the Colonial period, an extreme jealousy among the English iron manufacturers of any interference with their trade by the production of duplicates of their finished articles in Virginia for the satisfaction of the market there. Spotswood was fully aware of this feeling, and it was especially incumbent on him as governor to remove all occasion for it. Pig iron for shipment to England, therefore, made up the bulk of the output of his furnaces, and it was only a small quantity of iron articles in a more or less crude form which he ventured to sell to the people of Virginia, such as fenders, andirons, chimney backs, skillets, and boxes for cartwheels.

In the course of 1710-11 there arose such a state of poverty in the colony that the English Government's opposition to domestic manufactures was disregarded. It seems that about this time there had been a disposition in the General Assembly to discourage the further importation of African slaves, and the method adopted to effect this was to place a tax of five pounds sterling on the head of every Negro brought into Virginia. The constantly increasing number of black bondsmen had been promotive of a large addition to the volume of the annual tobacco crop, as there was no other employment to which their energies could be directed; and as the production of tobacco advanced in quantity, the price steadily fell, in consequence of the over-supply. The English Government, always subservient to the selfish demands of the English merchants, annulled the Assembly's statute, which sought, by a higher tax, to restrict the number of slaves imported. The stream of bondsmen pouring in continued in an even larger volume, and the crop of tobacco as a result went on expanding in size, while the price went on contracting in degree.

The planters became so discouraged by the smallness of the incomes derived from their only staple that they turned to manufacturing under their own roofs those articles of clothing which they had previously bought from the English traders. So great was the scale of this home production that, according to reports, in one county alone forty thousand yards of woolen, cotton, and linen cloth had in one year issued from the household looms. Spotswood, as the representative of the English Government, doubtless expressed his disapproval of this industry, but if he did so, no attention was paid to his perfunctory protest so long as the price of tobacco continued so low. He probably was not energetic in opposing the movement for domestic manufactures, because he expected it to die out just so soon as the main crop of the people should once more command a fair return.

Spotswood's attitude towards the sheriffs' slackness in enforcing the payment of the quitrents was much more vigorous. Here was a state of affairs that would continue indefinitely unless firmly halted. He urged upon the General Assembly's attention the advisability of passing a law which would call for the forfeiture of all land whose owners had during three years failed to deliver the amount due for these rents. In order to make easy the settlements of this fixed charge, he proposed a method far ahead of his time in financial wisdom—he suggested that for every hogshead of tobacco deposited in a public warehouse a certificate of receipt should be issued and that this certificate should be made legal tender. In advancing this suggestion Spotswood offered a plan that would assure, so soon as it was adopted, a perfectly stable currency, because that currency would be amply secured against every possibility of depreciation, except possibly through fire. No doubt this proposal would have been more favorably regarded by the General Assembly had it not been accompanied by a recommendation for the more rigid enforcement of the laws relating to the headright and the quitrent. In their opposition to both, that body went so far as to petition the King for the abolition of the headright altogether; and because Spotswood censured this act as equally unwise and futile, the Assembly endeavored to have him dismissed by trumping up numerous charges against him which, however, when referred to the English Government, he found no difficulty in refuting.

Having been accustomed to the mail facilities of England, which with all their serious deficiencies were the most satisfactory of that age, Spotswood was indefatigable in his exertions to make successful in Virginia the operation of the patent which Thomas Neale had obtained for the establishment of an intercolonial postoffice. The fees for transmission were prohibitive for most persons who were likely to find occasion to send letters. For the dispatch of one of a single sheet the sum of nine pence a mile had to be paid, if its destination was within the distance of eight miles; and four and a half pence in addition, when there was more ground to be traversed. This in modern values meant an outlay of about six shillings for the length of the first eight miles.

Like all his predecessors, Spotswood found himself, on the threshold of his administration, in opposition to the vestries' regulation that each clergyman's term should be limited to the provision of his contract on that point. He endeavored to ride down this rule, but the General Assembly positively refused to support him in the effort. They even went further than this. They denied that the right of permanent induction was possessed by the clergy in the colony, whatever might be the right of their fellows in England under the custom which had prevailed there almost immemorially. Commissary Blair with characteristic vigor promptly disputed the propriety of his action when he came forward to collate to a vacant benefice, and the controversy was made the more heated by the participation of the younger Philip Ludwell in it, with all the zeal and bitterness which had been shown by his father in the controversy with Jeffreys during the previous century. Very soon Spotswood found himself to be as impotent in this struggle as Nicholson had found himself to be in a prior one, for the question involved was too vital in its nature, in the view of the vestries and their congregations, for them to yield to mere official demand. Naturally, by keeping this check upon clergymen who might otherwise be lax, they assured such a performance of the ministerial duties in the different parishes as stood the highest test of practical fidelity and efficiency.

Spotswood's time was often employed more successfully in contending with much less civilized opponents than Blair and Ludwell. In 1717, in spite of the continuous attempts to put down piracy along the coast of Virginia, so many buccaneers infested the estuaries and bays within the Capes that they were said to have practically blockaded those inland waters. The Governor made up his mind, after repeated provocations, either to destroy them or to drive them away permanently. The *Shoreham* was still the guard ship, but sloops had proved to be more effective in such an enterprise as he now proposed to undertake.

There was a notorious outlaw named Teach prowling about the Carolina sounds at this time. In order to escape the legal consequences of his crimes he pretended to surrender his vessel and crew to the nearest local magistrate, and he thus obtained the certificate of immunity which had been offered by the authorities in case he should give himself up. But after a short period of desistance, Teach again called together his men—who had scattered themselves about the neighboring region—and going on board of his sloop, which he had been permitted to retain, he started at once upon a course of new depredations by stopping and rifling every trading vessel that crossed his bow. The news of these spoliations reached Spotswood's ears, and without hesitation he took steps to remove all chance of their repetition. Gathering up two or three small coasting vessels and manning them with sailors belonging to the royal service who happened to be at hand, he sent them after the sloop and its pirate crew. A fight ensued in which Teach himself was killed, together with some of his lawless followers. Teach's head was brought into the Chesapeake strung up to the bowsprit of his slayer's vessel.

It was not the fault of the firm yet conciliatory Spots-

PLATE XII. *From the portrait by Charles Bridges in the Virginia State Library,
Richmond, Virginia. Used by courtesy of the Governor of Virginia. Photo Cook.*

GOVERNOR ALEXANDER SPOTSWOOD

wood that during his administration there were occasional conflicts between the Virginians and the Indians. In September, 1711, the Tuscaroras, seated south of the border, rose unexpectedly and slew many of the settlers who had patented lands along the Pamlico and Neuse Rivers. There was reason to fear that some of the tribes residing within Virginia would hasten to join them in these murderous raids. Spotswood promptly dispatched a trained body of troops to intercept such a movement should it begin; and not satisfied with this step, he traveled through the trackless woods to the town of the Nottoways, in order to obtain the promise of their chiefs that they would not permit their warriors to take part in any such expedition.

Three years afterwards, in deep concern for the safety of the outlying settlements, Spotswood endeavored by peace treaties with the Tuscaroras, Nottoways, and Saponys, who occupied the part of Virginia situated next to the Carolina border, to raise a permanent barrier against the constantly threatened incursions of the alien and armed Indians that were so often skulking about the region. The native tribes were assigned an area of country supposed to spread over at least twenty-three thousand acres, but as acceptance would require their withdrawal from their original seats, the Saponys alone agreed to the arrangement. The Tuscaroras refused because they had decided to remove to North Carolina, in order to coalesce with the branch of their tribe which had long been established there. The Nottoways, deeply attached to their native town, positively declined to abandon it.

In order to increase his government's ability to deal successfully with these tribes, Spotswood erected a fort in the midst of the Sapony reservation, which he named Christanna and which was protected from open or furtive attack by a file of soldiers, supported by a band of tawny scouts who were instructed to patrol the surrounding forests without any intermission. The fort's importance was enhanced by the restriction to its confines of all trading between the English and the savages. It also became the site

127

of a school for Indian children, under the direction of an English clergyman; and with a view of augmenting the number of pupils, the superior advantage in bartering was granted to those Indian parents who had sent their offspring to this school to be regularly instructed.

Spotswood was always ready to respond to every appeal for help that he received from the adjacent colonies which were sinking under the blows of the tomahawk. In 1715, when the Indians were striking relentlessly at the settlers beyond the Virginian borders, he emptied the magazine at Jamestown of its store of powder and muskets and dispatched these materials of warfare, along with a large body of troops, to the rescue of his hotly pressed neighbors. He was so acutely alive to these constant incursions that in the winter of 1717-18 he hurried through the snow and rain to New York to stop the expedition which it was reported the Iroquois were about to launch against the tribes seated in the far southern Appalachian region. Before he could reach his destination the marauders had set out, but after a quick pursuit they were halted by a messenger from the north. The damage which they invariably inflicted in these raids, not only on the friendly Virginian Indians, but also on the whites, was subsequently reduced by their consenting to abandon the trail east of the Blue Ridge and to follow only the one running to the west of those mountains.

The energetic spirit and alert intelligence of Spotswood must, from the very first day after his arrival in Virginia, have been deeply interested in the mystery of the land situated back of that great wall which was known to close the western horizon. He was not the first to feel this curiosity, nor the first to seek to explore the heart of the secret. It is thought that the Jesuits had traversed the Valley early in 1632. At least this is the inference to be drawn from their maps. William Claiborne and his followers had not long afterwards turned their faces towards the same goal, but only to fail. Edward Bland and his fellow-explorers had pressed as far as the modern New River. Loederer, in 1669-70, had reached a point still more remote in that silent

128

wilderness. Abraham Wood only a short time subsequently had marched in the same direction, but the record of his journey reveals no conspicuous discovery.

The Valley at this time was the hunting ground of the different tribes and apparently was not permanently inhabited, with the exception of a few villages occupied by the Shawnees and Tuscaroras. The chief reason for this deserted condition was to be found in the periodic traversals of the trails by the terrible Iroquois warriors of the north, who carried the torch in one bloody hand and the tomahawk in the other. In 1706 Louis Michell is thought to have visited the lower reaches of the beautiful Shenandoah River; and either in Michell's company or alone, De Graffenried, one of the pioneers of Carolina, had seen with his own eyes all the charms of that verdant paradise. It was during his sojourn at Williamsburg previous to May, 1712, that he further inflamed Spotswood's curiosity about the great Valley by giving a vivid description of all that it had to offer to hasten its settlement.

But it was not until 1716 that Spotswood himself undertook that western journey which, from his distant day down to our own, has been celebrated in verse and prose as one of the romantic episodes in the long history of explorations in the primitive American wilderness. The genius of Fontaine, Ticknor, and Carruthers has caught and preserved for us some of the freshness of that tour of the forests and mountains. But there is a more classic record of this event than even these writers have furnished. Under the rule requiring the College of William and Mary to submit a copy of an original Latin poem as its annual quitrent for the land in its possession, one of its professors celebrated Spotswood's passage of the Blue Ridge in the language and meter of Rome; and these verses were solemnly presented to him by the academic authorities a few months after his return.

What was the object of the expedition which he so successfully carried out? It was to cross a chain of mountains which for a generation had silently lifted its peaks to the sky in sight of the wandering trappers who had threaded the woods of Piedmont. Some brave explorers had passed it further south, as we have seen; some had crept down from the north behind the barrier; but none so far had gone straight to the base of that towering chain in its central division, and from its top, at that point, looked down on the lower reaches of the Shenandoah.

Spotsylvania County, which ran up to this base and beyond, had been carved out of the region along the tributaries of the Rappahannock with the avowed purpose of raising a wall against the fierce inroads of the united Indians and French troops from the forts at Kaskaskia, Detroit, and Vincennes. The earliest colonists to plant themselves within this area were Germans, who began to come in 1714 and who were still its only white inhabitants when Spotswood mounted his horse at Williamsburg on August 20 to start upon his adventurous journey. At the hour when this journey began, the Governor was attended by John Fontaine, a member of a Huguenot family which had settled in Virginia only the year before. Fontaine was doubtless glad to resume the life of travel which had had its first stage in the recent voyage from England.

The expedition upon which Spotswood now entered was to last twenty-eight days to and fro, and it was to call for the traversal of four hundred and thirty-eight miles. Stopping at the homes of Colonel Bassett and of his own son-in-law, Moore, he next drew rein at the front gate of Robert Beverley, the historian; and from that spot the little party accompanied by Beverley turned westward up the valley of the Rappahannock River. But it was not until Spotswood dismounted at Germanna that he was joined by the entire cavalcade which was to ride with him to the crest of the Ridge. It consisted of a small band of gentlemen, two companies of trained forest rangers, and several Indian scouts who were thoroughly at ease in threading a trackless wilderness and in detecting traces of the presence of lurking savages. The entire party embraced as many as fifty persons, and the procession which they formed in making their way through the woods more or less in single file was further

130

strung out by a long trail of pack horses, carrying on their backs camp equipment, hampers of provisions, and an extraordinary quantity of liquors of all kinds. At night the members of the company sheltered themselves under the canvas of their tents, if the weather was menacing, or slept in the open, if the skies were cloudless.

The journey from day to day had all the charm of primeval woodland scenery and the scented freshness of forest air, but it was varied only by the recurrence of petty incidents. An unexpected contact with a hornet's nest and the stings of its occupants, or the hiss of a coiled rattlesnake were the only dangers which the band seems to have had to face. Nor did the men run any risk of starvation. On the contrary, they fared abundantly on the flesh of deer, bear, and turkey, which the rangers killed from hour to hour. The woods they traversed grew so thickly around them, and the foliage was so dense over their heads that a distant view was unobtainable; and probably not until they reached the foot of the mountains did they become aware of the nearness of the Ridge. By the fifth of September they had arrived at the crest, and here they encamped for the night.

They descended the next day to the valley of the pastoral stream which flowed northward along the western base of the chain. This they had the bad taste to christen the Euphrates, perhaps because they were unaware of its exquisite Indian appellation. On its bank Spotswood buried a bottle enclosing a formal document stating that he had taken possession of the surrounding country in the name of the King. When dinner had been finished, the first toast offered was to his Royal Majesty, and this was tossed off in champagne to the accompaniment of an explosion of musketry. "The Princess' health," Ensign Fontaine tells us, "was next drunk in Burgundy, and a volley fired, and all the rest of the Royal Family in claret, with a volley. We drank the Governor's health, and fired another. We had several sorts of liquors, viz., Virginia red wine and white wine, Irish usquebaugh, brandy, stout, two sorts of rum, champaigne, canary, cherry punch, water, and cider." Before dinner the company had

131

amused themselves with hunting, fishing, and swimming, but afterwards they were perhaps in a condition only to lie down and sleep. The rangers do not appear to have lingered with the gentlemen of the party, but in a few hours were off for the exploration of the Valley.

On the following morning the journey towards Germanna began, and that place was reached at the end of three days, with the record, strange to say, of but one incident of bibulousness on the route; on at least one occasion a bowl of punch was broached; but probably this had nothing to do with Major Beverley's rolling with his horse down a hillock or with Mr. Clouder's falling head foremost into a stream.

In anticipation of the success of the exploration, Spotswood had for its commemoration ordered a considerable number of miniature golden horseshoes to be made—a stroke of poetic sentiment—and one of these, set with diamonds, he gave to each of the gentlemen who had accompanied him. On each horseshoe was engraved the motto, *sic juvat transcendere montes*. Thrifty even when gratifying his sense of romance, Spotswood had expected the royal treasury to defray the expense of these beautiful baubles, but this being refused, he cheerfully assumed the cost himself. It is not known whether a single one of these horseshoes is now in existence. The name applied to their recipients, "Knights of the Golden Horseshoe," is still remembered.

After his retirement from the office of lieutenant-governor, Spotswood made his home at Germanna, where he had built a mansion of such large and handsome proportions that it was popularly known as the Palace. Here, in the enjoyment of the society of his wife, children, and visiting friends, and in the supervision of his mines and plantation crops, and in the perusal of books, he looked forward to many years of usefulness and contentment. And that anticipation was to be fully realized. This serene life was not interrupted until 1740, when war was declared between England and Spain. Spotswood was then, with the rank of major general, appointed to the command of the regiment which the colony contributed to the English forces. While stopping at Annapolis—from which he and his troops were to embark to take part in the expedition against Porto Bello —he suddenly passed away in his sixty-fourth year. To the last he had shown his interest in education and in the College of William and Mary by bequeathing that seat of learning all his books, maps, and mathematical instruments.

"Innocent in his private life," says the historian Burk, "unimpeached in his administration of government; a friend to the liberties of the Colony, without losing sight of the interest of the Mother Country; a skilful and enterprising soldier—he appears a star of no ordinary magnitude amidst the darkness with which he was surrounded."

Spotswood was charged by his enemies with aristocratic pride in criticizing the unexclusive suffrage law, but this simply meant that he thought men of property likely to be more conservative in exercising their right, if it was left to these alone, than would be a mixed and turbulent class which had not possessed the qualities necessary for the acquisition of even a moderate degree of pecuniary independence. If he was sometimes impatient with the parsimony of the General Assembly, it was because that attitude on their part was not, in his opinion, justified whenever the best interests of the community called for a more liberal policy.

The most winning picture of Spotswood in his private life is to be found in the description which Colonel Byrd gave of his visit to Germanna in 1732. "I arrived," he records, "about three o'clock, and found only Mrs. Spotswood at home, who received her old acquaintance with many a gracious smile. I was carried into a room elegantly set off with Pier Glasses, the latter of which came sometime after to an odd misfortune. Amongst other favourite animals that cheered the Lady's Solitude, a brace of tame Deer ran familiarly about the House, and one of these came to stare at me as a Stranger. But unluckily spying her own Figure in the Glass, she made a spring over the tea table that stood under it, and shattered the glass to pieces, and falling back upon

133

the tea table, made a terrible fracas among the China. This Exploit was so sudden, and accompany'd with such a noise, that it surpriz'd me, and perfectly frightened Mrs. Spotswood. But 'twas worth all the damage to shew the Moderation and good humor with which she bore this disaster. In the Evening, the noble Colonel came home from his mines, who saluted me very civilly; and Mrs. Spotswood's sister, Miss Thaky, who had been to meet him *en cavalier*, was so kind too as to bid me welcome. We talked over a Legend of Old Storys, supped about 9, and then prattl'd with the Ladys til 'twas time for a travellour to retire. In the mean time, I observed my old Friend to be very uxorious, and exceedingly fond of his children. This was so opposite to the maxims he used to preach up before he was marry'd, that I cou'd not forbear rubbing up the memory of them. But he gave a very good natur'd turn to his change of Sentiments by alleging that whoever brings a poor Gentlewoman into so solitary a place, from her friends and acquaintance, would be ungrateful not to use her and all that belongs to her, with all possible Tenderness."

Chapter X

COLONEL WILLIAM BYRD

In 1651 there arrived in Virginia, as a member of the Parliamentary commission appointed to receive its surrender, Captain Thomas Stegge. This was not his first sight of that region, for as early as 1637 he had seated himself there in order to engage to greater advantage in the profitable tobacco trade of the colony. This occupation, however, did not absorb all his thoughts and energies, since six years afterwards he was Speaker of the General Assembly, and somewhat later on, a member of the Council. It is to be inferred from his advancement to those honors that he was a man of something more than business shrewdness in his ability to stamp so deeply on his contemporaries the influence of his personality. He had in fact risen by the force of his own mind and character to the highest positions in the colony open to a resident citizen.

When Captain Stegge died he was survived by two children. One was a son, who resided in view of the great falls of the James, on a site now included within the boundaries of the modern city of Richmond. The other was a daughter, who had married John Byrd, a prosperous English banker or goldsmith, as men of that calling were then designated. John Byrd, whose home was in London, seems to have had ancestral connection with at least one family of high social standing among the country gentry.

The younger Stegge ran the same career as his thrifty father. He added to his inherited fortune by foresight and economy. He was also an officer in the ranks of the militia, a member of the Council, and, rising higher than his father in posts of pecuniary profit, the colonial auditor-general. This position could have been secured only by the possession of influence with the British Board of Trade. In his last will Stegge provided for the descent of his estate to his sister's son, the first William Byrd, who by this time had reached the age of eighteen, but who even then bore himself with the gravity of more advanced years. There was something additional which his uncle had left to him that in its direct effect on his career was to prove as valuable as the lands he had inherited—this was the transmitted friendship of two very powerful men, namely, Sir William Berkeley and Thomas Ludwell. Ludwell had been earnestly requested by Stegge in the text of his will to show his nephew the kindness which he had always bestowed on the grateful testator.

When the first William Byrd arrived in Virginia, he was in the possession of these three great advantages: the large fortune which had fallen to him through his uncle; the conspicuous friends to whom he had been recommended; and the high social position which had become his portion through the standing of his generous relative. These advantages made him a very eligible suitor, and it was not very long before he was happily married. His wife was the daughter of Colonel Warham Horsemanden, who had been a distinguished officer in the royalist army, but who, like so many other followers of Charles I of military rank, had left England after his royal master's death and purchased a plantation in Virginia. Here, however, he did not remain permanently, as the lure of his native country was too strong to be resisted.

The elder Byrd displayed a keen practical shrewdness from the threshold of his active life. He was not satisfied simply to hold on to his inherited estate. He determined to increase it, and to accomplish this purpose he turned to the pursuits of a country merchant and an Indian trader.

It was as an Indian trader that he was most successful. Year after year he sent out to remote posts in the dark forests on the frontier a train of peddlers and pack horses to exchange guns, ammunition, and other English goods for the furs and similar articles which the savages were eager to offer in return. They traveled as far over the rough aboriginal trails as the towns of the Catawbas and the Cherokees in the remote southern regions. Many traders joined with the elder Byrd in dispatching to these towns and to the towns of other tribes as many as one hundred pack horses in a single expedition. In the traffic of his numerous stores every kind of household merchandise was sold; and he also disposed there of the Negroes and white servants whom he had imported for that purpose. He further swelled his fortune by speculative purchases of tobacco on the plantations for shipment to Bristol or London. But these ventures did not always prove to be profitable, for the price of the commodity, after its arrival in England, was often very low in spite of the fact that the freight rate of importation had been extremely high.

The elder Byrd's general career followed the path which had been laid down by his kinsmen and predecessors, the two Stegges. He was appointed an officer of high rank in the militia; he was elected a burgess; he was nominated to the Council; and he was commissioned receiver of the quitrents. At first he was fully in sympathy with the plans of Nathaniel Bacon, because he, like Bacon, had plantations on the frontier which were exposed to the raids of the Indians; but he turned back to Berkeley when he found that Bacon intended practically to upset the colonial administration by reforming it.

He endeavored without success to obtain the King's permission to assume jurisdiction over a wide area of country near the falls in the James and to garrison it with a troop of fifty men. Not discouraged by his failure to secure this privilege, he petitioned the English authorities for a monopoly of the Indian trade, with a promise of a large tribute to the royal treasury. But this request also fell to the ground. As some compensation for these disappointments he was able to secure the appointment of auditor, which carried with it the office and profits also of receiver-general. His duty in these positions was to collect all moneys to which the King was entitled in Virginia. These funds were derived from the quitrents, from the export tax on tobacco, and from fines and escheats. Towards the close of life he was admitted to a seat in the Council, and by upright character, business capacity, the possession of wealth, and the enjoyment of official dignity, he occupied a position of distinction in the community at large.

After his marriage, the elder Byrd seems to have resided in a house situated at the falls in the James. It had been built by his uncle and had descended to him along with the rest of his uncle's estate. This house stood on such a low spot that it was exposed to destructive overflow whenever there was a freshet in the river, and this fact finally led him to erect a mansion of imposing size on higher ground at no great distance away. This house was still standing in good repair when the place was visited by an English traveler about one hundred years afterwards, who described it as an "elegant villa" even for that richer time. The center of the structure consisted of two stories, with a wing of a single story on each side.

The locality of the falls was at this time known as the World's End. Like navigation, the settlements appear to have halted here, as if balked for further progress by the masses of rock that filled the bed of the roaring stream.

In spite of the comforts and spaciousness of the mansion which they had built, the elder Byrd and his wife became dissatisfied with the spot. In the first place, it was open to Indian incursions; and in the second, it had grown lonely from the fact that the elder children had been sent to England to be educated. The falls at that date were too far away from the homes of people occupying the social position of the Byrds to afford them constant visitors by the exercise of a hospitable spirit. In the end they decided to establish themselves in a neighborhood which possessed more social advantages. Twenty miles down the river the elder Byrd had purchased of the Bland family the Westover estate, which embraced an area of about twelve hundred acres at the time of the sale, but which acquired in later years additions of importance. Only a few miles below Westover was the head of navigation for vessels engaged in the transportation of tobacco oversea. Mrs. Byrd had a personal acquaintance with the countryside through the fact that her father had resided here before his return to England.

The mansion which the elder Byrd erected was not the one that, still standing, has been so long celebrated in Virginia's social annals. The original building was constructed of wood, but it was fitted up with the handsome furniture which even then was brought over in large quantities from London. It was under this roof that the elder Byrd replanted his family in 1691. Two of his daughters were now at school in England. One of these, in the end, found a husband there; but the other returned to Virginia to become the wife of Robert Beverley and to die before she had passed her seventeenth birthday, leaving but one memorial of her former existence in the fragment of her tombstone, which still survives. Byrd's wife, of loyal Cavalier stock, also sank to the grave in 1699. In his own last hour he would have been alone but for the presence of his housekeeper and valet, and his friend and neighbor, William Randolph, who had been hurriedly summoned to his bedside.

The entire estate, with the exception of a few small legacies left to his daughter, was by his will to become the property of his only son, who bore the same given name as himself. It consisted in one particular alone of over twenty-six thousand acres of land, dispersed in separate tracts lying among the several counties.

The second and great William Byrd entered upon his majority with far more advantages than had fallen to his father's lot at the same age. Perhaps the most striking difference in their respective inheritances from nature lay in the fact that the son had not only as much capacity for acquisition as the father, but a power of enjoyment in many ways far superior to anything within the latter's grasp. The elder Byrd belonged to the type which in modern

139

COLONEL WILLIAM BYRD

America devotes itself to the accumulation of money, with only a languid interest in aspirations lying without that pale. His surviving letters reveal that he hardly had a thought for any side of the primitive world about him beyond what could be turned to his own pecuniary profit. There is no trace of intellectual curiosity in these letters, and its absence is not fully explained by the fact that they are simply links in a business correspondence. A keen practical shrewdness sticks out of every line.

The mellow geniality of the son was in conspicuous contrast with the methodical dryness of the father. But that the son was able to nourish all his natural powers and develop his inborn tastes was due to the elder Byrd's success in using his purely practical qualifications. With all his absorption in increasing his estate, he must have valued an education that extended far beyond the province in which he himself was so eminent. At least he must have allowed himself to be so far influenced by his wife, the daughter of a Cavalier, as to send his son to England, to be entered at a school of a riper character than any primary school then to be found in Virginia.

The change from the colony, so barren of scholastic openings, to the mother country, so rich in opportunities for the study of the humanities, was not simply an educational venture in the pedagogic sense of the word, for the younger Byrd. It was also a social venture. The advantages were not to be merely intellectual; they were also to be social. He was to become as accomplished in the drawing-room as he was in the library, because his talent for making use of either sphere was equally extraordinary. Under these combined influences he very naturally flowered into a person of remarkable versatility.

The first part of his stay in England was passed at Purleigh in Essex under the general guardianship of his maternal grandfather, the royalist officer, a man held in consideration alike for birth, character, and achievement. But his actual teacher was a friend of the family who enjoyed a high reputation for scholarship. The elder Byrd,

140

as auditor of Virginia, had been in constant correspondence with William Blathwayt, the auditor-general of the colonies, who resided in London, and it is quite possible that through this fact Blathwayt was interested in the Virginian boy from the first hour of his arrival and introduced him into his own circle of English intimates. The most important of these was Sir Robert Southwell, who was to be so kind and useful to the young man during the whole of his sojourn in England.

The elder Byrd was determined that his son's benefit from an European education should not be limited to the English and ancient literatures. Some knowledge of foreign methods of business should also be acquired; and as the Dutch were the most highly trained merchants of that period, young Byrd was instructed by his father to spend a part of his time abroad in Holland in the study of such of its mercantile rules as would be serviceable to him when he should be called upon to manage his own inheritance. He was still a mere youth in years, and he failed to find his new Dutch associates as attractive socially as had been his English. But his father refused to permit him to go back to London unless he should promise to enter, so soon as he arrived there, the countinghouse of Perry and Lane, a firm very famous in the Virginia trade of those times. The young man, however, was more interested in intellectual pursuits than in mercantile, and soon after he returned to England from Holland he seems to have been able to combine the acquisition of a sound knowledge of law with the acquisition of an equally sound knowledge of business. He was in the course of time called to the English bar.

While a student in the Middle Temple, Byrd was thrown into intimate relations with Benjamin Lynde, who became many years afterwards chief justice of the highest court in the Massachusetts colony. In a letter addressed to his friend when both were elderly men, he laughingly confessed that the two together had led very jolly lives in London in the frequent pursuit of passing intrigues. "But," adds Byrd, "matrimony has atoned sufficiently for such backslidings, and now, I suppose, you have so little fellow feeling left for the haughty jades that you can order them a good whipping."

Byrd was too young during his first sojourn abroad to win a large company of distinguished friends. That was to take place afterwards, when he returned to London a matured man in possession of a large fortune. He was only twenty-two years old when his foot retouched his native shore, but even then, his appearance, bearing, and conversation indicated plainly the culture resulting from his contact with the great world of England.

Throughout the Colonial period the custom prevailed in Virginia, as it had long done in the mother country, of advancing young men of fortune, just reaching their majority, to seats in the House of Burgesses. Byrd was promptly chosen after his arrival at home to represent the county of Henrico; and so favorable was the impression which he made on his fellow members by his tactful and courteous bearing and by his talent for business, that he was named with John Povey to lay an address of the General Assembly before the English Board of Trade. In 1698 he was appointed by the Council to be the colony's agent in London, and this position he continued to hold until the Board decided in favor of Lieutenant-Governor Nicholson in a controversy raised by him over whether the Council and House of Burgesses had a right to submit petitions in London without making Byrd the principal spokesman.

As nature abhors a vacuum, so every prominent Virginian of that day abhorred a vacancy in office, and just so soon as it was found to exist, he rushed forward to fill it. When Byrd withdrew from the agency, he became a candidate for the secretaryship of the colony, which had recently lost its incumbent. At his solicitation the Board of Trade recommended him to the King, but without success. The language which that body used in bringing him before the royal eye was a clear proof of his ability to impress himself strongly on the minds of men, even when he was still young in years. "Mr. Byrd," they said, "is a person of good character, unblamable conduct, and known loyalty to his Majesty and his government, and has had the advantage of a liberal education and knowledge of the laws of England." While sojourning in London in the service of the Virginian authorities, Byrd, now in the flush of his attractive physical appearance, charming manners, and sprightly conversation, made the most of the social pleasures open to him in the capital's fashionable drawing-rooms through intimate association with the most distinguished people in England. One of his faithful friends of this period was the Earl of Orrery, who, as the champion of a certain literary party, had raised the controversy which suggested to Swift the production of his famous satire, *The Battle of the Books.*

On his arrival in England Byrd had resumed his friendly intercourse with Sir Robert Southwell. Southwell had filled the honorable post of president of the Royal Society and continued to participate in its proceedings until his death in 1702. It is probable that he obtained admission for Byrd to this association. Byrd was so familiar with every aspect of nature in Virginia that he was not at a loss for an interesting subject to discuss before his fellow-members. The subject which he did select was entitled "An account of a negro boy that is dappled in several places of his body with white spots." Few of the persons who heard him read this paper had ever seen a Negro, and those who had seen one could only recall a creature of the blackest hue. Byrd's description of this strange object must have left a lively impression on the minds of his inquiring auditors. There is no record of his having submitted any other paper.

He remained in England until his father's death, which occurred in December, 1704, about seven years afterwards. On receiving information of this event, he gave up all the charming associations which had made his stay in England so delightful, and prepared for an early return to his home on the banks of the James. There could hardly be a more remarkable contrast within the limits of civilized life than that between his fashionable existence in London, in full enjoyment of all its excitements, and the round which was now to make up his daily occupations on a large Virginian plantation, situated on a mighty stream surrounded by forests and sparsely inhabited country estates.

But Byrd, not affected by the leap from the Thames to the James, started in with the energy of all Virginians in those times when a vacant office was in sight, to secure the posts which his father had occupied. He had already been appointed to the auditorship before he reached the colony, but as it was decided to separate this office from that of the receiver-general, he resigned the former and accepted the latter; and he was successful in getting a larger salary attached to its tenure. His aspiration to fill his father's seat in the Council was gratified in 1709; and he continued to occupy it during the next thirty-five years. Had not the life of Commissary Blair, the member who had been seated in that body longer than he, been protracted to eighty-seven, Byrd would have risen to the presidency of the Council at an earlier date.

While still a very young man, he had married a daughter of Colonel Parke, a Virginian who had won unusual social distinction in England and still greater military. Parke's social prominence rested primarily on his own remarkable social talents, but it was due in a measure to his birth, since his mother belonged to the famous Evelyn family of Wotton which has been eminent from a remote period down to the present day. So vigorous was his natural ability, so insinuating was his address, that Marlborough, the foremost captain of that age, made him a member of his personal staff and selected him to carry to Queen Anne the dispatches announcing the victory of Blenheim. And he was subsequently appointed to the governorship of the Leeward Islands, where he met his death on the breaking out of a furious riot.

Byrd's marriage to Parke's youngest daughter brought him into intimacy with the Custis family, a member of which was the husband of Parke's eldest daughter. The tie between Parke and himself, however, proved to be of little financial benefit. Mrs. Byrd's paternal inheritance was limited to one thousand pounds sterling, while her sister's embraced the whole of her father's large estate in Virginia. But Byrd's pecuniary connection with Colonel Parke did not end with his wife's small legacy. He very generously assumed the English debt of his deceased father-in-law; and this obligation kept him in more or less pinched circumstances until nearly the close of his life, in spite of his possession of a princely fortune.

In 1710 there arrived at Jamestown a man who by his political measures was destined to bring the spirit of acute controversy into Byrd's life during many years. This person was the celebrated Alexander Spotswood, who had been appointed lieutenant-governor of the colony by Lord Orkney, the nominal governor. Probably no official of his high rank in Virginia ever took over the reins of administration without some friction with the Council almost from the very start. Its members were always independent in spirit and often arrogant in word. So great was the height of power which they had already reached when Spotswood took the executive oath that they were hardly to be distinguished from an oligarchy. They were men who showed in their imposing bearing the influence of good birth, personal authority, and the possession of wealth. The families of Wormeley, Ludwell, Lee, Burwell, Carter, and Byrd were represented among them, and so closely related by ties of blood were they as a body that in many cases all were unable to participate in its proceedings without exposing themselves to the charge of partiality.

We have already seen how bitterly a majority of Nicholson's councilors aspersed his conduct, and how this led to a quarrel that was disgraceful to both sides. Andros had run upon the same snag. It was also Spotswood's luck to find himself confronted with the like antagonism just as soon as he sought to carry out the reform of certain evils which bore with peculiar hardness on the interests of the King. There was at this time, for instance, a total lack of precision in defining the bounds of the patents, and gross irregularities also marked the annual collection of the quitrents. As to the patents, the only condition attached to them when issued was that a house should be erected on the soil embraced within any one of them, before the end of three years; and a small area of ground was also to be put in tillage. Spotswood materially added to this condition by persuading the General Assembly to insert a clause in the law to the effect that all land so acquired should also escheat if the quitrents had remained unpaid during a period of three years. But there was another evil which he thought should be removed. As the case now stood, the tobacco turned over to the sheriffs was not sold to advantage, simply because the deputies of these officials were lax in performing their duty. The tobacco, indeed, passed through so many hands before it reached the receiver-general that the fees seriously curtailed its volume, to the proportionate loss of the royal treasury. Byrd was personally interested, as receiver-general, in every proposal that was designed to cut out this defect. This led him to submit a plan which he anticipated would work successfully, but Spotswood with some heat rejected it and brought in a plan of his own. The principal features of the latter were: first, that the quitrents should be collected by the sheriffs themselves, and not by their deputies, at places selected by the county courts; and, secondly, that these rents should be paid in sterling money or in foreign coin or with notes secured by deposits of tobacco in the warehouses.

As Spotswood's plan had in it more to commend it, the members of the Council preferred it to the one which Byrd had drafted. The only two ballots cast against it were cast by Byrd and Ludwell. Byrd afterwards drew up an elaborate defense of his action, but Spotswood was unquestionably right in condemning the "gross mismanagements and the fraudulent collections" that took place under the prevailing system. "That these should exist," he said, "was no reflection at present on the integrity of the sheriffs, the first gentlemen in the country"; but, he added, it was a reflection on their deputies, who actually collected the rents and who were supposed to deliver them in full to their superior officers. If the fidelity of the sheriffs themselves was involved at all, it was only through the fact that they accepted their subordinates' accounts without inquiring into the accuracy of the figures. As Byrd's duty as receiver-general was limited to taking over the sheriffs' returns, no question of neglect could be raised against him should these returns prove to be fraudulent, in consequence of the deputies' delinquencies.

Spotswood was so much pleased with the success of the new law passed at his suggestion, he asserted that "one-third of the crown lands in Virginia had, in one year, yielded a greater revenue than the whole did formerly."

In 1713 Byrd obtained leave from the Council to transfer the functions of receiver-general to his deputy while he was absent in England, which he now intended to visit. During his stay there he protested before the Board of Trade against the diversion of the quitrents to the English treasury; and he was listened to with favorable attention. This fact increased his influence in Virginia, since the proposal was looked upon there with a feeling of keen disapproval. And he was also successful in persuading the Board to repeal two laws which Spotswood had induced the General Assembly to adopt. One of these had authorized the payment of all debts in tobacco; the other had created a company to monopolize the Indian trade.

Some time previous to 1716 Byrd sold the office of receiver-general because he thought that by doing so he would be the better able to meet the attacks of Spotswood, who was now strongly antagonistic to him, owing to the controversies which had arisen between them in the past. Spotswood, who was a somewhat unscrupulous fighter, did not hesitate to use the supposed shortcomings of the receiver-generalship under Byrd's management to weaken the hold which the latter had secured on the good will of the Board of Trade. Byrd revealed rather sour feeling in resigning the office by asserting that the incumbent "must either be a slave to Spotswood's humor, must fawn on him, jump over a stick whenever he was bid, or else he must have so much trouble loaded on him as to make his place uneasy. In short, such a man must be either the Governor's dog or his ass, neither of which stations suit in the least with my constitution."

But Spotswood was not satisfied with the passage of the laws already mentioned, which had caused Byrd so much disquiet. He now proposed another innovation that was destined to arouse even greater animosities than those which had sprung from the question of putting an end to the frauds in the collection and payment of the quitrents. Hitherto the courts of oyer and terminer, which met for the punishment of serious crimes, had been held separately from the general court, but up to this time, the judges of these by-courts had been drafted from the members of the general court. Spotswood came to the conclusion that they would subserve their purpose better should they be composed in part of councilors and in part of outsiders. It is possible that he expected in this way to add some trained lawyers to the body of these judges. Perhaps in a somewhat factious spirit, Byrd among others protested against the introduction of this change as calculated to add too much to the present power of the lieutenant-governor by enlarging the sphere of his patronage. The courts of oyer and terminer, he said, would meet often, and in each instance of their convening Spotswood and his successor—if the proposed innovation were carried out—would have the opportunity to appoint an entirely different set of satellites.

Spotswood boldly submitted his plan to the Board of Trade, which decided in favor of its adoption, provided that it was not repugnant to the tenor of any existing statute. A counter-petition was sent over by the Council, and in this document the burgesses also joined, at the same time appointing Byrd to serve as their private agent in London. When Byrd found that the Board of Trade was opposed to the position taken by the Council and burgesses, he appealed directly to the King, but without success. In the meanwhile, the attorney-general had delivered an opinion to the effect that Spotswood had the right to nominate the members of the courts of oyer and terminer. But a compromise was afterwards effected between the lieutenant-

PLATE XIII. *From a portrait by Kneller, 1702, recently found in England. Used by courtesy of the owner, Mr. William Byrd, New York City. Photo Cook.*

COLONEL WILLIAM BYRD, 2nd

governor and his antagonists which permitted him to name the judges of these courts, but which required him to restrict his nominations to the members of the Council.

Spotswood's personal hostility to Byrd, however, was not appeased by the adoption of this rule. In February, 1719, he urged the Board of Trade to remove his opponent from his seat in the Council on the pretended ground that he had by his long absence from Virginia forfeited his place in that body. The question was referred to the Privy Council, over which the King presided in person, and its decision was in favor of Byrd's retention of his office. Not long after his return to Virginia he became reconciled to Spotswood, a man with whom he had much in common; and this kindly feeling continued until Spotswood's death many years afterwards. The amity of their later intercourse is clearly revealed in Byrd's lively description of his visit to Germanna, to which we have already referred. The two men came together on that occasion with a warmth of cordiality that could have had its origin only in their genuine esteem for each other.

The long sojourn in London which Byrd was compelled to make while performing the duties of his agency was from a social point of view the most brilliant part of his successful life. There was, however, one feature at the beginning of that sojourn which left his spirit ill at ease. He was devoted to the members of his family, and yet he was accompanied by none of them when he set out, because he anticipated that he would not be long absent from home. Finding, however, that he was likely to be kept in England for an indefinite period, he wrote to his wife to come out to him, but hardly had she arrived in London, when she succumbed to smallpox, the furtive scourge of the time. She had brought with her a little daughter, born after Byrd had set sail for England.

In the course of the following year his daughter Evelyn joined him. Byrd gave the most loving attention to her education, and she grew up to be a very charming woman. She was beautiful in face, graceful in figure, sprightly in mind, and amiable in spirit. The high position which her father occupied in English society was shared by her, and she won the friendship of persons of the first order of distinction in that society. There has descended a tradition of a love story which associates her name with that of the brilliant Lord Peterborough, a celebrated man of fashion about town and also a skillful officer in the field. For reasons which have never been disclosed, the affair ended in a separation that left the beautiful young Virginian a maid for life. Perhaps it is this fact, coupled with the tranquil background of the Old World Westover, and a speaking portrait, which have thrown such an extraordinary veil of romance around her memory.

Byrd remained in London until 1726 and, like his daughter, contracted while there friendships with the most celebrated Englishmen of that period. A long list of portraits, transferred to his home in the colony, testified to the distinction of these personal associates on the other side of the water. These portraits preserved, with all the fidelity of life, the faces of Lords Orrery, Oxford, Halifax, and Egmont, the Duke of Argyle, Colonel Parke, Sir Robert Southwell, and William Blathwayt, and among the ladies of prominence the features of Lady Southwell and Lady Betty Cromwell. And in the midst of these were to be seen the portraits of himself, his wives, and children, all the work of the famous London painters of those artistic times.

Byrd had taken as his second spouse Maria Taylor of Kensington, a lady with many accomplishments and of great charm of person and sweetness of temper, who seems to have stood with perfect equanimity the change from the numerous excitements of London to the seclusion of a Virginian plantation.

Byrd never returned to England again. The remainder of his useful and brilliant life was passed in the colony, in the happy and rational pursuit of all those serious occupations and lively amusements which made up the daily routine of a Virginian country gentleman of that period. "We live here in peace and plenty," he wrote, "in innocence and security, fearing no enemy from abroad or robbers at home. What can we poor hermits do who know of no intrigues but such as are carried on by the amorous turtles, or some such innocent lovers?"

He was keenly interested in watching over his numerous slaves, in building houses, in breeding livestock, and in following the growth of his crops. Especially was he well informed as to the quality of soils and timber, for he was the proprietor of 179,440 acres, much of which was under cultivation, but far more in primeval forest. He had inherited 26,231 acres of this land from his father, and the rest he had acquired by patent or purchase. His holdings embraced vast territories along the James, the Pamunkey, the Roanoke, the Dan, the Staunton, and the Meherrin. In 1742 he obtained a patent to a single tract on the Dan which spread over an area of not less than 105,000 acres of savannas and woods. He did not expect to cultivate all these lands. His purpose in taking them up was to sell them to immigrants, but he was unsuccessful in accomplishing this on a large scale. He particularly regretted his failure to establish a Swiss colony in the region of the Dan.

Byrd derived much pleasure from the pursuit of gardening. "A garden, a grove, and a purling stream," he said in one of his letters, "are the innocent scenes that divert my leisure." He was also interested in experiments to improve the quality and increase the abundance of his fruits; and he tested the efficacy of many forest herbs in cases requiring medical treatment.

He possessed all the accomplishments of the gentlemen of that day in the provinces of riding, shooting, and hunting. He served with fidelity as a member of the vestry of his parish and was a staunch supporter of the established Anglican church. He never slackened in the performance of his duty as a member of the Council, and he filled his seat so long that he outlived all his original associates in that body. His attainment of its presidency was only delayed, as we have already mentioned, by the longevity of Commissary Blair.

COLONEL WILLIAM BYRD

But Byrd was something more than a loyal churchman, a skillful planter, an experienced sportsman, a patriotic statesman, and a founder of towns, for it was he who laid off the sites for the modern cities of Richmond and Petersburg. His taste in every department of life was that of a man of the world and of the finest education of his day. His mansion at Westover, whether it was looked at from without or from within, whether considered in its architecture, in its furnishings, in its decoration, or in its situation on the banks of the James, was comparable with the most beautiful homes of its size to be found in England. His library, collected principally by his own discernment, was perhaps the largest, the choicest, and most varied that existed in the American colonies.

But above all, Byrd was the most remarkable writer, with the exception of Franklin, of the Colonial age. He was a voluminous correspondent, and the Englishmen with whom he exchanged letters at great length so frequently were among the first figures of those times, such as Sir Hans Sloane, Mark Catesby, Peter Collinson, General Oglethorpe, and Lords Egmont, Carteret, and Orrery. These letters of Byrd were full of the delightful qualities of ease, gayety, humor, and information.

His convictions on all subjects are expressed in these pages with the most engaging frankness. Like that great country gentleman of the next century, General John H. Cocke, Byrd was impressed very unfavorably by the practical effect of the institution of slavery, and he was one of the first to congratulate Oglethorpe on his action in shutting that institution out of the confines of Georgia. Slavery in his opinion was especially open to condemnation for its relaxing moral influence on the character of the white people; but above all, he said, it degraded manual labor by leaving the cultivation of the soil and practically all other work chiefly to the hands of Negroes. He thought, too, that the presence of so many bondsmen of the most primitive instincts necessarily created constant apprehension of that most appalling of all catastrophes—an uprising of slaves;

152

and this, too, without there being any justification for it in their treatment, for he denied that the Virginian Negroes were subject to any real roughness of discipline, "unless," he added, "they happen to fall into the hands of a brute, who always passes for a monster."

But slavery was only one of the topics which Byrd discussed in these letters. His themes run over almost every interest of the human mind, all presented by him with a sprightliness of expression which greatly enhanced the force of their intrinsic appeal. This quality of sprightliness was revealed in an equal degree in all the narratives of his travels, whether relating to the running of the boundary line between Carolina and Virginia or to the journey to the Land of Eden, or to the mines at Germanna. The former two works give a most graphic description of the diversified region that extended from the James westward to the foot of the mountains. The tour to the mines led him through a country which was inhabited, although only sparsely, but the two tours towards the Roanoke and the Dan carried him over a land which still remained almost everywhere in the condition in which it had lain for uncounted centuries. Its forests, its savannas, its streams, its vegetable life, and its animal life are detailed with charming minuteness in the pages of these narratives. All reflect the grace and lucidity of his literary style, the keenness of his observation, the vivacity of his spirit, and the kindness of his disposition. There is a flavor pervading every paragraph that is reminiscent of the English classics of the eighteenth century, but with an idiosyncracy of its own. Pure description is saved from dryness by a sense of humor that never fails to invest the subject with an unexpected brightness. If its similes are sometimes to the modern taste a little risqué, they are always preserved from grossness by the natural gayety of the writer and by his innate refinement.

It was not strange in the smallest degree that he should be known as the "black swan" of his family. In the whole history of the community there is not to be discovered a man of more varied accomplishments, more versatile tastes, more polished deportment, more winning temper than he. If we possessed no other proof of the intrinsic soundness and the diverse charm of the plantation life of Virginia in the Colonial age, we should have only to point in silence to the romantic figure of the younger William Byrd, who looks down the intervening centuries, invested with all the elegance and culture of the Old World, combined with the kindly simplicity, the unspoilt manliness, and the noble freedom of the New.

Chapter XI

COLONEL GEORGE WASHINGTON

F<small>ROM YOUTH</small> to old age, Washington, following the habit of his Virginian ancestors and his Virginian contemporaries, spent the greater part of his time out of doors. His official functions kept him during one interval of his life more under roof than was congenial to his tastes; but even during this period, which embraced the eight years of his presidency, it was noticeable that he left Philadelphia for his home in Virginia as often as he could do so without neglect of his public duties, and while there he passed most of his hours on horseback attending to his farms.

It was not simply a longing for the quiet pleasures of the fireside at Mount Vernon that influenced him, whenever he had the opportunity, to set out for the banks of the Potomac. It was his interest in the operations of his plantations; the allurement of his own fields, forests, and streams; the excitement of the fox hunt—it was all these that rose up before his mind's eye to make his purely official work appear dull and dry in comparison. The life which he led at Mount Vernon indoors differed hardly at all in spirit from the life which he led at Philadelphia indoors, so far as the social side was involved. His beautiful home was so crowded with visitors after his permanent retirement from office that he possessed there during his last years quite as little privacy as he did in the capital during his presidency. Indeed, it became necessary for him to secure the assistance of kinsmen to relieve him of the chief burden of the personal entertainment of his guests. But he did not experience this

cramped feeling for one moment while he was superintend-
ing the sowing and planting or taking part in the other
business with his plantation managers and servants, for
both kept him for hours daily under the canopy of the
heavens.

The most characteristic spirit of the colonial plantation
life of Virginia in Washington's youth, as in his maturity,
was this devotion to outdoor pursuits and recreations. Their
powerful influence on his own personality was very clear
proof that they were not naturally productive of coarseness
or frivolity. As a boy there was not a sport suitable to his
age in which he was not deeply versed. The old legend of
the cherry tree symbolizes his skill in handling a hatchet;
he did not shrink from climbing to the height of even the
Natural Bridge; he could swim with the easy confidence of
one of his mother's ducks; he knew where the best fishing
holes in the Rappahannock River near by were situated;
he could keep on the back of a fractious colt which no one
else dared to ride; he had no rival in a foot race or horse
race; he could, with his gun, bring down deer or bird with
an unfailing aim; he could find his way about the forests
with the success of an Indian, owing to his knowledge of
woodcraft; and he could foretell the weather with the
shrewdness of a modern meteorologist. In short, he was an
accomplished country lad who had passed the most fruitful
hours of his young life beyond the domestic doorway.

It was from this intercourse with the world of the far-
spreading skies and the teeming earth in all their aspects
that he had gained far more knowledge than he had acquired from books. His principal education, indeed, was
obtained in the academy of the unspoiled country extending along the banks of the majestic Potomac and Rappahannock, and not from the log schoolhouse of some local
clerical pedagogue. Until his last hour, although he improved in English scholarship as he advanced in life, he
continued more or less infirm in his orthography. But he
never exhibited the slightest ignorance of those manly accomplishments which in the highest circle of colonial

Virginia were thought to be as essential to a gentleman's equipment as all that he could learn from the pages of textbooks.

It was Washington's destiny to be associated from boyhood to death with objects or scenes, whether physical, military, or political, that stood out, like his own character, with extraordinary vastness. His first intelligent gaze fell on the shining waterscape of the Potomac River as it flowed so majestically not far from the spot of his birth. The Rappahannock, too, was so broad a stream that the tradition of his ability to throw a stone across it near Fredericksburg has always been regarded worthy of perpetual memory. It was in sight of these two streams that he passed his childhood and youth. Then, as a surveyor, he became familiar with that brooding wilderness which spread away in forest to the western limits of the Northern Neck. Only the sky could give an equal impression of boundlessness. Then followed the perilous mission to the upper Ohio Valley, a region that was apparently still wider in extent. The operations of the Revolutionary War seem to be small in comparison with the maneuvers of modern campaigns, but what was lacking in volume in the number of the participants was made up by the immensity of the ground traversed in the prosecution of hostilities. The far-reaching country between Quebec and Savannah embraced a very large part of North America, and in the very center of its numerous battlefields towered the figure of Washington. And a similar association with vastness is perceptible when we contemplate his work of founding a government that in time was to extend its jurisdiction from the rays of the rising sun, as they first fell on the continent, to the last rays of the same orb as it sank behind the globe three thousand miles away.

It is hard for us to conceive of Washington as taking up some conventional profession in his youth, for this would have confined his energies to a town, or at least to a well-settled rural community. A wider scope than this seemed to be necessary for the free play of a spirit as full of primitive energy as his. It is therefore no cause for surprise to find that at the age of fourteen he was eager to take to seafaring, an ambition in which he was thwarted only by the opposition of his mother and uncle. It is possible that the broad reaches of the Potomac and Rappahannock, which he knew so intimately in these early years, had planted this aspiration in his breast; or it may be that his frequent association with the sea captains of the day who navigated the merchantmen sailing between the Virginian wharves and the English ports had suggested this hazardous profession. But the dry land, and not the ocean, was to be the scene of his achievements.

The first step which he took at the beginning of his career was one really more congenial with his tastes and more suitable to his powers than voyages backwards and forwards between the New World and the Old. We have mentioned that he had shown from boyhood the strongest relish for all the sports, recreations, and serious occupations of a rural existence; that he was familiar with the horse, the gun, and the fishing line; that he was deeply versed in the art of exploring unerringly the dark woods or managing a boat, and that he could endure without inconvenience the successive changes of the seasons and the fickleness of the weather. These natural and cultivated aptitudes came powerfully to his help when he was selected by the proprietor of the Northern Neck to employ his skill as a surveyor—which he had acquired in a desultory way—to lay off certain patents to frontier lands which that proprietor had granted. Through his brother Lawrence's marriage to William Fairfax's daughter he had formed the acquaintance of this titled family, and his early entrance into practical life had been made possible by its patronage.

In the performance of the duties of this new occupation Washington and his assistants traversed, in the course of the next few years, the vast area of the magnificent western region included in Lord Fairfax's principality. He became as familiar with the virgin domain of the Piedmont and the Shenandoah Valley as he already was with the long-established plantations of the country adjacent to the banks

158

of the lower Potomac and Rappahannock. His strong taste for life in the open air was more than gratified; his manly spirit was confirmed and further nourished; his ability to cope with the confusing intricacies of the forests was increased; and his capacity for dealing with the Indians and the frontiersmen, equally impatient of restraints, was more fully developed. It was a life exactly adapted to the cultivation of his native military instincts, for it gave him experience in controlling and using men; it sharpened his eye for the lay of land, as bearing on offensive or defensive tactics; and it invigorated his frame for the future hardships and privations of the camp and the march.

That Washington's fitness for an active military life was early recognized was proved by the fact that Governor Dinwiddie appointed him to the command of one of the four military districts into which the colony was divided in 1752. This imposed on him the duty of maintaining the military organization and supervising the accouterment of eleven counties. At this time he had barely reached his twentieth or twenty-first year, but young as he was, he also carried on his shoulders the burdensome management of his deceased brother's estate and the general direction of his mother's plantation operations.

The most acute question at that time was raised by the advance of the French from the valley of the Ohio towards the towering barrier of the serrated Alleghenies. That this advance was inevitable was foreseen as long ahead as 1735 by the shrewd William Byrd, who during this year pointed out the advantages which that nation would acquire by taking possession of these mountains. They would in this way, he said, be able to seize the mines and carry off all the ore; they could engross the enormous trade in furs which had grown up between the English and the Indians on the western flank of the chain; and finally, in order to confirm the allegiance of the savages and ward off English attack from the east, they could easily build impregnable forts in every important mountain pass.

Had immediate attention been paid to this pregnant warning, the French would not have had the time to construct the line of fortifications which they raised from Lake Erie southward in order to block the westward rush of emigrants from the English colonies. In 1742 a somewhat feeble effort had been made by treaty to transfer to these emigrants the right to occupy all that region situated between the Alleghenies and the eastern bank of the Ohio River. But in spite of the supposed guarantee of a safe settlement in that quarter, the Indians continued to intrude, if not for the actual purpose of murdering the white inhabitants, as in 1738, when Orange County was invaded by them, at least for the purpose of striking a blow at some distant tribe like the Cherokees, as was the case later on, when the Iroquois passed through the Valley of Virginia and came in fierce conflict with the local militia at Balcony Falls.

The pecuniary advantage of organizing a company to take over the settlement of the far western lands was clearly foreseen by a little group of Virginian and Maryland citizens in 1749. Among the incorporators were such men as Governor Dinwiddie, George Mason, Thomas Lee, and Lawrence and Augustine Washington. Christopher Gist, who had been appointed to be the Company's agent, was sent out to explore the valley of the Ohio. Reaching that stream, he passed over to the north bank and pushed forward through the wilderness adjacent to the river on that side as far as a point opposite the present site of Louisville, and there returning to the south bank, he made his way back to the scene of his original crossing. On both banks he found an immense sweep of primeval forest, but this umbrageous scenery was here and there broken by parklike savannas, overgrown with the rankest grasses and frequented by countless herds of bison and elk. The report he submitted upon the beauty, fertility, and vastness of the country which he passed through led the Company to secure from the Indian tribes who inhabited it the right to grant patents to the most desirable lands within its area.

The election of Lawrence Washington to the presidency of the Company was directly influential in arousing the

160

WASHINGTON AT THE AGE OF TWENTY-FIVE

PLATE XIV. *"From a miniature on ivory presented by Washington to his niece Harriet, and now belonging to her daughter's family."* Copied from the Fairfax Scrapbook in the Virginia State Library, Richmond, Virginia. Used by courtesy of the Governor of Virginia. Photo Cook.

COLONEL GEORGE WASHINGTON AT TWENTY-FIVE

interest of his younger brother George in this new scene for exploration and settlement. The work of surveying which he had done on the eastern flank of the Alleghenies was in time to be done by others on the western slopes.

In 1752 Dinwiddie was chosen deputy-governor of Virginia, and he had not been long seated at Williamsburg before he recognized that the most threatening public condition which he had to face and, if practicable, remove, was the impending advance of the French towards the Alleghenies from the west. It was he who divided the colony into four military districts, as has already been mentioned; and this was done as the first step to place it in a stronger position to resist the approaching invaders, who were now claiming the western country, not by the right of peaceful penetration, but by right of La Salle's explorations south of Canada. A visible proof of this asserted right to possession of all this vast region was presented in the tablets of bronze, so inscribed, which the French scouts buried in the ground at the mouth of every important tributary flowing into the Ohio River. The government of Virginia could not admit the justice of this claim without consenting to the erection of a permanent wall of forts and bayonets, which would be a far more effective instrument for stopping the English movement westward than the menacing crags of the Alleghenies.

Dinwiddie planted himself firmly on the treaties with the Indians as giving the Virginians the right to occupy all the lands in the region of the Ohio and its principal affluents. He decided that his first act in his proposed policy of resistance should be to send an emissary to the French commander at Vincennes near Lake Erie, in order to deliver a remonstrance against the intrusion of French troops into territory belonging to the English King. Washington, as we have seen, had been appointed to the military control of one of the four districts into which Virginia had been divided; and it was to him that Dinwiddie now turned, without apparently having previously debated in his own mind the possible superior fitness of any other person for the per-

161

formance of the delicate and dangerous purpose to be accomplished. This confidence was amply fulfilled.

Young as Washington was at this time, he had already acquired a solid reputation for good judgment, firm courage, and power to command men. Moreover, his experience in surveying the wild lands of Lord Fairfax—which increased his knowledge of woodcraft in general and gave him an inkling as to the character of the region beyond the Alleghenies—and also his ability to defy fatigue and to endure privation seemed to point him out conspicuously for the mission of traversing mountain and plain, savanna and forest, which had to be covered in the journey to Vincennes.

Setting out from Winchester with Jacob Van Braam, a French interpreter, and joined on the banks of the Cumberland by Gist and an escort of four men, he pressed on through driving rains and blinding snows, over streams in freshet and along rough woodland trails, until the spot was reached where the Ohio was formed by the confluence of the Allegheny and Monongahela rivers, destined soon to become so famous in the French and Indian War as Fort Duquesne. Washington's trained eye recognized at once the strategic advantage of the place as a site for a powerful fortification, but he quickly resumed his journey towards the north; and he did not halt again until he had delivered the letter of remonstrance to St. Pierre, the French general in charge of the armed post at Vincennes. This letter was read, and a reply in opposition was soon drafted and handed to Washington for transmission to Dinwiddie. He did not linger after receiving it, for already a successful effort had been made to tamper with the loyalty of some of the Indian chiefs who had accompanied his party as guides on the northward trail.

It was not until Washington and his companions had arrived at Venango that they were able to continue their journey on horseback, as the path between Vincennes and that post had been too rough for them to travel in this less fatiguing manner. But in a short time they were compelled to dismount again, owing to the obstructions of rocks and streams in the way, and having lifted all their baggage and accouterments to the backs of the overwearied animals now led by hand, they took up the march once more. So slow was the progress, however, that Washington, having first chosen Gist to accompany him, decided to go on ahead of the party to hasten his arrival at Williamsburg. He and his companion left their horses behind and plunged into the thick forest on foot. The costume which Washington now wore was the costume of the frontier—moccasins, buckskin trousers, and Indian matchcoat. On his back he carried his pack, and in his hand his rifle.

It was not long before the two men ran unexpectedly into a band of French Indians, one of whom Washington selected to serve as his guide through that unknown region; but this act was to prove almost fatal to either Gist or himself, for while they were afterwards crashing through the dark thickets, the treacherous guide fired at close quarters at one or the other, only to miss his mark. Gist would have shot him down at once without mercy, but Washington stepped in and saved the savage's life and at nightfall permitted him to vanish into the woods. The two travelers themselves, under cover of darkness, pressed on towards the Allegheny River.

When the banks of that stream were reached, with a hatchet as the sole implement in their possession, they began the construction of a log raft, but it sank as soon as they had taken their places on board of it. A second was quickly built and proved sufficiently staunch to bear up their weight; but in their strenuous effort to keep her free of the running ice, Washington was thrown into the water by the jamming of his pole. After he fell into the stream, however, he was able to seize one end of the raft and thus drift with the current, with his head above the surface, until the rude vessel grounded on an island. A keen wind was blowing down the river and the air was bitingly cold. No fire could be lighted to warm the two drenched and shivering men, and thus they passed the night. Washington escaped all harm from the exposure, but Gist suffered frostbite in both hands and feet. After many perils they were able to get as far as a small English trading post which had been established in that remote region. When Washington finally reached Williamsburg, he had traversed fifteen hundred miles through the wilderness in winter, over flooded rivers, and here and there tracked by murderous Indians. He had been absent for a period of ninety days.

The tone of Pierre's letter convinced Governor Dinwiddie that the French had no intention whatever of yielding one foot of ground which they occupied in the west, and that unless they were halted by military force, they would continue their advance towards the western slopes of the Alleghenies. Under the leadership of Colonel Fry and Lieutenant Colonel Washington, a regiment numbering three hundred men was sent off to the confluence of the Allegheny and Monongahela rivers, with instructions to complete the fort situated at that point, which, it was supposed, the Ohio Company had already begun. A large body of volunteers from New York and South Carolina were expected to coöperate with the Virginia troops. Washington, in command of two companies, marched ahead, and on arriving at Great Meadows in April, 1754, was chagrined to hear that the men who had been employed to construct the fort had been captured by the French and their place taken by French builders. The fort had been finished by them and was now held by a garrison of that nation.

Between Great Meadows and Fort Duquesne a hostile detachment had planted itself for the purpose of watching the movements of the Virginians, but within a short time its commander was surprised by a night march of Washington, the commander himself and ten of his men were killed, and many others were intercepted and carried off prisoners. By the end of April Colonel Fry was dead, and Washington had taken his place at the head. He decided to retreat to Great Meadows, as he did not think that he could in his present position successfully resist the attack in force now threatened from Fort Duquesne.

At Great Meadows a fortification had been built which

now received the name of Fort Necessity. It labored under the disadvantage of being surrounded by a screen of leaves, with an undergrowth of grasses, which would afford shelter to the Indian allies of the French in discharging their guns at the garrison. This ground was promptly occupied by the enemy and effectively used. To render the situation worse, a heavy rain filled the defensive ditches with water, which made them untenable, while many of the colonial soldiers took to drink and were soon entirely incapable of firing a gun. At this crisis a messenger from the French commander came forward under a flag of truce, and so liberal were the terms of capitulation offered his little army that Washington considered it wise to accept them. His troops were permitted to retain their weapons and baggage and to leave the fort with their own colors flying. Owing to the destruction of the pack horses for conversion into food during the siege, most of the baggage had to be abandoned. That the difficulties of his position fully justified the course which Washington pursued was admitted by the General Assembly, which went so far as to adopt a resolution of appreciation of the good judgment which he had shown in saving his troops from the humiliation of an actual surrender.

The Virginian people were not discouraged by the upshot. This was revealed in the great activity which they now exhibited in increasing their forces for renewed operations in the field. The number of companies was augmented from five to ten, and twenty thousand pounds were appropriated for a more vigorous prosecution of the war. Maryland, New York, and England swelled this sum by generous additional contributions.

A cause of friction at this time between officers of the colonial regiments and the officers by British appointment was the inequality in rank that separated them. A captain, major, or colonel belonging to the former, for instance, had to give way to officers bearing these titles who happened to be serving under commissions granted by the English military establishment in the colonies. Men who were subordinate in rank to Washington in the campaign of Great Meadows assumed a command higher than his own after the reorganization of the army, simply because they could show the royal signature. Washington, finding himself reduced to a mere captaincy, resigned and withdrew to Mount Vernon. In order to remove this conflict, Dinwiddie required that all the new companies which had been raised by Virginia should be organized without any connection with the British regulars stationed in America.

The first step to retrieve the failure to hold back the French was taken by sending a small body of troops under Colonel Innes to Winchester. But it accomplished nothing beyond erecting a stronghold on the north branch of the Potomac, afterwards known as Fort Cumberland. It was now expected that the English Government would dispatch oversea a disciplined and well equipped army to assist the colonists; and this anticipation in the end proved to be correct. General Braddock arrived with a considerable body of trained soldiers, which was afterwards swelled by several companies of Virginian and Maryland infantry, a company of Virginian light-horse, and a little band of Indian scouts. New York furnished two companies only. The army embraced about twenty-two hundred soldiers in all, but they were bound togther by few influences that produce an effective military force, for the men were different in origin, and they were commanded by an officer, full of personal courage, it is true, but lamentably ignorant of the country and of the methods of warfare unavoidably called for there, if success was to be won.

The march of these incongruous troops began at Alexandria and from that city continued by way of Frederick and Winchester to Fort Cumberland. Washington had, in consequence of Dinwiddie's urgent advice, received an appointment on Braddock's staff. Having traversed the western region before, he knew the difficulties which it would offer to transportation; and this led him to suggest to his superior officer the use of pack horses instead of wagons as a means of conveying the baggage and provisions; but no attention was paid to his advice. A roadbed had to be opened up with

166

the axe through the forests all the way to the Monongahela River in order to create an avenue for these lumbering vehicles, which were able to get over only five miles of ground in the course of twenty-four hours. Small detachments of men, sent on ahead to reconnoiter, were in some instances intercepted and killed by the stealthy French and Indian scouts.

The banks of the Monongahela were reached not far from the site of Fort Duquesne. In the meanwhile, Washington had been suffering so severely from an attack of fever that he had been constrained to follow in a wagon in the remote rear, but before the final march upon the fort began, he had pushed forward, although still unwell, and joined the main army. The troops, strung out in a serpent-like line as they advanced along the green banks of the stream, made a picturesque spectacle with the red coats of the regulars, the brown buckskins of the volunteers, and the glitter of the muskets and bayonets blending their different colors to decorate the scene.

Leaving the valley behind, the army began to ascend the bordering high ground in three divisions; one, of three hundred men, in front; another, of two hundred, close behind this; and the third, composed of the wagons and the bulk of the forces, following at a short interval. The van very soon entered a heavily wooded country full of dark ravines on either flank of the rough pioneer highway. Suddenly this detachment was met with a hot fire from the invisible enemy dispersed among the trees. This was the moment when these troops, now well in front, should have taken to the same woods and fought the foe after the Indian manner. Such would have been the course had Washington been in command, but, unluckily for the colonial cause, he was not.

Braddock was of the stiffest type of the English martinet, and in his courage, pride, and ignorance, he considered it an act of cowardice for even a part of his troops to scatter like a covey of partridges in order to carry out such a slinking method of warfare. In the open field he could very soon have driven back the far inferior French and Indian force

167

by the use of European tactics, but in insisting on the rigid maintenance of his lines on the road, in full sight of his hidden opponents, he simply exposed his unfortunate soldiers to a rain of missiles, to which they could make no effective response. In vain a cannon was used to shell the ravines, but no real execution could be done by this weapon, as none of the enemy could be seen to fire at. As the men in advance shrank back in consternation under the impact of bullets from invisible guns, reinforcements were hurried up, only in their turn to stagger back before the same destructive storm. A general panic now broke out which Braddock, rushing recklessly forward, tried hopelessly to stem. While the troops in the front ranks, now thoroughly demoralized, were rapidly disintegrating, a band of Indians stole in a circuit through the woods to the rear, and throwing themselves with piercing war cries on the baggage train, killed or drove off the wagoners. In vain the men who had charge of a cannon in that quarter endeavored to shatter the band, but in the end they themselves were compelled to turn and flee.

In the meanwhile, the brave British officers were frantically striving to force their troops to retreat with some regard to order, but the confusion had become uncontrollable, and the soldiers who were not too much overcome by fear to turn tail cast their guns down in the road and took to their heels. Everything that might impede their flight was abandoned—the muskets, the artillery, the ammunition, the baggage. "They ran," said Washington, in after years, in recalling the scene, "like sheep pursued by dogs. An attempt to rally them was as unsuccessful as if we had tried to stop the wild bears of the mountains, or the rivulets, with our feet, for they would break by in spite of every effort to prevent it."

By this hour, Braddock had been fatally wounded, probably by one of his own men who had resented his fatal obstinacy even on the battlefield. After exhibiting prodigies of personal valor, he was saved from immediate death by the fidelity of Colonel Orme of his staff, with the unselfish aid of several American officers, conspicuous among whom was Colonel Stewart of the Virginian troops. The latter force, throughout the terrible conflict, had retained their steady presence of mind. At the first shot they had dispersed in the ravines, in order to meet the fire of the fugitive enemy by a counter-fire from behind logs and growing trees. A party of eighty of them, who had made a breastwork of fallen timber, lost fifty of their number by a fusillade of bullets poured out at them by the regulars, under the impression that they were a detachment of the enemy.

How severely the Virginians as a separate detachment had suffered was shown by the history of one of their companies. Every one of its officers perished, and only a single officer of another survived. Washington had been so exposed throughout the battle, while carrying Braddock's orders from point to point, that two horses had been shot under him; and his coat also had been penetrated by numerous bullets. Twenty-six of the British officers out of a total number of eighty-six were slain, and thirty-seven were wounded. As many of the rank and file were killed or wounded as composed the entire force of Frenchmen and Indians who took part in the shambles.

During the remainder of that day, throughout the succeeding night, and far into the next day, the British regulars continued their helter-skelter flight, although there was not the smallest indication that the enemy were in pursuit. Braddock, closely escorted by Washington, was borne along the rude highway in a springless farm wagon, to which he had been helplessly lifted. For a long time he uttered not a word, as if lost in a stupor of regret or surprise; but a few hours before he died, he was heard to mutter mournfully, "Who would have thought it! Who would have thought it!" He was buried beside or beneath the road over which he had marched only a few days before in all the splendor of a military progress, confident of success in his campaign, and assured of promotion to higher rank as a reward for his services. Washington read the ritual for interment over the lonely grave and then resumed his journey towards Mount

Vernon, no doubt full of sorrowful meditation over the fate of his brave but intractable commander.

Consternation throughout the colony followed the sanguinary failure at Fort Duquesne. An eastward movement of the people residing near the Allegheny and Blue Ridge Mountains began. "Scarcely do I know a neighborhood," said a witness of this flight at the time it occurred, "but what has lost some families, not idlers, vagrants, and pests of society, but men of worth and property, whom it was evil for any community to lose." The famous Presbyterian apostle of that day, the Reverend Samuel Davies, strove with noble energy by his personal influence to encourage the people exposed to the marauding and murderous Indians to hold their ground. In a powerful address which he delivered in the presence of a large body of volunteers who had been organized for the defense of the threatened communities, he prophetically exclaimed: "I cannot but hope that Providence has raised up that heroic youth, Colonel Washington, whom hitherto Providence has preserved in so signal a manner—for some important service for his country."

Washington was in command of all the forces in Virginia who were under arms at this critical moment and ready to take the field. Winchester was the only post along the northwestern frontier that had not been abandoned; and here, in October, 1755, he undertook in person to bring a large body of raw troops under the repressive discipline which was so urgently needed to whip them into military shape. The difference between him and the infatuated Braddock was shown in the extraordinary pains which he put himself to in order to prepare these soldiers for the peculiar running forest tactics which had to be employed, if the Indian method of warfare was to be successfully countered. He was convinced that it was only in this way that the region between the Blue Ridge and the Ohio River could be permanently cleared of the savages, who even now were harrying that part of the former population which had been unable to escape across the mountains. "The supplicating tears of the women and the moving petitions of the men," he exclaimed, referring to this remnant, "melt me into such deadly sorrow that I solemnly declare, if I know my own mind, I would offer myself a willing sacrifice to the butchering enemy, provided that this would contribute to the people's ease."

Washington now advised, as a further means of protection, that a series of forts should be built in a straight line, beginning at the point where Capon River entered the Potomac, and extending as far as Mayo's River in the county of Halifax on the Carolina border. Within a short time fourteen of these fortifications were erected, with dimensions of sixty feet square, with two bastions respectively, and all spacious enough to give room for the housing of a garrison ranging from fifty to seventy men. In the case of some of the forts the distance to the next did not exceed twelve miles, and in no instance was this interval greater than twenty-five.

All these precautionary measures proved to be effective for only a short period. In 1758 the raids of the French and Indians along the frontiers began again, and it was thought necessary to put a stop to them by the destruction of Fort Duquesne, the starting point of all these incursions. By June of that year Washington's regiment had arrived at Fort Cumberland. General Forbes was in command of all the troops which had been assembled for this expedition. Like Braddock, he deliberately ignored Washington's urgent warning in sending Major Grant ahead of the main column to begin the assault on the French stronghold situated at the confluence of the Allegheny and Monongahela rivers. The troops under his order fell into an ambuscade as they approached the fort; the commander himself was captured; and about two hundred and seventy-three of his officers and privates were slain. The Virginians who happened to be enrolled in this detachment lost five of their officers out of a total of eight, but they were able to drive off the enemy when an attempt was made to seize the baggage.

When news of this disaster was brought to General Forbes's main army in the rear, a slow forward movement

171

of that body began, with the impatient Washington in the van, in command of seven thousand men. When the Ohio River was reached—after the lapse of two months, largely occupied in making a new highway through the Wilderness, instead of following the Braddock Road as Washington advised—the site of the fort was still fifty miles distant. The campaign was about to be abandoned for the winter when the scouts came into camp and reported that the fort was thinly manned and that the Indian allies of the French were now dispersed among their own towns. At once an advance was ordered, and when the now sanguine troops arrived at Fort Duquesne, it was found to be on fire and without a single defender, owing to the fact that the garrison had taken to boats and stolen away down the Ohio River. The stronghold was renamed Fort Pitt, and the army returned to the East.

Washington was soon elected to the General Assembly, and on his taking his seat in that body, a resolution was offered and unanimously adopted, commending the successful part which he had played in the war. He was so overcome by this public tribute to his services that he could only stammer a reply. "Sit down, Mr. Washington," said the presiding officer noticing his confusion, "sit down. Your modesty equals your valor, and that surpasses the power of any language I possess to describe."

Chapter XII

PATRICK HENRY

THROUGH HIS father, John Henry, who had settled and
married in the Virginian county of Hanover, Patrick Henry
was of Scotch descent; and through his grandmother, a
Dabney or Daubeny, he had a cross current of Huguenot
blood in his veins. On the paternal side he shared the blood
of at least two families of Scotland which enjoyed, either
then or afterwards, unusual intellectual distinction. These
were the Broughams and the Robertsons. His grandmother,
Jean Robertson, was an aunt of the celebrated historian
of the same surname, while her niece was the grandmother
of Lord Brougham, so famous at a later date in the
history of English politics and jurisprudence. A cousin of
John Henry was at one time an editor of the *Gentleman's
Magazine.*

It will be thus perceived that Patrick Henry's Scotch ancestors counted in their ranks men of genius and learning,
but they could not lay any claim to a higher social rank
than that occupied by persons belonging to the middle
class. And even after his emigration to Virginia, Patrick's
father, although influential and respected in his community,
could hardly be said to enjoy the social distinction possessed
by the historic families of the colony. He served as county
surveyor, colonel of militia, vestryman, and presiding magistrate. In all the relations of life he was a useful and an
exemplary citizen, but not so high above the general level
of his neighbors as to be devoid of a fellow-feeling with the
humblest. Probably he had in his disposition a larger vein

of native loyalty than the great orator, his son. "There are those alive," records a contemporary of the latter, "who have seen John Henry at the head of his regiment celebrating the birthday of George III with as much enthusiasm as Patrick afterwards displayed in resisting the encroachments of that monarch."

But it was not from his Scotch forebears that Patrick Henry is supposed to have inherited his powers of eloquence. The Winstons, from whom his mother was descended, a family of the sturdiest British stock, numbered among themselves at least one distinguished orator. This was his great uncle, William Winston, whose reputation for ability as a speaker lingered very long in the traditions of the county of Hanover. The famous Dolly Madison, the most charming mistress who ever reigned over the White House, was a kinswoman of Patrick Henry through the Winston branch of the family tree. Her power to persuade and delight with her tongue possibly was traceable to the same source as her cousin's eloquence.

Henry was born at Studley, about sixteen miles north of Richmond, the future scene of his most dazzling display of oratorical genius, and not far from the Slashes, the birthplace of Henry Clay. He was one of a family of ten children, seven of them sisters, who continued to be the objects of his tenderest affection throughout his life. He is commonly thought to have been something of a saunterer in his youth, with a decided aversion to study; and yet he is known to have relished the Latin classics and had even mastered some Greek. But his gun, and not his book, was the favorite companion of his leisure, and the quiet forest was his constant resort. Here, on the banks of a stream into which he had pitched his fishing hook, he would sit by the hour, with a contemplative eye on his cork; or, prone on his back, he would follow the circling of the buzzards in the open domain of the sky far overhead. It was perhaps in some lonely spot like this that he read his Vergil and Livy and Tristram Shandy, the three masterpieces which never lost their zest for him.

174

During twelve months Patrick served as a clerk in a roadside store, and then, with money supplied by his father, he set up with his brother as a rural merchant. The story of his life in this incongruous calling was not unlike that of Abraham Lincoln when similarly employed—he is said to have been more interested in the debates which he provoked among his bucolic customers than in the sale of his sugar, molasses, calico, and farming implements. Unluckily, when these were disposed of, he found that it was not so easy to collect the sums due by the purchasers. Indeed, it required but a year to exhaust the resources of the firm. Happily, he had by this time found a wife whose father, Colonel Shelton, was the keeper of the tavern at the county courthouse and also—and this was more important at the moment—the owner of a plantation. At Colonel Shelton's advice Patrick turned from the management of the store to the cultivation of this land, which he carried out largely with his own hands; and he also dug the ditches and hewed down the woods. But in the intervals of these hard labors he continued to indulge his irresistible taste for shooting, hunting, and fishing.

His house was destroyed by fire, and Patrick, now the father of a family of very young children, determined once more to unite farming pursuits with mercantile. Assisted by a single clerk, he endeavored to carry on his store without desisting from his planting operations; but in 1760, when he was twenty-four years of age, he was constrained to close the store, and what was worse, he was left in debt. Jefferson met him at this period of his life and described his bearing as notable for its lack of polish, which was natural enough in the light of his previous rough occupation. He was also reported by the same hypercritical observer, about that time, as delighting in music, dancing, and pleasantry, proof at least that his mishaps had not soured his spirit. This taste for music continued to the end of his life. By constant practice he became an excellent performer on the violin.

Henry now wisely, as the event demonstrated, decided

175

to study law. The only textbook in his reach was *Coke-on-Lyttleton,* which he mastered from the first page to the last. It is said that he came before the Board of Examiners after a preparation for his proposed calling that had not been prolonged beyond six weeks. Wythe, a member of this Board, refused to sign his application for a license; but Sir John Randolph, having searchingly tested his general knowledge, remarked, "Mr. Henry, if your industry be only half equal to your genius, I augur that you will do well, and become an ornament and an honor to your profession." Robert Carter consented to sign only upon receiving a promise of careful additional study in the future.

Having placed his family in his father-in-law's tavern, where he himself would sometimes act as Colonel Shelton's substitute in the latter's absence, he concentrated his principal energies on the acquisition of a law practice; and in this effort he was gradually successful. Such business as he obtained was at first limited to Hanover and the adjacent counties, but no case of importance arose in his professional career until he was employed as counsel for the defense in the suit which has come to be known in history as the Parsons' Cause, the first scene, as time was to reveal, in the drama of the American Revolution. In 1696 the stipend of the clergymen had been increased from 13,330 pounds of tobacco to 16,000. The act granting this addition was confirmed by the General Assembly in 1748. Tobacco in time advanced about 50 per cent in value; a period of poverty then followed; and the clergy complained that their salaries did not afford them a comfortable subsistence. They therefore petitioned for higher payment.

The General Assembly, aware that the people at large were suffering from the burden of the existing taxes, required that all debts should be paid in money figures, tobacco being rated arbitrarily at two pence the pound. This was in contravention of the law of 1748 so far as the clergy were involved, and to make the plan valid it was necessary to obtain the King's approval; but as the new act was to run for only ten months, the royal veto—if that was to follow

—could, as the Assembly knew, be received only at the eleventh hour. A short crop was harvested in 1758, and the price rose in consequence. The burgesses now adopted the Two Penny Act a second time, to continue in force for a period short of twelve months. The clergy in their resentment sent an emissary to England, under whose influence the King vetoed the measure. When news of that fact reached Virginia, the parsons decided to take legal steps to recover the large difference between their respective salaries as then paid in tobacco valued arbitrarily at only two pennies a pound, and those salaries as they should have been paid in the high-priced tobacco of the prevailing market, according to the original act, now automatically restored in force. This amounted in each instance to some two hundred and sixty-seven pounds sterling. It was claimed by the clergy that this additional sum was due to each of them by contract with their vestries.

The Reverend Mr. Maury, the rector of a large parish, confident, like his fellow-clergymen, of the justice of his cause now that the offending act had been annulled, brought the subject in dispute into Hanover Court for a decision. Associated with the cause was John Lewis, who opened the case by showing that the collectors of the tax had acted in harmony with the law as it then existed. But, replied the counsel for Maury, the King has made that law null and void by his formal disapproval. A demurrer was then entered and sustained by the Court, in spite of the popular sentiment in favor of the validity of the old act. The question was then suddenly sprung by the defense: did any damage really result to the plaintiff? This point called for the verdict of a jury, and as the one now summoned was composed of men in sympathy with the prevailing feeling represented by the defense, its members were peculiarly open to a popular appeal. And it was soon revealed that this appeal was to be made by the greatest orator who had appeared in the history of the colonies. The argument was deferred for several days, and when it began, a multitude from the country around had assembled. Numerous clergymen, confident of triumph after the demurrer had been decided in Maury's favor, very ostentatiously took seats on the bench beside the magistrates, whose presiding officer was John Henry, the father of Patrick. Patrick had persuaded his uncle to return home, "because," said he, "your appearance here might strike such an awe in me as to prevent me from doing justice to my clients."

When the counsel for Mr. Maury had presented his case, Henry arose to speak. His manner was awkward and his expression abashed, while his words came disjointed and confused from his lips. His father was ready to shrink in shame out of sight, but Henry, soon recovering his self-possession, was able to put forth for the first time all those astonishing powers as a public speaker with which he had been endowed by nature. His attitude became lofty, his gestures easy, graceful, and commanding, and his voice clear and strong, with a strange appeal in its tone that was irresistible to the minds of his hearers. The eyes of every spectator were riveted upon the countenance of the now inspired orator; tears poured down his father's cheeks; and the jurymen leaned forward in their seats and listened as if entranced.

The substance of Henry's argument was that there was a mutual obligation binding the King to the people and the people to the King. If the covenant between the two was broken by the King, then the people were released from their implied contract to sustain and obey him. The law of 1758 was a reasonable measure that had the approval and support of the Governor, the Council, and the House of Burgesses, and the King, in disallowing it, disregarded his responsibility to his subjects. He ceased to be their father. He became their oppressor.

A cry of treason arose at the utterance of these plain bold words, but the justices gave no attention to it. Henry, without pausing, next launched an attack on the clergymen who were seated on the bench. He did not address them directly but pointed his reflections by glancing towards them from time to time. It is the true function of the clerical office, he said, to safeguard the people in spiritual matters un-

178

regulated by secular laws. If that office failed to do this, it failed in everything and was of no use to the community at large. Fortunately, the power of the clergy was not equal to their will, "for if it were," Henry added, "these rapacious harpies would snatch from the hearth of their honest parishoner his last hoe-cake; from the widow and her orphan children, her last milch cow; and the last bed, nay the last blanket, from the lying-in-woman."

At these words the clergymen rose in confusion and hastened from the courtroom. Henry continued his argument at length and closed with the question: would the jury rivet the bonds under which the people were already groaning? Find for the plaintiff, he exclaimed, but only for one farthing. That will be sufficient. The jury responded to the appeal by bringing in a verdict for one penny damages. An ovation to Henry followed, and he was borne out of the courthouse on the shoulders of the excited and enthusiastic throng. It became a proverbial expression in that part of Virginia, in after years, whenever admiration of a public speaker was to be voiced in the most exalted way, "He is almost equal to Patrick when he pleaded against the parsons."

But Henry's reputation, in spite of this triumph, was for a time confined to his native county. There were no newspapers in that age to spread abroad knowledge of his newly revealed powers. When he appeared next in a cause it was at Williamsburg in the contested election case of Nathaniel Dandridge. No one there had had any previous information about him, and owing to his rather negligent dress and undistinguished carriage, he was at first treated with indifference, if not with contempt. But when he began to unroll his argument, this impression changed to one of amazed admiration.

Henry became a member of the House of Burgesses for the first time in 1765. Nearly every family of high social position in Virginia was represented among its one hundred and eighteen members. There were in the body men long known for their remarkable talents and patriotic services.

The presence of George Wythe, Benjamin. Harrison, Edmund Pendleton, Richard Henry Lee, Paul Carrington, and Archibald Cary alone would have conferred on it lasting eminence. Henry had hardly been in his seat during three days when he rose to question the propriety of the forced loan offer which was proposed by Speaker Robinson in order to save himself from the criminal consequences of his careless handling of a large amount of government funds, for the safekeeping of which he was responsible as treasurer. Through the influence of Robinson's friends, a relief bill was passed in the House of Burgesses, but it was thrown out in the Council.

All menace to the Americans from the French had been removed by the triumph of Wolfe at Quebec, and yet the necessity of retaining an English military force on the continent was admitted. This fact led the British Government to decide that a part of the expense of maintaining this force should be borne by the people of the several colonies. Especially just did this policy seem to the English when the cost of defeating the French had not yet been fully defrayed by Parliament. The Navigation Acts were also constantly violated in New England to British loss. To raise money in America, Parliament imposed a stamp tax, and to uphold the Navigation Acts, writs of assistance were permitted to be issued. The first of these measures was odious because the colonists had always exercised the sole right of taxing themselves; the second was also odious because the officers of the law were empowered to break into any house they chose. The eloquent Otis in Massachusetts came forward to denounce the writs of assistance; Henry, in Virginia, with still greater effect fulminated against the stamp tax.

Before Henry threw himself into opposition to that tax, the public's general attitude had been one simply of remonstrance. The leaders in the General Assembly—Bland, Peyton Randolph, Edmund Pendleton, Wythe, and Richard Henry Lee—were moderate in spirit and cautious in speech. If they ever uttered a bold sentence against any English measure injurious to the colonists, it was tempered by a loyal one. They were satisfied simply to send a protest to Parliament or the King. The possibility of actual resistance under any circumstances did not apparently occur to their minds. Henry was now twenty-nine years of age. He had no traditions behind him of that sort of devotion to the throne which was fostered in so many Virginian families by generations of wealth and prominence. He was intrepid in soul and easily aroused to fierce invective by both private and public wrongs. He looked upon the Stamp Act as unjustifiable from every point of view, and he was filled with astonishment when he found that the House intended to adjourn without voicing the smallest degree of condemnation of its tyranny. George Johnston, also perceiving this purpose, urged that body, while sitting as a committee of the whole, to take the Act under debate, and this gave Henry the opportunity to introduce a series of resolutions in denunciation of the measure which he had hastily written down on a flyleaf of an old copy of *Coke-on-Lyttleton*.

The substance of these memorable resolutions was that the subjects of the King in Virginia were entitled by their ancient charters to all the privileges, prerogatives, and immunities which were possessed by the English people; that the exclusive right of taxation belonged to them acting by themselves or by their chosen representatives; and that an assumption of this right by any person or persons besides the General Assembly tended towards the destruction of both American and British liberty.

The debate which followed the reading of these resolutions was described by Jefferson, who, still a college student, was present in the lobby, as "most bloody." The conservative leaders of the body urged the adoption of a moderate and conciliatory tone, but their influence was swept away by Henry's passionate declamation. "His torrents of sublime eloquence," to use another of Jefferson's expressions, prevailed, and even the last resolution, the most outspoken of the series, was temporarily sustained. It was in the course of this flaming discussion that Henry exclaimed:

181

"Tarquin and Caesar had each his Brutus, Charles the First, his Cromwell, and George the Third—" Here he paused. Cries of "Treason, treason," resounded in all parts of the chamber. Assuming a more lofty attitude, and with a look of unshaken determination, he closed the sentence, "and George the Third may profit by their examples."

This speech, as Henry himself afterwards said, was the first to be raised against the earliest unconcealed scheme to tax America from London. Alone, unadvised, and unassisted, he drafted, presented, and supported his own resolutions. Although the fifth and most extreme of them all was rescinded at the next meeting of the Assembly, it became known in time to the people of all the colonies and had a powerful influence in strengthening the spirit of popular resistance.

He left town for the back country so soon as the House adjourned. Through a contemporary description we have a glimpse of him as he passed along the street on his way homeward, wearing a pair of leather breeches, and carrying his shabby saddlebags on his arm, while he led by the bridle a horse which was lean enough to have been born and reared in the upland pine barrens.

In 1768 Henry, who had hitherto been residing in Louisa County, returned to Hanover, where he had purchased the famous old mansion known as Scotchtown. Here he passed the ensuing five years of his phenomenally busy career. He was still a member of the General Assembly, in which body he led the opposition to the wing headed by Edmund Pendleton. The course of events was soon to reveal that there was no kind private feeling between the two to soften their political antagonism. Indeed, the only public men with whom Henry was in close personal and political association during the period of agitation which preceded the rupture with Great Britain, were a few liberals like Jefferson, Richard Henry Lee, and Lightfoot Lee. "We were all sensible," Jefferson has recorded, "that the most urgent of all measures was that of coming to an understanding with the other Colonies to consider the British claims as the common cause

PLATE XV. *From an engraving after the painting by Rothermel of the scene when the orator provoked protesting cries of "Treason! Treason!" Photo Cook.*

PATRICK HENRY BEFORE
THE HOUSE OF BURGESSES

of all, and produce unanimity of action; and that, for this purpose, a committee of correspondence in each Colony would be the best instrument for intercommunication."

Four resolutions were drafted at a private conference between Henry, Carr, Jefferson, and others in sympathy with them, and submitted to the House; and this was the immediate signal for the dissolution of that body by the governor. The resolutions, however, led to the formation of the committees which had been proposed at the conference, and were the real forerunner of the Continental Congress. Henry was a member of the Virginia committee. How overwhelming was his eloquence in support of the colonial cause at this time is proved by the impression which it made on one of the earliest and most careful of observers. "He is," said Mason, "by far the most powerful speaker I ever heard. Every word he utters, not only engages, but commands, the attention; and your passions are no longer your own when he addresses them. But his eloquence is the smallest part of his merit. He is, in my opinion, the first man on his continent as well in ability as in public virtue."

In June, 1774, there arrived at Williamsburg the news that the port of Boston had been closed, and this announcement at once aroused the bolder spirits in the General Assembly —among whom Henry was preëminent—to the necessity of spurring the people on to a more resolute resistance. Steps were first taken to assure the appointment of a general day of fasting and prayer for the purpose of imploring Providence to avert from America the calamities of civil war; to inspire its people with firmness in support of their rights, and to turn the hearts of King and Parliament to moderation and justice. For passing the act which named a day for this public invocation to Heaven, Botetourt dissolved the Assembly. At an adjourned meeting its leading members recommended the formation of an association and the nomination, by the intercolonial committee of correspondence, of delegates to assemble in a continental congress in order to suggest measures for the protection of the common interests.

PATRICK HENRY

After the Virginia Convention organized in August, 1774, Henry was one of the first delegates selected to serve in this general Congress, which had been formally summoned to come together in Philadelphia. Roger Atkinson said of him at this time that he was a "very devil in politics, and a son of thunder," and that he was certain to "shake" the new body whose sessions he was about to attend. In the journey to Philadelphia he was accompanied at the start by Pendleton only, but, stopping at Mount Vernon on the way, he was there joined by Washington. The Virginia delegates were the foremost men in the colonies in fortune, talents, and political standing alike. When the Convention was ready for business, Henry quietly took the floor so soon as he found that there was no eager disposition among the members to express the wrongs which had been inflicted on the American people by the British Government. Beginning in his customary halting fashion, he quickly rose to the height of his powers of eloquence and closed with the memorable words: "The distinctions between Virginians, Pennsylvanians, New Yorkers, and New Englanders are no more. I am not a Virginian, but an American."

After this first inspiring call to action, Congress no longer hesitated, but proceeded to adopt a Declaration of Rights, a Petition to the King, and an agreement in favor of non-importation, non-exportation, and non-consumption—all measures that pointed unmistakably to a resolute resistance. When Henry was afterwards asked to name the foremost men in the Convention, he replied with characteristic generosity: "Rutledge, if you speak of eloquence, is by far the greatest orator, but Colonel Washington, who has no pretension to eloquence, is a man of more solid judgment and information than any one on the floor."

Henry predicted sometime before the second Virginia Convention assembled to take decisive steps towards defense that England would push the colonies to extremities; that she would consent to no accommodation of the existing antagonism; and that hostilities might break out at any hour. "How can America without arms, without ammunition, without ships, oppose such a power successfully?" he was asked. "She cannot alone," was the reply. "But," he continued, as he rose with animation from his chair, "where is France, where is Spain, where is Holland, the natural enemies of Great Britain? Will Louis XVI be asleep all this while? Believe me, no." He asserted with the firmest conviction that France would intervene with arms and supplies so soon as national independence had been formally declared. A letter from Joseph Hawley was read to him by John Adams, in which Hawley used the words: "After all, we must fight." In tones of great vehemence, Henry exclaimed, on hearing these words, "By God, I am of that man's opinion."

As soon as he arrived at home on his return from Philadelphia, he called the militia of Hanover together and urged upon them the duty of preparing for war in defense of their rights; and he earnestly recommended the formation at once of volunteer companies. But he quickly found out that the people at large were not easily aroused to a sense of the impending danger. This was the general state of public opinion in Virginia when the Convention of March, 1775, assembled in St. John's Church in Richmond. Henry, taking the initiative with characteristic decisiveness, submitted three resolutions. The third was the most important of all. It demanded that the colony should be immediately put in a posture of defense by arming, drilling, and disciplining the number of men who would be required for that purpose. Not until then had any colonial leader frankly expressed in public the imperative need of an unconditional declaration by all the colonies of war upon Great Britain. The general impression had been simply that war could not be avoided unless that Government was willing to recede. Henry alone seems to have thought that a rupture of the existing peaceable relations with the mother country was inevitable. "He left us all far behind," said Jefferson of the orator's action at this crisis. The truth of this statement is proved by the tenor of the wonderful speech which he delivered before the Convention. "Gentlemen may cry 'peace,

185

peace,' but there is no peace," he exclaimed. "The war is actually begun. The next gale that will sweep from the North will bring to our ears the clash of resounding arms. Is life so dear, or peace so sweet, as to be purchased at the expense of chains and slavery? Forbid it, Almighty God! I know not what course others may take, but as for me, give me liberty or give me death."

Henry did not wait to receive specific orders from the Convention, but struck the first blow by organizing the militia of Hanover for a march on Williamsburg to make reprisals on the royal treasury there for the powder that had been removed by Dunmore to the custody of a British ship. He had become convinced that the British authorities were planning to obtain possession of all the powder in all the colonies. Was this not the object of the excursion to Concord? What other purpose could the enemy have had in emptying the Powder Horn at the Virginia capital?

The volunteers who came forward at Henry's summons promptly chose him to be their commander, and they were stopped in their march on Williamsburg only by the receiver-general's timely payment of a compensatory sum for the powder which had been carried off by Dunmore. The latter, finding his position insecure, fled from his palace to the British ships and in time began that course of depredation along the shores of the Chesapeake and its tributaries which has made his name one of infamy in American history. In the meanwhile, Henry had attended the Congress at Philadelphia which appointed Washington to the post of commander in chief of the Continental armies. While there, he was elected a member of the Virginia Convention, which, before he could arrive from the north, had assembled on July 17 to organize a regular army for the general military service. Three regiments, each one a thousand strong, were authorized to be raised, in addition to a large force of minute men and buckskin men from the frontiers.

On taking his seat, Henry found that in his absence he had been elected to the colonelcy of the First Regiment, and Woodford of the Second. Apparently the Third was not yet

formed. Henry was soon advanced to the rank of commander
in chief of the Virginia forces as a whole. The general direction of affairs was placed in the hands of the Committee
of Safety, and it was to their orders that the new commander was subject. Unfortunately for his military ambition, some of these men were personally hostile to him, while
others were sincerely doubtful of his military talents.

By September 20 Henry had assumed control of his troops
at Williamsburg. These gradually increased in number to
nine companies of regulars. As the entire body of these
troops was to be ultimately enrolled in the Continental line,
the majority of the Committee of Safety, who were un-
friendly to Henry, determined to hold him back from active
service until a Continental officer of higher rank should arrive on the ground to take over the command. Dunmore
continued to ravage the shores of the Bay and rivers, with
Norfolk as his headquarters, but instead of sending Henry
to dispossess him, the Committee of Safety instructed Woodford to do so. Woodford claimed that under these circumstances he was not required to accept Henry as his military
superior, and he was stiffened in this mutinous attitude by
his victory at Great Bridge. When Henry, irritated justly
by his subordinate's refractoriness, complained to the Committee of Safety, they coldly asserted their right to direct
all operations just as they preferred. In claiming this
right—which they did under the sly influence of Pendleton's
personal hostility—they laid themselves open to the rebuke
of the Convention then in session at Williamsburg.

But Henry's position had become so unpleasant to him
that when Congress recommissioned him colonel of the First
Battalion, which had now been taken over by the Central
Government, along with five other Virginia battalions, he
resigned his post so soon as he found that he was to be
under the orders of a Continental brigadier. The troops
formerly subject to him put on mourning when they were
informed of his intention to retire; and they would have
deserted the ranks in a body had he not persuaded them to
remain. They indignantly denied the assertion of their col-

187

onel's enemies that he had neglected to enforce discipline among the soldiers of his regiment.

In May, 1776, the fifth Virginia Convention assembled. In the meanwhile, the public sentiment of all the colonies had, under the operation of different influences, been hardening in favor of a formal proclamation of separation from Great Britain. On May 14 General Nelson read a series of resolutions in Henry's handwriting, calling upon the Virginian delegates in Congress to procure a clear and full declaration of independence; and these were adopted by the Convention without dissent and carried off to Philadelphia by special messenger. In obedience to their tenor, Richard Henry Lee submitted the immortal demand that the United Colonies should be declared "free and independent states." A constitution for the new commonwealth was next adopted, which contained the famous Bill of Rights written by Mason, with Henry's aid in at least two of its most important articles. It was afterwards said of this document that it was "the history of England in miniature."

Henry was the first to fill the office of governor of Virginia under the new régime; and after the completion of this term he was repeatedly elected to the same position. On the occasion of his first inauguration, democrat as he was, he wore a scarlet coat, black smallclothes, and a dressed wig. There were now four hundred thousand people in the state over which he presided. During his absence from Williamsburg, caused by sickness, Jefferson brought forward the measures which aimed to abolish entail, primogeniture, and the established church in Virginia. There is no reason to think that the Governor disapproved of these radical changes. At one time, when the tide of bad fortune seemed to be running strongly against the Continental armies, a report was spread abroad that Henry was secretly under consideration for the revolutionary post of dictator; but whether this was so or not, there is no proof that he countenanced such a suggestion. When the fiery Archibald Cary heard of the rumor, he exclaimed to the Governor's brother-in-law, in the spirit of an old Roman, "Tell him that the

PLATE XVI. *From a portrait by Sully. Photo Gramstorff.*

PATRICK HENRY

day of his appointment will be the day of his death, for he shall feel my dagger in his breast before the sunset of that day." How little popular credence was put in the report was revealed in Henry's reëlection without opposition.

He had always taken a keen interest in the protection of the western country from Indian invasion, and under this influence he quickly responded to George Rogers Clark's request for a large amount of powder for use in its defense by that heroic officer. In 1777, Clark returned to Williamsburg with a plan for the expulsion of all the English garrisons from the chain of forts which they occupied north of the Ohio River. Jefferson, Wythe, and Mason warmly approved this plan, and so earnestly did Henry recommend it in a special message to the General Assembly that this body voted in favor of supplying the soldiers and money necessary for the success of the proposed expedition. With one hundred and eighty men Clark, after a campaign of incredible hardships, captured all the English forts and sent the English governor a prisoner to Williamsburg.

The splendid domain thus won was turned over to the Union by Virginia to make the signatories to the Articles of Confederation embrace all the states. France had refused to enter into an alliance with America until this was effected, and it had not been effected simply because Maryland had positively declined to sign until Virginia should convey to the states as a whole her right to the conquered territory in the Northwest. Maryland's signature completed the circle, and thus the French requirement was fulfilled.

Probably Henry never in the course of his illustrious career gave a more remarkable proof of his genius as a speaker than in the Convention of 1788, which was summoned to ratify the National Constitution. He advocated the rejection of the instrument because he was convinced that it would confer on the Central Government powers that would gradually destroy the authority of the separate states, upon which, in his opinion, the liberty of the people depended. He was defeated, as we shall see, on the main issue, but he at least compelled the ultimate adoption of ten

189

amendments which removed most of the objections to the instrument that he had so forcibly urged.

It seems that Henry had, while a member of Congress, supported a series of resolutions in support of the supposed functions of that body, which, at the time, were thought to be coercive; but this lenient attitude towards centralization on his part was completely altered by the later proposal of New England, under the scheming influence of the furtive Spanish envoy, to close the Mississippi River for twenty-five or thirty years. From that hour he showed himself to be suspicious and jealous of the power of the Federal Government—so far, indeed, that he declined to become a member of the Philadelphia Convention which drafted the Constitution, because he wished to have a free hand, should he disapprove its provisions.

The Virginia Convention sat for twenty-three days. Henry was on his feet at least once on eighteen of these days; and on some days he spoke not less than three times. In one instance he occupied the floor for a period of seven hours. Arrayed against him were Madison, Edmund Randolph, Marshall, Pendleton, and Wythe. His principal supporter was George Mason. He summarized his conclusions when he exclaimed in debate, "The dissolution of the Union is most abhorrent to my mind. The first thing I have at heart is American liberty; the second thing, is American Union. I see great jeopardy in this new government. I see none from our present one, the Confederation, which has carried us through a long and dangerous War, and secured us territory greater than any European monarch possesses. If a wrong step be now made, the Republic may be lost forever."

An incident occurred in the course of this debate which illustrated Henry's affectionate nature. Observing that a son, whom he had left at home to protect the family during his own absence, had come into the hall, he grew apprehensive lest some calamity to his domestic circle had happened. He halted abruptly in his argument, stooped to the ear of a friend sitting near, and in an agitated whisper begged him to go and inquire. The news was brought back that Mrs.

Henry had given birth to a son and that both mother and child were doing well.

The second incident was of a more general character. While inveighing against the dangers to follow the adoption of the Constitution, he exclaimed, "I see it; I feel it; I see beings of a higher order anxious concerning our decision." "When, lo," says Wirt, "a storm at that instant arose, which shook the whole building, and the spirits he had called seemed to come at his bidding. Nor did his eloquence or the storm immediately cease, but availing himself of the incident with a master's art, he seemed to mix in the fight of his ethereal auxiliaries, and rising on the wings of the tempest, to seize upon the artillery of heaven, and direct its fiercest thunders against the heads of his adversaries. The scene became insupportable, and the House rose without the formality of an adjournment, the members rushing from their seats with precipitation and confusion."

In the end the Federalists perceived that it would be unwise to force a vote without a recommendation in favor of amendments. The resolution to ratify with this provision was adopted by a majority of ten. Ultimately, ten of the seventeen amendments which were first proposed became a part of the framework of the Constitution.

Henry now thought that his political career was terminated, and he started out with characteristic energy to augment his fortune by renewing his practice at the bar, which had been seriously interrupted. This course had become more and more imperative with the steady increase in the number of his children. It has been said of him that the cradle never ceased to rock under his roof. Throughout his life from his majority down, he had shown a disposition to move from place to place. His practice, in consequence, was carried on in many counties in succession. First, he was a citizen of Hanover; then of Louisa; then of Henry; then of Prince Edward; then of Campbell; and finally, of Charlotte. He died at Red Hill in the latter county. As long as his strength survived, during these closing years, he was always ready to accept a retainer, most frequently in the county courts, but sometimes in the Federal. He traveled long distances to attend. In these last court scenes he exhibited as much power of eloquence as he had done on the rostrum. Especially was this so in the British Debt Cause, which also brought out all his capacity for reasoning and all his resources of professional learning.

Many amusing anecdotes were told of his skill in outwitting the opposing counsel and bringing their clients into ridicule. The most famous of all these stories relates to Johnny Hook, who had entered suit for the recovery of the amount due him for supplying meat to the Continental troops—especially during the Yorktown campaign. Henry, who was engaged for the defense, "painted," says Wirt, "the distresses of the American army exposed almost naked to the rigor of a winter's sky, and marking the frozen ground over which they marched with the blood of their unshod feet. 'Where was the man,' he exclaimed, 'who had an American heart in his bosom who would not have thrown open his fields, his barns, his cellars, the doors of his house, the portals of his breast, to receive with open arms the meanest soldier in that little band of famished patriots? Where is the man? There he stands.' Henry then carried the jury by the powers of his imagination to the plains around York; he depicted the surrender in the most noble and glowing colors of his eloquence. The audience saw before their eyes the humiliation and dejection of the British as they marched out of their trenches. They saw the triumph which lighted up every patriot's face, and heard the shouts of victory, and the cry of 'Washington and Liberty.' 'But hark! What notes of discord are these which disturb the general joy, and silence the acclamations of victory? They are the notes of Johnny Hook hoarsely bawling through the American Camp, 'beef! beef! beef!' "

Henry was to appear in one more political scene before the curtain fell. When the Constitution was finally ratified by all the states, it was perfectly logical on his part, after the position which he had taken before its adoption, to look upon the Union as a consolidated government, and not as a mere congeries of sovereign commonwealths, as so many asserted. It was this conviction which led him to comply with Washington's urgent request in 1799 that he should become the candidate for a seat in the General Assembly of Virginia, in order to combat the opposition which prevailed in the state of the idea of a supreme central administration. This opposition was fostered by the great influence of the States' Rights party.

Henry caused it to be announced that he would address the people at Charlotte Courthouse. When he arrived there, he was received by a concourse of admirers who stuck to his elbow until the public exercises began. A Baptist preacher who was present was offended by this excessive homage. "Why do you follow Mr. Henry about," he cried out to the crowd. "He is no god." "No," said Mr. Henry, deeply moved by both the scene and the remark. "No, indeed, my friend. I am but a poor worm of the dust—as fleeting and insubstantial as the shadow of the cloud that flies over yonder fields, and is remembered no more." "The tone with which this was uttered," a bystander has recorded, "and the look which accompanied it, affected every heart and silenced every voice."

Henry had to be lifted to the rostrum when the speaking was about to start, and he stood before his audience bowed with age and infirmities. But in a few moments after the opening of his address, says one who was present, a wonderful transformation of the whole man was observed. "He stood erect; his eyes beamed with a light that was almost supernatural; his features glowed with the hue and fire of youth, and his voice rang clear and melodious, with the intonations of some grand musical instrument whose notes filled the area and fell distinctly and delightfully upon the ears of the most distant of the thousands gathered before him."

John Randolph was present in the audience and later on spoke to the people as a candidate for Congress on a platform which supported the principles embodied by Madison and Jefferson in the famous Virginia and Kentucky Resolutions. The youthful statesman, so soon to win such great distinction, dined with the old Revolutionary orator. "You call me father," said Henry in parting with him. "Then, my son, I have something to say to thee: keep justice, keep truth, and you will live to think differently." But Randolph alone of all his associates in the famous group of original advocates of States' Rights never swerved from the convictions expressed on the occasion of this first public address.

Although elected to the General Assembly, Henry was too infirm to take his seat. In recent years he had declined to accept the nomination to the Federal Senate; had refused the tender of the post of minister to Spain and also to France; and had rejected the offer of the secretaryship of State and the chief-justiceship of the Supreme Court. He died with words of religious faith on his lips. "How wretched I should be at this moment," he whispered, "if I had not made my peace with God." His body reposes in the garden of Red Hill, and the sole inscription upon the face of his tombstone is "His Fame His Only Epitaph."

Chapter XIII

THOMAS JEFFERSON—THE FIRST PHASE

How DID Jefferson acquire the spirit which has made him the most illustrious apostle of intellectual, religious, and political freedom who has appeared in American history? There were certain influences in his life during childhood and boyhood that must have subtly tended to foster in his mind a liberal outlook from the beginning. For instance, he was born on the edge of what was then an interminable wilderness towards the west. In 1735, when Peter Jefferson patented a large tract of land on the banks of the Rivanna in the shadow of the Monticello Mountain, a region of thick forest lay between his new home at Shadwell and the Blue Ridge, broken at long intervals only by grassy savannas. Occasionally a trapper threaded the copses along the winding and brawling streams to find a colony of beavers; or a lonely hunter followed up the trail of a bear or buffalo feeding on the steep hillsides. Traces of the aborigines were still to be discerned. Jefferson never forgot the night scenes in the camps of the Indians, who in his boyhood halted on his father's land while journeying to Williamsburg to confer with the colonial governor.

The entire region westward was visible from the slopes above Shadwell as far as the Blue Ridge, and even after Jefferson had left his childhood behind, the curling smoke of few farm cabins was to be detected ascending from the bosom of the endless sea of foliage. The susceptible years of his boyhood were passed in the midst of a rural nature which as yet had been only here and there slightly gashed by the axe of the settler. It was not possible for an observant eye and receptive mind—such as he possessed even in youth—to look closely on that vast panorama of forest without drinking in unconsciously the spirit of liberty which lurked in its wild recesses. It seems logical enough, therefore, that he should have believed so firmly in the natural rights of man—those rights which are independent of laws and customs and civilization itself.

The life which Jefferson led as a boy was not that of a son of the modern frontiersman. He was never called upon to split rails like the youthful Lincoln, or to help to hew down the superabundant trees, or to break up the virgin ground with the plough, or to milk the cows, or to drive the horses to pasture. Peter Jefferson owned numerous slaves, and upon them fell the burden of carving out a complete homestead in the remote corner of the woods. While Thomas, still a child, was sojourning for a few years at Tuckahoe on James River with his parents and maternal kinsmen, in the midst of all the refined influences of a beautiful colonial home, the iron muscles of these bondsmen were clearing the primeval timber from the low grounds and uplands of Shadwell, building cabins, and turning up the soil with the hoe and ploughshare.

When Jefferson returned to his birthplace in his ninth year, the surrounding region was still sparsely inhabited; in a physical sense, it was still but little removed from the condition of the western wilderness; but the atmosphere of the reoccupied mansion on the Rivanna was as full of social charm, moral wholesomeness, and intellectual culture, as the atmosphere of the most famous residences in the oldest counties of Tidewater.

But it was something more valuable than the sentimental advantage of respectable birth which Jefferson inherited from his father. First, a good name. Peter Jefferson was greatly esteemed as a skillful surveyor, an upright magistrate, a faithful burgess, an honest man. Secondly, a robust frame. No slave in Peter Jefferson's possession could lift so heavy a hogshead as he; no rival with the sextant could lay off a patent through underbrush and across rocky gorges with so little fatigue by nightfall. Thirdly, and, far above all, liberal opinions. Peter Jefferson's sympathies were always on the side of the people at large, and he had the reputation of being the staunchest and frankest Whig in his district. Since Thomas Jefferson was in his fourteenth year when his father died, the generous principles of that father had had ample time to stamp themselves indelibly on his mind and spirit. The whole tenor of his public life was to show the influence of this fact unmistakably.

To his mother, on the other hand, was traceable those refined instincts which made him, at the very time he was formulating the principles of our New World democracy, a man of the most fastidious tastes and the most polished bearing. She was a member of the Randolph family, who, before their emigration to Virginia, had been allied with the best blood of England and Scotland and, what was more to be valued, had in that kingdom been long celebrated for their services to the church, their acquirements as scholars, and their excursions into the romantic domain of poetry. In Virginia their genius for success had not deserted them— they had filled numerous public offices and accumulated large estates in slaves and lands. Indeed, there was no family connection in the colony in the eighteenth century which surpassed them in the amount of property owned, in social influence, or in public usefulness.

How did Jefferson acquire, by the time that he had reached maturity, a fund of classical, scientific, and general information such as few persons with every advantage for study and observation possess at the end of a long life? As he was directly indebted to his father for his vigorous frame, liberal outlook, and sense of probity, so to that parent also was due his first relish for books. It was Peter Jefferson's habit, when at home from his surveys, to amuse himself at night by the fireside in reading Shakespeare, Pope, Swift, and Addison; and his wife and children were always called upon to listen to his recital of his favorite passages. The son's first lessons in the ancient tongues were learned from a Scotch clergyman who then filled a pulpit in a parish not far from Shadwell. One of the last wishes expressed by his dying father was that the classical education thus so happily begun should be continued to the final stage of the ripest scholarship; and how keenly Thomas Jefferson valued this opportunity to advance to that stage is disclosed in the statement made by him towards the end of his life, that if he had to choose between the advantage derived from the classical education which his father had been so solicitous to give him and the benefit from the estate inherited from that father, his decision would unhesitatingly be in favor of the former.

Two years of acquisition were passed by Jefferson under the tuition of the Reverend James Maury, who confirmed and increased the young student's relish for the works of the ancient poets and historians. He then entered the College of William and Mary, which was second to no seat of learning on the continent in the variety and thoroughness of its instruction.

Although Jefferson is reported to have been at this period of his life somewhat awkward in his gait, this fault of immaturity stood no more than his large fund of scholarship in the way of his taking part in all the amusements of the place and hour. On his mother's side, he was through the Randolphs a near kinsman of the foremost personages of that lively society; and they quickly and cordially drew him into all the dissipations and recreations of their circle. But in after life he used to say he was very grateful that his thoughts at that period had not been completely diverted by these charming pleasure-lovers from all the serious purposes which had brought him from Shadwell to Williamsburg. In fact, he was saved from demoralization by the gravity which was native to his character, in spite of his admiration for a spirited race horse, his taste for sprightly conversation, and his weakness for flirtations with young ladies who were the toasts of the idle hour. It was this elemental trait in his disposition which, young as he was, prompted him to seek the company of the ablest and most accomplished men in the little capital. "Under temptation and difficulties," he remarked in his later commentary on these years at college, "I would ask myself: what would Dr. Small, Mr. Wythe, and Mr. Peyton Randolph do in this situation?"

Small, a Scotchman of fine native talents, ripe attainments, and singular persuasiveness of tongue, was so deeply impressed by the youthful Jefferson that he admitted him to constant intercourse on a footing of perfect intellectual equality. The pupil often asserted, after he had become famous, that Small had "fixed the destinies" of his life by the lectures which he delivered in the college and still more by his informing conversation in private. That learned professor perhaps only confirmed the taste for scientific observation and the bent towards utilitarian philosophy which were really inborn characteristics of the future President. But the most permanent effect of the latter's association with Small was the broadening of those liberal opinions which, as we have seen, he had inherited from his father. Quite possibly, too, it was due principally to Small's influence that his religious views became more latitudinarian than the clergyman of the established church, to which he belonged, approved. Nor were his convictions ever again restored to orthodoxy.

Hardly second in importance to Jefferson's fruitful association with Small was his intimate intercourse with Fauquier and Wythe. Fauquier was a disciple of the skeptical Bolingbroke, and it has been conjectured that his influence in undermining Jefferson's original religious opinions was only a little less effective than Small's. But Fauquier's was also felt in more beneficial directions. He was a thorough man of the world, witty, fastidious, graceful, and urbane, with a taste for the classics and a decided aptitude for music. Around his dinner table Small, Wythe, Jefferson, and himself constantly met, a congenial group in spite of Jefferson's youth; and on these occasions the conversation would run the whole gamut of science and literature, with excursions every now and then into lighter and more frivolous avenues of talk.

It was in the field of jurisprudence that Jefferson was most deeply indebted to Wythe, for after the completion of his academic course he became the private pupil of that distinguished lawyer. The rule then followed by the youthful aspirant for the bar was to enter a regular practitioner's office and there pursue his studies under his superior's general supervision. During a period of five years Jefferson sat, as it were, at Wythe's feet, a privilege as fruitful in its personal influence as in its professional. At this time he left his bed daily at dawn and continued his application to his books during fourteen hours, with only short intervals reserved for his meals and moderate exercise. The best proof of the thoroughness of his training for the bar is to be found in certain opinions of a distinctly legal character which he drafted while Secretary of State.

Jefferson came of age in 1764, when the peace of the colonies was so rudely shaken by the British policy following the signing of the Treaty of Paris. Fresh from the liberal companionship of Small and Wythe, deeply versed in the interpretation of the law of Coke and Lyttleton, remembering the Whig principles of his father, and inspired by the freedom of his native mountains, he, young as he was, instinctively resented the declaration of the British Parliament that it possessed both the right and the power to tax the American people without their consent.

The substance of the famous resolutions which Henry offered in 1765 probably did not go as far as Jefferson wished, if the tenor of his own later *Summary View* can be taken as a proof; but how thoroughly he approved of their spirit was shown by his course just as soon as he began to take an active part in the political affairs of the colony. It was not until two years had passed that he became a member of the bar, which brought him into intimate relations with the most influential public men of the community; and it was not until two years later still that he was elected to a seat in the House of Burgesses. Now for the first time he was able to utter his opinions from a height that was bound to draw attention to them. He had not become alienated from all the

PLATE XVII. *From an original engraving in the possession of the author.*
KING GEORGE THE THIRD

conservative members of his mother's family, the Randolphs, many of whom remained loyal to Great Britain throughout the Revolutionary War.

During Jefferson's first session in the House Botetourt dissolved that body because of its sympathy with the action which Massachusetts had recently taken in opposition to the measures of the British Government. Jefferson was one of the members who retired to the Raleigh Tavern and drew up articles of association recommending to the people of all the colonies the policy of refusing to buy British merchandise. When the *Gaspee* was burned in 1773, Henry, Lee, Carr, and himself and a few others were irritated by the failure of so many of the colonies to show a proper spirit of resistance to British aggression, and in order to foster a firmer disposition, they met again in the Raleigh Tavern and drafted a series of resolutions in favor of the appointment of a committee of correspondence in each colony, whose duty it should be to promote unity by constant intercommunication. The resolutions also recommended the holding of a convention, in which all the colonies should be represented, and which should lay down the course that it would be proper for all to pursue.

The earliest of his public papers bearing on the rising controversy between Great Britain and her American colonies was the instructions given by the freeholders of Albemarle County in July, 1773, to their two newly elected burgesses, one of whom was Jefferson himself. These instructions, which were certainly written by him, sounded a note for the first time that was to run through all his Revolutionary documents of a later composition, namely, that the people of the colonies possessed not only the charter rights to be governed by the laws of their own assemblies alone, but the "common right of mankind" to be so governed, independently of all charters; that these joint natural and legal rights had been invaded by Parliament in numerous instances in the course of recent years, to the imperilment of the rights of the British Empire as a whole; and that the people of Albemarle County would always be ready to unite with their fellow-subjects throughout that Empire in executing the powers which God himself had given for the reestablishment of these rights, whenever overthrown.

This doctrine of natural rights—which was simply an abstruse idea of the philosophers of the eighteenth century, without any real connection with the purely legal aspects of Parliamentary taxation—was now heard for the first time in the controversy. Hundreds of resolutions were passed by the Virginian counties in this crisis in presentation of their views, but in Albemarle alone was the justification for resistance based primarily on natural law and natural rights. In the remainder, the position taken by Patrick Henry in his address upon the Stamp Act was simply a legal, constitutional question to be decided. The spokesmen of the counties did not perplex their minds by the application to that question of the idealistic principles of political speculators. They concerned themselves only with the British Parliament's assertion of the legal right to tax them. They did not think themselves called upon to claim, as Jefferson had done in so many words, that this body had no natural right to exercise any sort of control over any department of their affairs or any branch of their interests.

Jefferson stated in after life that he was upheld in this extreme view by but one man of influence in the community, George Wythe. All the others, however liberal and outspoken, while denying Parliament's right to tax the colonies without their consent, acknowledged its right to impose duties for the regulation of trade.

It was not long before there opened up to Jefferson a much more conspicuous opportunity to reiterate the same radical principle of action. The celebrated *Summary View of the Rights of British America* was drafted by him for the Convention which met at Williamsburg in August, 1773, just a few weeks after the passage of the resolutions of Albemarle County, to which we have already referred. Doubtless its text had been drawn up before these resolutions were adopted and had really inspired their composition. The *Summary View* was not read by Jefferson in person to the committee of the Convention which passed on documents of that nature before reporting, or refusing to report, them to the Convention itself. It was brought to the committee's attention by one of his friends, as he had been detained on the road to Williamsburg by an attack of sudden and severe illness. That this revolutionary paper was not given out by the committee at all was only what was to be expected in the then conservative state of popular sentiment. Jefferson himself candidly admitted at a later date that his radical expressions were not at the time good for the patriot cause, and wisdom, he thought, had therefore been shown by the committee in declining to make them public. In fact, not even the boldest spirits in the Convention were then prepared to assent to his cool statement that Virginia, Hanover, and England stood on a footing of political equality, because all three were simply provinces of the British Empire; and that the only ligature joining these provinces to each other was their common allegiance to George the Third. Virginians, Hanoverians, Englishmen—all were fellow-subjects of the King, but all were independent of each other. Upset the monarchy, as in Cromwell's time, and the last political tie between them would at once be loosed.

The members of the Convention of 1773 were wise in refusing to base the justice of their protest on so extreme a suggestion—a suggestion, indeed, that disclosed the sympathy of Jefferson's mind with the idealistic principles of John Locke and his disciples, and with that radical spirit which led ultimately to the excesses of the French Revolution. In the present great dependencies of the British Empire—Canada, South Africa, Australia, and New Zealand—we perceive the exact relation which he asserted had existed from the beginning between Great Britain and her American colonies, a relation of practical independence in every way, except in allegiance to the Throne. But this relation in our own times has been brought about, not by a clearer conception of the natural rights of people, but by the growth of those dependencies in wealth and power.

A copy of the *Summary View* found its way to London,

was warmly approved by Whigs like Edmund Burke, but was looked upon by the Government as so seditious a document that the name of its author was included in a bill of attainder. This, however, was afterwards suppressed. Such was one of the facts which kept alive in Jefferson's breast his undisguised dislike of the British.

In June, after drafting the Convention's reply to Lord North's conciliatory proposals, he made the first national stride in his political career by becoming a member of Congress. For this election he was indebted, unlike most of the public men of his time, not to talents as a speaker, but to skill as a writer, coupled with shrewdness and boldness in private conferences. And he was also known to possess a fund of scientific knowledge and to be deeply versed in polite letters. His career in Congress followed the general line of his previous career in the House of Burgesses—there he continued to hold and express the same convictions touching the true relation of Parliament to the colonies which he had laid before the committee of the first Convention at Williamsburg. In the growing struggle with Great Britain he stood alone in Congress in the assertion of the doctrine of Natural Rights, while the other members leaned upon the legal rights of all transplanted Englishmen. Their moderation in insisting upon these latter rights and in offering the sole fact of their violation as a justification for resistance, was very conservatively expressed by John Dickinson in July, 1770, in the report which he and Jefferson submitted to Congress on the sixth day of that month. Only a few sentences of Jefferson's original draft were retained in the text of that document. At this time he, no more than Dickinson or Americans in general, had reached the stage when he either expected or desired a severance from Great Britain.

Looking at the conservative attitude of the leaders in the movement of resistance at this hour—that attitude which was really directed, not to the conquest of separation from, but only to the conquest of conciliation with, the infatuated mother country—we discern how fully they deserved Chatham's noble eulogium for their prudence of utterance, their restraint of feeling, and yet their iron firmness of purpose. Especially reluctant were the Virginians to break away from England. They still spoke of it as "home." Not for a single hour had they as a community lost their consciousness of their identity in blood, in language, in moral principles, in religious creed, in laws, in literature, in national reasons for pride, with the inhabitants of the island across the Atlantic. They, too, were Englishmen, and as such, members of the greatest empire in the world, participants in its material advantages and political prestige, and possessors in common of the fame of all its heroes, sages, statesmen, and philosophers.

But events were now following fast upon each other's heels, and the loyalty to the mother country, even among the Virginians, was very rapidly growing cold and unresponsive. In the winter of 1775-76, imposing majorities in both Houses of Parliament approved the King's speech stupidly counseling a vigorous war upon his subjects oversea. American vessels and cargoes were to be confiscated; no foreign ship was to be permitted to enter an American port to engage in trade; while commissioners, backed by a formidable fleet and a strong force of British and Hessian soldiers, were to be sent out to the colonies to receive the assurance of their humble and confidently expected submission.

Hardly had news of the British plans for their subjugation reached the Americans when Paine's epochal pamphlet, *Common Sense*, was published, to increase further the indignant surprise which they then felt. Now for the first time the opinion became general that a formal declaration of independence could no longer be avoided. In May, 1776, Congress adopted a resolution advising each colony to set up a state government for the administration of its own affairs; and on the same day the Convention then sitting in Virginia instructed its delegates in Philadelphia to declare publicly in favor of an immediate separation from Great Britain. It has been surmised that Jefferson—who had been absent in Virginia until the fifteenth of May—had been influential in causing the Convention to take this bold step.

When Congress chose a committee to draft the Declaration, it was he who obtained the largest number of ballots. It has been presumed that his reputation as a writer was the real reason for his winning such a signal honor, but it is quite probable that the uncompromising opinions which he had always expressed had an almost equal share in bringing about his appointment. His selection by his colleagues to draft the new charter of liberty carried with it many possibilities of personal danger, since the men who were then directing the course of events knew perfectly well that, should the movement of resistance ultimately fail, it was the author of the Declaration and the commander of the armies who would feel the heaviest weight of the avenging British arm.

Like the *Summary View*, the Declaration of Independence bases the right of separation on the natural right of a community to govern itself; but at the same time Jefferson recognized that what he described as "a decent respect for the opinion of mankind" required him to present the practical motives which justified the exercise of that natural right. The Americans as a people put very slim reliance on the political philosophy of the opening paragraph of that great document as a really acceptable reason for a revolution— the right of self-determination was even more of a glittering theory then than it has proved itself to be in our own day— but supported by the long array of grievances which Jefferson marshaled, that philosophy assumed a practical complexion; and this practical complexion has only deepened with the progress of time, for what was more or less idealism in the eyes of Jefferson's colleagues has, in the eyes of later generations, become—largely through the constant recital of the doctrines of the great Declaration—the accepted principles of the American people, but by no means as yet of the whole world.

What are these principles for which we are so much indebted to the author of this document? First, the equality of all men, if not in the eyes of nature—as Jefferson asserted—in the eyes of the law. Second, the right of all men to life, liberty, and the pursuit of happiness; third, government was instituted to protect this inalienable right; and fourth, the exercise of the powers of government, without the consent of the governed, is tyranny, and only the governed can legally prescribe what those powers should be.

There were two consequences of the Declaration of Independence which we may touch upon here. In the first place, it alone made certain the coöperation of other nations in securing that permanent separation from Great Britain on which the American people were not at first resolved. As long as the colonies declined to throw off their allegiance to the King, there could be no inducement for foreign countries to lend their aid, since such a policy looked, not to actual independence, but to a mere redress of grievances.

In the second place, the Declaration of Independence was an indictment, not of a whole people, it is true, but what is almost equally poignant, of the representative of a whole people. That indictment could never be forgotten—perhaps could never be forgiven—by the British, whether they were successful in the struggle to conquer their colonies or not. Its author must always be a sinister figure in their eyes. Washington, Hamilton, and Franklin have long been reinstated in the kindly view of the English people, while Jefferson has rarely won a fair estimate of his merits from their writers and speakers; and he continues, in spite of the friendship which time has fostered between the two nations, the one statesman of the Revolution who has never with them lost his unpopularity. In some measure this fact is due to his preëminence as the father of American democracy, which for a long period was so antipathetic to the social and political system of the English Commonwealth; but it is also largely attributable to the existence of the Declaration, which was the first signpost to mark the political and social divergence of the paths of Great Britain and the United States.

Jefferson accepted a nomination to the House of Delegates in 1777 because he was anxious to remove from the statute book of Virginia certain laws which had been as influential in maintaining the English character of his native community as the original English strain in its blood or its unbroken intercourse with the mother country oversea. He was particularly solicitous to assist in abolishing entail and primogeniture and in pulling down the established church—regulations which had been adopted in continuation of the English system in Virginia and which, in spite of their supposed injustice, had done so much to nurture for the future crisis of the Revolution and for the national period to follow, the greatest body of statesmen that has, within so short a time and so narrow an area, appeared in the Western Hemisphere.

The majority of the General Assembly were churchmen and large landowners, and the several bills which were introduced by Jefferson and his backers for the radical destruction of these props of their social framework aroused a hostility against Jefferson himself, as the leader, which was to pursue him until the end of his life. As a matter of fact, the revocation of these laws was the logical result of the change from a monarchical to a republican form of government. That revocation would have come had no such man as Jefferson been born on earth. It was the first practical step towards the democratization of the community, now inevitable. By doing away with the priority or the monopoly of personal and institutional claims, it placed all the members of every family and the different religious denominations on a footing of absolute equality.

In our own age, with its now old inheritance of the democratic tradition, the system introduced seems to be axiomatic enough, although the aristocratic system which prevailed in colonial Virginia still prevails in England, in spite of the existence in that Kingdom of as large a body of dissenters in proportion to population as was to be found in the community oversea when Jefferson, a Deist, and Madison, a Presbyterian, first laid their axes at the root of the Anglican establishment there. England has always affirmed that as religion was a bulwark of society, it was entitled to the formal recognition of the State, even to the point of being made a great department of the general government.

On the other hand, in the eyes of Jefferson—a man who had no real faith in any religion—the association of Church and State was a crime against the cause of freedom in all its aspects; and he went at its destruction in a spirit that was more suggestive of an American Voltaire than of a great reformer who acts under the pressure of necessity, but who retains a deep sympathy with the spiritual aspirations of mankind.

In a mood of greater calmness and moderation, and with the assistance of Wythe and Pendleton, he undertook the revision of the general laws of the new commonwealth. The wise regulations which were to govern the future naturalization of foreigners had their initiation with Jefferson; so did the elaborate and farsighted scheme drawn up for the erection of a public school system, which provided for a university at the top for the whole state, classical academies in the middle ground for each district, and primary schools for each township.

Jefferson recommended that all slaves born in Virginia after a certain date should be set free on reaching a designated age and, having been first given a mechanical education, should be deported to Africa. But he soon came to the conclusion that public opinion was not yet ripe enough for the acceptance of this proposal. Still he never lost the conviction—which time was to confirm—that all the slaves would ultimately be emancipated and that delay in granting them liberty would only aggravate the evils which would inevitably accompany the act of setting them free.

The first executive position which Jefferson filled was the office of governor of Virginia. Did he demonstrate his unfitness for this post as flagrantly as his enemies openly asserted during his life and as his detractors have done since his death? It is well known that a demand for his impeachment was submitted by one of his own neighbors at Monticello at the session which the General Assembly, driven pell-mell across the Blue Ridge by Tarleton's troops, held in Staunton. The gravamen of the charge was (1) that he had not put the state in a condition of defense after he had been warned by Washington of a threatened invasion from the south by land or water; (2) that he had not made full use of the military resources at his command; (3) that he,considered his own personal safety too tenderly when the British soldiers were approaching Richmond; (4) that he retired from Monticello to Carter's Mountain near by too hastily when red-coated dragoons had been sighted in the streets of Charlottesville below; and (5) that he had withdrawn from the office of governor when he found that its difficulties and dangers were rapidly increasing.

In order to meet these serious accusations in person, Jefferson sought election to the House of Delegates, and when they came up in the course of that body's proceedings, he replied fully, frankly, and quietly to every one of them from his seat. How convincing his answers were is proved by the resolution adopted unanimously by the House and the Senate in eulogy of the uprightness and patriotism which he had shown in the performance of all the duties of the office at the most exacting hour in the history of the war. His right to this commendation cannot be disputed in the light of the fact that he had done as well as the limited means for the defense at his disposal allowed. Virginia, following Washington's recommendations, had perhaps been too generous in sending her troops for the common advantage beyond her borders; and when the avalanche of Cornwallis' army fell upon her own soil, she was not in a position to meet the invasion with the force that she could have mustered had she previously shown herself to be solicitous only for her own protection.

But with due allowance for this diversion of strength, there is reason to think that Jefferson was not personally sufficiently equipped to win the reputation of a very capable war governor. That he himself was conscious of his own deficiencies in the tenure of that office during those violent times is indicated by the opinion which he afterwards expressed, namely, that its duties called for military training and experience in the course of a period of conflict. And such were the qualifications possessed by Nelson, who suc-

ceeded him, and who proved, in consequence, a more satisfactory executive.

It was not long before Jefferson was again elected to a
seat in Congress. Among the important measures which he
suggested, as a member of that body, was the appointment
of a committee which during the recess should exercise all
the executive powers of the Government. A committee so
chosen did undertake this duty, but soon falling into wran-
gles and factions, voluntarily resigned its delegated functions in disgust.

Dissatisfied with the plan of division which Robert Morris
had reported for the coinage, Jefferson recommended the
adoption of the dollar as the unit, and in the end this solu-
tion was accepted.

During his term as governor, he had signed the bill passed
by the General Assembly for the cession to the United States
of all title to the Northwest Territory, then held by Virginia
as the result of the successful campaign of George Rogers
Clark. Jefferson was appointed by Congress a member of
the committee selected to draft a plan of administration for
this great empire beyond the Ohio. The plan which he drew
up was afterwards used in the composition of the celebrated
ordinance that prohibited the introduction of slavery into
all that region after 1800. This was the first effective blow
struck for the ultimate extinction of this institution on the
American continent.

Chapter XIV

GEORGE MASON

THE FOUNDER of the Mason family in Virginia, the first
George Mason, who gave his Christian name to the eldest
son of several generations of his descendants, was, before
his departure from England, a gallant royalist officer in the
civil wars. He took part in the fatal battle of Worcester as
the commander of a troop of horse; and after that overwhelming defeat, fearing that he would be arrested by the
Roundheads, he fled in disguise oversea. He had the year
before been preceded thither by a large body of persons who,
having been ardent partisans of the unfortunate Charles,
decided that it would be prudent for them to look for a
refuge among the loyal planters seated in the valleys of the
James, Rappahannock, and Potomac. In one ship alone, during the year 1649, some three hundred and thirty of the beheaded monarch's followers set sail for the Chesapeake.

When the first George Mason was planning to leave the
Kingdom secretly, he, too, was doubtless influenced in choosing Virginia as an asylum by his cognizance of its people's
devotion to the memory of the martyr of Whitehall, and
by their stubborn refusal to bow before the supremacy of
Parliament. The fanatical loyalty of Sir William Berkeley
was known to every royalist in England; and all were certain that after they had passed the Atlantic they would receive from his government a welcome that would do much
to soften their poignant recollection of their misfortunes.

When the emigrant, George Mason, arrived in Virginia,
he turned his face towards what was then looked upon as

the most promising part of the colony in which to settle, namely, the Northern Neck, which included within its fertile boundaries the valleys of the Rappahannock and Potomac. He picked out a broad area for a patent at Accohick, on the banks of the latter stream, which at that point resembled an arm of the Bay in width from margin to margin. In the neighborhood of the spot where he built his dwelling house, there resided the Cavaliers, Colonel Fowke, Sir Thomas Lunsford, and Captain Giles Brent. Indeed, the country spread out between the two rivers had drawn to its soil a considerable number of gentlemen who, before they abandoned England, had belonged to the Royalist party. Colonel Gerard Fowke was one of the most conspicuous of these. He was a member of the Fowke family of Brewood and Gunston Halls, standing in Brewood Parish, in the west division of the Kingdom near the little hamlet of Gunston. Gunston Hall subsequently became the property of the Giffards, celebrated in history as the owners of the Boscabell Oak, in the foliage of which the second Charles hid himself in order to evade the gaze of the Roundheads scouring the fields below. It was through the intermarriage of the Masons and Fowkes that Gunston was adopted as the name for the famous family seat on the Potomac, so long associated with the life of George Mason of the Revolution. Colonel George Fowke was the paternal ancestor of the great patriot, who was fourth in descent from the original Mason of the same name.

The first Colonel George Mason very soon exhibited, like all the foremost Virginians of that age, a capacity for acquiring lucrative public offices. He was first appointed to the post of sheriff of Stafford County; then he became the clerk of its court; and, finally, he rose to the very honorable position of county-lieutenant. These offices were filled only by men who could justly claim that they belonged to the class of gentlemen, a class which then enjoyed certain distinct advantages in both social and political life, although these advantages were without the actual sanction of law.

Mason, like his neighbors, Fowke, Brent, and others, was

not disposed to observe scrupulously the rights of the savage tribes seated in the neighborhood of his estate; and on one occasion he was summoned to court to answer a charge of this character laid by the King of Potomac. The Indians, although often imposed upon, were only too frequently themselves the aggressors.

It was in a frontier incident involving the two races that Bacon's Rebellion began. Previous to that event, a servant belonging to Thomas Matthews' plantation in Stafford had been killed by a band of Doeg marauders. Colonel Mason and Captain Brent, on hearing of this murder, raised a troop of horse, crossed the Potomac, and then separated and set out in pursuit. Captain Brent was the first to succeed in coming up with one band of the savages, and the chief and ten of his followers were shot down before they could escape. A son of the chief, about ten years of age, was led away in captivity. Colonel Mason, in the meanwhile, had overtaken a second band, which in turn was attacked and nearly destroyed before it was learned that its members belonged to a friendly tribe.

The little prisoner, on reaching Colonel Mason's house, fell into a trance, in which condition, at Captain Brent's suggestion, he was baptized when it was found that every physical remedy had failed to restore him. We are told by the chronicler that while Mrs. Mason was gazing at the boy, he slowly unclosed his eyes and perceptibly breathed, "whereat she ran for a cordial, which he took from a spoon, gaping for more, and so, by degrees, recovered, though, before his baptism, they had often tried the same means, but could, by no means, wrench open his teeth."

Following the precedent so general in Virginia's political history at this time, the second George Mason succeeded his father in the various offices which the parent had occupied; and like his father, too, he found a fierce pleasure in fighting the numerous bands of Indians who were so often skulking within the confines of the settlements or sneaking along the borders. The third George seems to have pursued the beaten path of his father and grandfather, so far as the acquisition

214

of office and the accumulation of landed property were concerned. He appears to have been less aggressive in temper. At least he left behind him no record as a soldier in Indian warfare; but this was probably due to the fact that the savages had, by the time of his appearance on the scene, been pushed further back behind the mountains.

It is an indication of the colony's advance in years and stability that the fourth George Mason was born under the roof which had already sheltered two generations of his forebears. This George was the greatest member of the family, the eminent Revolutionary patriot whose name is so celebrated in the universal history of human rights. As his father died intestate, he inherited all the paternal landed estate; but his widowed mother, a woman of determined spirit and vigorous sense, was able in time to save enough out of her own income to transmit to her younger children an ample competence.

The education of George Mason seems to have been obtained entirely from tutors, but he was so fortunate as to possess in his father and also in an uncle, John Mercer—with whom he was thrown in almost daily intimacy at this early period of his life—kinsmen remarkable for taste and scholarship. Mercer had gathered together a private library of excellent quality, to which his nephew had constant access, and of which he did not fail to make the amplest use. In the meanwhile, he was acquiring a stock of physical strength by his pursuit of all the sports at that time so popular with the boys of the colonial plantations. He shot deer, squirrels, and wild turkeys in the woods, and ducks, geese, and swan on the rivers; and no doubt, young as he was, he followed the hounds with his father and his father's neighbors. The streams were full of fish of all kinds, and the youthful rodsman was often seen reclining on the bank. The broad bosom of the Potomac and the wide mouths of the creeks flowing into its waters offered exceptionally fine courses for his sailboat, which he had early learned to manage with confident skill.

During these years of study and diversion Mason did not

suffer from lack of companions. In the long line of estates bordering the Potomac there were numerous families of good birth, intellectual culture, refined manners, and ample fortune. With many of these he was united by ties of cousinship, for by the time that his life began, Virginia had been settled long enough to allow of frequent marriages between the families residing in the same region of country. There were many persons of his youthful age in the general circle to which these families belonged, and the exchange of visits and the sharing of sports by them from season to season were easy and constant. The combined educational, social, and recreational advantages which Mason thus enjoyed before arriving at his majority left a permanent impression on his receptive and sympathetic nature.

He came of age in 1745. Few men of his generation in the colony entered upon active life with so fair a promise of happiness and usefulness. Youth was in his possession, robust health, a competent fortune, a handsome face, a graceful figure, high social station, an intellect of the noblest order, a careful literary training, and a temper notable for its sweetness and equableness. He remained a bachelor only five years. In 1750 he married Anne Eilbeck, the daughter of Colonel William Eilbeck of Maryland. Mason's father had owned a plantation adjacent to the Eilbeck estate, on which he spent much time, and there he ultimately died. It was owing to this proximity that the son made his first acquaintance with the young lady of the house. As she was only sixteen years of age at the hour of the union, their association must have begun as children.

It was at Gunston Hall, on the Virginia side of the Potomac, that their married life was passed. This famous mansion was completed about 1758. It was situated on the banks of the great stream, and in its noble surroundings of water and forest, and in its embellishments of sward, shrubbery, and flowers, was as beautiful a family seat as was to be found in Virginia in those times.

The first connection of George Mason's name with any branch of public affairs arose from his becoming a member of the Ohio Company, organized in 1749 for the settlement of the valley of the Ohio River and the prosecution of trade with the Indians in that region. The first men in the colony were actively interested in this enterprise. Thomas Lee, President of the Council, was the leading spirit in pushing its interests, and with him were associated such influential citizens as Lawrence Washington, Governor Dinwiddie, and John Mercer, an uncle of George Mason. It was not long before the Company was obstructed in its purpose by the interference of the French, who were looking to the absorption of all that part of the West into their own dominion. This scheme culminated in the building of a series of forts which halted all further English immigration until Fort Duquesne had been finally captured and the French forces permanently expelled from that entire region.

George Mason's sole part in political life before the Revolution was in the membership of the House of Burgesses. Apparently, at that time he filled the office for but one term. He represented the county of Fairfax. In early manhood he seems to have been devoid of any ambition to acquire public distinction; and this characteristic continued more or less throughout his life. Only a sense of duty made him responsive to the call of his fellow-citizens. In spite of the extraordinary eminence which he had won as a public servant, in his last will he advised his sons to prefer the happiness of independence and a private station to the vexations and disappointments of public business. This attitude of mind, which seems unworthy of so great a man, was probably due to the fact that he was throughout his years of maturity a chronic sufferer from gout, which made it difficult for him to endure the hardships of traversing the highways of those times. It required at least five days to reach Williamsburg by carriage—a journey not to be borne with equanimity by a man tortured with pain.

There is no indication in Mason's life that he loved ease for the sake of ease alone or that he was indulgent of self. But it remains a fact that, while he left a deep impression on the political history of his day, his achievements were not so numerous or his reputation so national as his solid powers as a public speaker, his sagacity as a political counselor, and the profound respect in which he was as a man held by his contemporaries seemed to call for. His taste for country life offered him a far greater enjoyment than the excitements of a political career. Established under his own roof at Gunston Hall, surrounded by the members of his family and visiting friends, and occupied with the operations of his landed property and with the welfare of his bondsmen, he had not the smallest desire to be drawn into the political current of the colony for the mere purpose of his own advancement or diversion.

The Gunston Hall plantation was really a small principality, like all the large plantations in the vicinity. It was a community that was fully self-contained, except that a foreign market had to be found for the tobacco. There were the slaves engaged in cultivating the staple crops of each season; in manufacturing, on the domestic looms, the cloths which they wore in winter or summer; in building the cabins in which they dwelt; and in fashioning the implements that they used. The entire list of artisans was represented— stonecutters, carpenters, blacksmiths, saddlers, weavers, knitters, and tailors. There were hunters and fishermen to supply the master's table, gardeners to tend the mansion grounds and the flower and kitchen enclosure, shepherds and herdsmen to overlook the livestock, and grooms to care for the stable. The round of workingmen and helpers was complete.

Along the banks of the Potomac, whether towards the falls or the mouth of the river, rose in Mason's middle life, as in his youth, a succession of country homes occupied by Fairfaxes, Washingtons, Lees, Alexanders, Lomaxes, Carters, Tayloes, and numerous other families of distinction. The distance between these mansions was not so great as to discourage an almost daily exchange of visits. Throughout the year there was a series of dances, dinners, and races to bring the members of this gentry constantly together, and there is no evidence that Mason, in the quiet period preceding the passage of the Stamp Act, did not take part in this round of amusements, except when temporarily disabled by one of those recurring attacks of gout which were directly traceable to his ancestors' love of good cheer.

From the round of duties and pleasures which made up his daily plantation life Mason was abruptly aroused, in the spring of 1764, by the news of Parliament's Declaratory Act, passed in March for the purpose of asserting its right to tax the people of the colonies, although they were unrepresented in that body. The special tax imposed later on under this Act's authority was the notorious Stamp Tax adopted in the winter of 1765-66. The first public utterance of opposition to it was raised in Westmoreland County. The signers of that memorable protest were all friends of Mason and were aware that he was in sympathy with their action. The justices of Stafford County, also his friends, resigned their commissions rather than obey the demand that they should uphold the detested measure.

The commotion which followed the effort to put the Stamp Act in force in all the colonies led to its repeal, but the principle set forth was reasserted by Parliament. This principle Mason very vigorously combatted in the earliest of all his political writings. In a public letter by him, bearing the signature of "Virginia Planter," he conveyed to the British people a solemn warning against the calamities that would certainly follow a second attempt to impose a Parliamentary tax on the American people. But the infatuated British Government refused to listen. In 1767 a new revenue act was passed, which in turn had to be repealed; but the principle asserted was left intact by the retention of the duty on tea.

It was Mason who drafted the resolutions in favor of nonimportation that were carried to Williamsburg by Washington. In the great measures which were soon adopted in that town by the bold group of patriots under the influence of the news that the Boston Port Bill had passed—such as the expression of sympathy with the people of that town, the proposal that a general congress should be called, and the appointment of a day of fasting and prayer—he had no official pari, for he was not at that time a member of the House of Burgesses, although he happened then to be visiting Williamsburg on private business. There is reason, however, to think that he was invited to join in the patriots' most intimate councils. It was on this occasion that he was thrown for the first time in the company of Patrick Henry, for whom he entertained thereafter an ardent admiration and a deep affection.

During the summer of 1774 there were held in all the counties public meetings in favor of adopting a policy of non-intercourse and also of summoning a continental congress. The resolutions passed in Fairfax were drawn by Mason, and they set forth with convincing force the reasons for using a non-intercourse method to compel Parliament to recede from the arbitrary position which it had assumed. The resolutions contained a most luminous presentation of all the principles and facts that entered into the controversy between Great Britain and the colonies, and when the Convention met at Williamsburg in August, they were used as the basis of the association organized by that body and of the later association organized by the general Congress in Philadelphia, when it assembled in the ensuing September.

Jefferson, as we have seen in our account of the contemporary Albemarle resolutions, had taken the radical and more or less idealistic position that the colonies possessed the right of self-government, not so much by charter right, as by natural right, and with this natural right Parliament could not legally interfere. In the Fairfax Resolutions Mason did not declare, like Jefferson, that the colonies were independent of Parliament, nor did he deny that body's constitutional right to legislate for the general concern. Indeed, he admitted that it was only proper that England should derive definite advantages from the colonies in return for the military protection which it had given. But these advantages, he said, should stop with trade and commerce. The regulation of internal policies and grants of money belonged to the jurisdiction of the colonial assemblies. If Parliamentary usurpations had at any time been

G. MASON.

PLATE XVIII. *From an old etching. Fridenberg Galleries.*

GEORGE MASON

tolerated, it was simply because it was thought to be expedient to do so at that particular hour.

Mason was not a member of the first Continental Congress. His indisposition to seek or accept conspicuous public office held him back now, as it was so often to do afterwards, although his ability and sympathy with the patriot cause were known to all. He finally consented to his nomination to the Virginia Convention of July, 1775, which organized the minute regiments to take the place of the independent companies recruited by the counties. In this body he succeeded Washington, so soon to be chosen commander in chief of all the Continental armies. There were special reasons why Mason now desired to remain in retirement. Recently he had lost his wife, and he thought that his very young children were entitled to his first consideration. This was another evidence of the contentment with which, had he been left to his own wishes, he would have continued indefinitely in the background, while Virginians of talents inferior to his own were rising to fame in both Williamsburg and Philadelphia. But he was always prompt to advance the cause of the colonies by the use of his powerful tongue and pen. He was not so ardent, however, in action. When his son applied for service in the standing army which it was proposed to raise by a levy of fifty men in each county, Mason refused to approve the step, on the ground that a militia "was the only true, natural, and safe defense of a free country." He accepted his own appointment to the Committee of Safety, on which fell the government of the colony before the Commonwealth was established, but owing to ill health, he withdrew after a brief tenure of the position. All the energies which he could command were soon concentrated on the defense of the shores of the Potomac near Gunston and Mount Vernon against invasion. This he endeavored to make successful by the use of row galleys heavily armed. But his heart evidently sighed for more peaceful times. "May God grant," he wrote to Washington in 1776, "a return of those halcyon days, when every man may sit down at his ease under the shade of his own vine and his own fig tree, and enjoy the sweets of domestic life; or if this be too much, may he be pleased to inspire us with spirit and resolution to bear our present and future suffering becoming men determined to transmit to our posterity unimpaired the blessings we have received from our ancestors."

The last convention to assemble in Virginia before the termination of the Colonial era was in May, 1776; and of this body Mason was a member. It was this Convention that drafted the instructions to the Virginian delegation in Congress to bring in resolutions pronouncing the United Colonies to be free and independent states. And a committee was also chosen to frame a declaration of rights and a state constitution.

Mason was appointed a member of this committee, which was one of supreme importance. Its chairman was Colonel Archibald Cary. On May 24 Cary read the Declaration of Rights, which had been written by Mason, and its text was fully discussed during three days in the course of the following month. After a few small alterations, it was finally adopted. On the twenty-fourth of June Colonel Cary reported the new Constitution for Virginia; and this, too, had been drafted by Mason. Of the three great state papers which were produced by this Convention two were the fruits of his pen. The third, the instructions for the submission in Congress of resolutions in favor of a national Declaration of Independence, had been submitted and approved before he was able to take his seat.

The greatest of all these documents was the Declaration of Rights, which was the first state paper of that character to be adopted in America. Today it forms a part of the fundamental law of nearly all the commonwealths of the Union. The principles which it specified as the basis of free government were as follows: man has a natural and inherent right to the enjoyment of life and liberty; rulers and magistrates can legitimately derive their powers only from the people, and to the people they are at all times amenable; a majority of the people have the right to abolish their form of government, should it turn out to be incompetent; the only just title to public office is public service; legislative, executive, and judicial functions shall be separate; delegated bodies shall be chosen, not by restricted, but by universal, suffrage; no taxes can be validly laid without popular assent; ordinances cannot lawfully be passed or suspended without the approval of the people's representatives; in a criminal prosecution the accused shall have the right to be told the nature of the charge against him and to be confronted by his accuser and witnesses; he shall have the right also to submit evidence in his own favor, but himself to be exempt from testifying, should he so prefer; the verdict against him to be valid must be unanimous; he cannot justly be deprived of his liberty except by the law of the land or the judgment of his peers; excessive bail, excessive fines, and cruel and unusual punishments shall be inadmissible; the press shall be free; the natural and safe defense of a free state is a well-regulated militia; standing armies, except during war, are dangerous; at all times the military power shall be subordinate to the civil power; justice, moderation, temperance, and frugality are the four civic virtues which should control the administration of public affairs; religious liberty is the apex of the State.

It has been said of the Virginia Bill of Rights that "it was a condensed, logical, and luminous summary of the great principles of freedom inherited by Americans from their British ancestors. It was the extracted essence of Magna Carta, the Petition of Rights, the Acts of the Long Parliament, and the Doctrines of the Revolution of 1688, as expounded by Locke, distilled and concentrated through the alembic of George Mason's own powerful and discriminating mind."

The principles set forth in this celebrated document are reflected in the Declaration of Independence, which is admitted to be the most memorable state paper ever drafted in the history of the Western Hemisphere.

The body of the State Constitution was composed by Mason, but the preamble was the production of Jefferson's pen. This document is said to have been the first written constitution adopted by a free state. Both Mason and Jefferson were members of the first General Assembly to convene after that document became law. This Assembly witnessed the introduction of the great reforms relating to the church, primogeniture, and education which have contributed so much to Jefferson's fame. In formulating these memorable innovations he had Mason's invaluable assistance. How high was his opinion of his coadjutor is revealed in his own words: "Mason," he said, "was of the first order of wisdom among those who acted on the theatre of the Revolution; of expansive mind, profound judgment, cogent in argument, learned in the lore of our former constitution, and earnest for Republican change on Democratical principles. His elocution was neither flowery nor smooth, but his manner was most impressive, and strengthened by a dash of biting sarcasm when provocation made it seasonable."

Mason was chosen, along with Jefferson, Wythe, Thomas Ludwell Lee, and Pendleton, to recast the existing statutes, but he refused to accept the appointment on the ground that he had not been trained to the profession of law. In 1777 he also refused a nomination to Congress. In a letter which he wrote at this time to a kinsman in England he said, "I have constantly declined acting in any other public character than that of an independent representative of the people in the House of Delegates, where I still remain, from a consciousness of being able to do my country more service there than in any other department. . . . If I can only live to see the American Union firmly fixed and free government well-established in our Western land, and can leave to my children but a crust of bread and liberty, I shall die satisfied." This epochal consummation he was destined to witness. But it is a remarkable fact that he declined to approve the great instrument which created the Federal Union and which has been so powerful in holding it together. His opposition to the document in the National Convention which drafted it, and in the Virginia Convention which ratified it, had its motive in an irrepressible feeling of apprehension lest consolidation, pushed too far, should jeopardize the freedom of the American people at large and of the Virginian people in particular. He wished the Union to be formed, but he did not think that it would be wise to draw the bonds between the states too tightly together. Under no circumstances would he tolerate any encroachment on the sovereignty of his native commonwealth.

In consenting to his appointment by the General Assembly to a seat in the Convention at Philadelphia, Mason was departing from the rule which had hitherto governed his course in relation to national bodies. Probably his work of drafting the Virginia Constitution inclined him to share in the proceedings which were to formulate the Constitution for the United States. He took a very active part in the deliberations of the Convention, made many suggestions of value, but on the whole was less successful than Madison in leaving the impression of his political ideas on his audience. In the end he refused to sign the instrument, on the general ground that he did not think it offered sufficient safeguards for the rights of the Southern commonwealths. As it was in substance a compromise between the conflicting interests of the two great divisions of the Union, he was doubtful of its stability and permanence under the test of practical operation. He was of the opinion that the document should be submitted to the ballot in each state as a far better way than the state convention for finding out with accuracy whether the Constitution was acceptable to the majority of the people.

When the Virginia Convention assembled in 1788 to ratify the Constitution, the views which Mason held about it were widely known and caused alarm among those who favored the instrument. "He is growing every day more bitter and outrageous in his effort to carry his point," wrote Madison in April, "and in all probability, in the end, will be thrown by the violence of his passions into the politics of Mr. Henry." Henry was the supreme leader of the opposition. Public sentiment at this time seems to have been running against both Henry and Mason. Indeed, it was reported that Mason had been warned not to enter

GEORGE MASON

Alexandria, situated not far from his home, as there was reason to expect that he would there be assaulted by a mob. But instead of heeding the threat, he quickly mounted his horse and rode straight to that town. Taking a position on the steps of the courthouse, he called to the sheriff to announce at once that George Mason would address the people. A large crowd in no friendly mood quickly ran together in front of him to hear him voice his objections to the Constitution, and although he spoke at times in very denunciatory language, he was listened to attentively and respectfully; and when he closed, he was permitted to withdraw from the scene without molestation. Had the public opposition to his views been as strong as it was said at that time to be, he would not have been chosen to represent Fairfax County in the impending ratification Convention.

His eagerness to precipitate the conflict over ratification was shown by the fact that he was the first speaker to take the floor when the Convention opened. "In one instant," we learn from Grigsby, the historian of that Convention, "the insensible hum of the body was hushed, and the eyes of all were fixed on him. His once raven hair was as white as snow. His stalwart figure, attired in deep mourning, was still erect; his black eyes fairly flashed forth the flame that burned in his bosom; the tones of his voice were deliberate and full. He was now sixty-two years old. From his entrance into public life, he was confessedly the first man in every assembly of which he was a member, though rarely seen on the floor except on great occasions."

Mason urged that the Constitution should be discussed clause by clause before the final vote should be taken. He was convinced that if each clause were discussed separately and then, before being passed on, were submitted to a vote, the approval of even one would be used to influence the Convention to adopt the rest in succession, and when the Constitution had been thus ratified clause by clause, it would be ratified as a whole. In the debates that followed, the protagonists on the one side were himself, Henry, Grayson, Monroe, Harrison, and Tyler; and on the other Wythe,

226

Madison, Marshall, Pendleton, Nicholas, Innes, and Edmund Randolph. There were three generations of Virginian statesmen represented in these two opposing and keenly antagonistic wings.

On the motion of Judge Tyler the Convention resolved itself into a committee of the whole, and the discussion of the Constitution then began, with the venerable Wythe in the chair. The first surprise in the opening debate was the reversal of the position which Randolph had taken in the Philadelphia Convention—he now expressed himself in favor of ratification. Mason in his second speech was keenly critical of the taxing power that had been granted to Congress. He thought that this power should be limited to the duties on imports. It was his opinion also that the provision relating to representation in that body was neither free nor full.

During the next few days following this speech he was employed in drawing up a bill of rights and a series of amendments. On the eleventh he delivered his third speech, in which he dwelt upon the need of such a bill as he had just drafted to serve as a safeguard for the welfare of the people at large, and also the need of amendments to supplement this bill. He objected to the clause in the Constitution relating to the militia, advocating an amendment that would forbid the militia of each state from marching beyond the borders of adjacent states. He censured the bestowal on Congress of the right to control elections, as this would tend to destroy responsibility; and he expressed apprehension about the supervision which that body was to exercise over the Federal District as certain to make it a popular sanctuary with all criminals.

He was deeply solicitous about the states' reserved powers. "Is there anything in this Constitution," he asked, "which secures to the States the powers which are said to be retained? Will any power remain to the States which are not expressly guarded and reserved?" He also opposed the clause which allowed the importation of slaves during the ensuing twenty years. He advocated the limitation of the president's incumbency to but one term, but, strangely enough, questioned the expediency of creating the office of vice-president. He was opposed to investing the president with so much authority—especially in his relation to the command of the army. That dignitary, he said, would have more power than the King of England. He thought that the provisions touching the federal judiciary would destroy "the dearest rights of the community" by curtailing the jurisdiction of the state courts. More than this, the federal judiciary would ultimately paralyze the functions of the state governments themselves. To no one would it be acceptable except to those who favored a national consolidated government.

In his final speech Mason put forth all his abilities to secure the adoption of such amendments as he considered essential to the public safety under the Constitution; but he frankly announced his determination to acquiesce in the Convention's decision on this point, whatever it might be.

When the debates ended, the vote was taken on a resolution calling for the passage of amendments previous to ratification, but it resulted in the negative by a majority of eight. A second resolution in favor of ratification, with subsequent amendments, passed in the affirmative by a majority of ten. The terms of ratification included the assertion of the right of secession whenever the powers under the Constitution should be perverted to the injury or oppression of the American people. The committee to prepare the amendments was composed of Mason, Henry, and Grayson for one side, and Madison, Marshall, and Randolph for the other. A bill of rights and also a series of amendments were subsequently reported. With a few exceptions these corresponded, in substance at least, with those prepared by Mason and agreed to by the committee of opposition to which he belonged. The Convention adjourned on the 27th.

In 1790 Mason was appointed by the Governor of Virginia to the office of United States senator made vacant by the death of Colonel William Grayson, but he refused to accept the honor. The remaining years of his life were comparatively uneventful. He died at Gunston Hall in 1792.

Chapter XV

RICHARD HENRY LEE

THE FIRST of the Lee family to seat himself in Virginia was Richard Lee, who left England during the Puritan ascendancy with the intention of founding a permanent home among the plantations of that colony. There he rose to a position of great influence and at one time filled the important offices of member of the Council and secretary of state. His son Richard was educated in London, inherited a large fortune from his father, succeeded him in the Council, and throughout life is said to have borne a reputation "for exact justice, and honesty, and unexceptionable loyalty." Thomas Lee, who belonged to the third generation in Virginia, long occupied the post of president of the Council and performed with distinction the duties of the governorship.

Such were the ancestors of Richard Henry Lee in the direct line, reaching back to the first of the name to plant himself on Virginian soil; and the honorable careers which all of them, one after another, ran there were in harmony with the importance of the family in the social and civic life of England. There the name ascended to the Norman Conquest, and in its transfer to the colony oversea—a land that was new as the mother country was old—it was destined to add greatly to its fame. The future patriot, Richard Henry Lee, aware of the conspicuous part which his great-grandfather, grandfather, and father had played in the history of Virginia, must even in youth have been unconsciously influenced by the tradition of the public service in which they had so prominently and so uprightly taken part. A determination to follow in their footsteps must have lodged in his mind from boyhood. The example set by his mother's ancestors in Virginia was equally stimulating, for during a long period they had furnished to the administration of public affairs in the colony a succession of distinguished leaders. The Ludwell name, indeed, was as closely identified with the local government as the name of Lee. Interest in that government, as we thus perceive, was an inheritance of Richard Henry Lee on both sides of his family. He offered another illustration of the fact that participation in the progress of the community at large was as much a matter of course for a young colonial Virginian of his birth, talents, and estate, as it was in England at that time for a young man of the same fortune, the same ability, and the same conspicuous descent.

There was one important physical tie that knitted him to the spirit of the local past as much as did its written history and its oral traditions. Stratford, under the roof of which he had been born, was one of the most stately mansions to be found in the colony. It was erected in a manner so solid that it has come down even to our own age unimpaired. Within its ample walls seventeen rooms were embraced; and these had been provided, not so much for the contingency of a large family, as for the reception of the successive bands of guests who were expected to be welcomed and entertained within its precincts when finished. The furniture, the ornaments, and the portraits which it contained, all pointed to the distinguished social connections of the family both in Virginia and in England. The atmosphere of the various apartments was the atmosphere of the contemporary English residences of the same size. Within the threshold hospitality in its most generous and lavish form was exercised, and all the domestic amenities were cultivated there. The life which the family led out of doors was the life which in those times was led by the proprietors of every large English landed estate. The horse, the gun, and the huntsman's horn drew the family sportsman to the field, and the announcement of popular speaking appealed to the graver interests of the inmates.

Such was the birthplace of Richard Henry Lee, and such were the social scenes which environed him in his youth.

He drew his first breath in a room in which his brother, the signer, Francis Lightfoot Lee, and also the great military commander, Robert E. Lee, were afterwards to be born. He was destined to live for nearly half a century before his allegiance to the Crown was dissolved by the Declaration of Independence. How strong was the ligament which bound his father to England was shown by his determination to enter his son, while still a mere lad, in an English school. Richard Henry's first introduction to study was through a tutor under the paternal roof. When informed that he was to become a scholar in a Yorkshire academy, he began to prepare himself physically for holding his own in the boxing bouts which formed a rough part of the life of the youths in attendance there. He was able to equip himself successfully for this purpose by a daily exchange of passes with a Negro boy of his own age. When his father found him engaged in this rough sport, he reproved him with severity but was quickly mollified when his son revealed the reason for the fisticuffs.

While in England Richard Henry Lee exhibited the taste and capacity of a faithful student. He took advantage of the tuition of the competent teachers under whom he sat there to acquire an unusual knowledge of the ancient languages, and he continued throughout life to read the classics with care and pleasure. Nor was his enjoyment of pure belles-lettres restricted to the Grecian and Roman tongues. He was a constant reader of Shakespeare, Milton, and other English writers of imagination. After his return from England—which occurred in his nineteenth year—he spent much of his time while residing with an elder brother in mastering the contents of many volumes of a political or philosophical cast. He was particularly interested in the treatises of Locke, Cudworth, and Grotius for the light which they threw on the principles of government and international law. Equally strong was the appeal which history made to his mind; and he early grew familiar with the works of the eminent ancient and modern writers in this province. He was not simply a general reader who turned over pages for mere passing recreation. He was also a discriminating one who sought to make a permanent addition to his stock of useful information. He was not a lawyer by profession, but few men at the bar of Virginia in those times were more deeply versed in the general principles of that science.

His interests in these early years, however, were not confined to the examination of a variety of intellectual subjects. Indeed, he was so far from being a mere student in his habits of life that he had a keen relish for society. From youth he enjoyed every kind of genial personal intercourse. Moreover, by the time that he had reached his majority he had become a careful man of business; and so great was the confidence felt in his judgment and discretion even then that he was often chosen by his friends to act as guardian or trustee. When the occasion for his military services arose, he was quick to volunteer. He raised, for instance, a company of his neighbors to join the force which Braddock had concentrated at Alexandria for the purpose of seizing Fort Duquesne and dispersing the French and Indians beyond the Alleghenies. Of this company Lee was chosen to be captain; but as Braddock was unwilling to receive the men as recruits—probably from their lack of training, which could not be given in so short a time—they retired to their homes.

It was a proof of the reputation for ability and integrity which Lee had soon won, in spite of his uneventful rural life, that he was in his twenty-fifth year elected to a seat on the Westmoreland County bench. This position at that time was the highest in the local government and as a rule was reserved only for men of mature years and large property. The jurisdiction of the court practically covered the entire field of law. A seat in that body called in a peculiar degree for the possession of wide experience and broad common sense. How satisfactorily Lee performed the duties of his membership and how constant he was in his attendance were shown by the desire of his associates for his appointment to the presidency of the bench and by their petition to the governor and council for his nomination to that office even before length of service made him eligible for it. His election to a seat in the House of Burgesses quickly followed. It is said that during this initial session Lee took no part in the debates of that body. This was not from a lack of interest in the proceedings or from a dearth of information touching the subjects under discussion. On the contrary, his silence was due exclusively to a distrust of his own capacity to express himself with ease, should he take the floor. This instance was one of the most notable on record of a man with extraordinary powers as a public speaker who had no confidence whatever in his possession of those powers before he had put them to a test. When he did venture to rise on his first occasion to do so it was only after the most laborious preparation of the substance and expression of the address to be delivered and after a rigid curtailment of its length. It dealt with the grossly immoral spirit, the physical atrocity, and the political evil of the slave trade. His presentation of the theme was vigorous, candid, and unanswerable. The point of view was from the loftiest height of humanity and statesmanship; and this attitude towards that question Lee maintained throughout life.

The impression made upon his hearers by this first utterance in the House was favorable without being extraordinary. It cannot be said that through its deliverance he leaped into fame and influence at once, after the manner of his future rival, Patrick Henry, in the Parsons' Cause. But a second occasion gave him the opportunity to display his wonderful oratorical ability in its fullest scope. His brother, who was not a fluent speaker, was called upon to introduce a resolution which was of special importance to the popular party in the Assembly. In the beginning he spoke with effect, but a question from a member of the opposition threw him into such confusion that he was finally compelled to resume his seat without completing what he had intended to say. At this moment, when his party associates were about to sink in despair, Richard Henry Lee, inflamed with

sympathy for his brother in his predicament, rose quickly
to his feet, took up the argument where it had been dropped,
and pressed it home with such clearness, such eloquence of
expression, and such elegance of gesture that at the end
of his remarks he was hailed as one of the foremost orators
in the House, if not already the foremost of all. He became
from this hour the leader of his party in that chamber, and
his influence was increased by his talent for practical business. Moreover, his personal bearing was so simple, so sincere, and so considerate that he won the good will of his
fellow-members without an effort.

That Lee was capable of the utmost boldness and firmness in defending the interests of the people at large was
shown by his action when there got abroad a suspicion that
Speaker Robinson had been guilty of defalcation of public
funds consigned to his custody. It was Lee who moved that
a committee should be appointed to inquire into the state
of the treasury. He did not falter when his proposal was
received with a black frown by the presiding officer of the
House, who was so directly involved in the delinquency, or
with looks of pretended contempt by his partisans on the
floor. Lee's spirit appeared by this conduct to be excited only
to keener indignation and reprobation, and he spoke with a
power that he had never before equaled.

It was not long before the attention of the colonists everywhere was diverted to a cause for anxiety which had arisen
in the mother country and which was destined shortly to
throw a cloud over the future of the American communities.
The Treaty of Paris had left England with a vast addition
to her outlying territory, but with such an accumulation of
debt as made her doubtful of her ability to pay, unless she
could obtain an increase of revenue through taxation of the
numerous groups of her subjects seated along the Atlantic
Coast in the West. The need of money was augmented by
the determination of the English Government to organize
and maintain permanently twenty new regiments in America.
"It was this plan," said Edmund Burke at the time, "which
first turned the eyes of English financiers to the Colonies."

"I well remember," he added, "that Mr. Townsend, in a brilliant harangue on this subject, did dazzle them [Parliament] by laying before their eyes the image of a revenue to be raised in America. Here began to dawn the first glimmerings of this new Colonial system." The general principle was announced in the 15th Act of 4 George III; and not long afterwards the practical application of the Act was made by the passage of a measure specifically imposing certain stamp duties on the colonists for the purpose of levying a revenue across the Atlantic payable into the British exchequer alone. The liberal statesmen of England of that day foresaw with clearness the consequences of this course on the part of the British Government; they protested against the adoption of such a policy; and they forewarned the people of the colonies of the evil which they might expect under its operation. Its inauguration was arranged to take place in November, 1765. Apparently this warning was not untimely.

There was not a more resolute or more persistent opponent of the Stamp Act than Richard Henry Lee. But this was not until he had grasped its real meaning, for it is an actual fact that at one period in its history he was an applicant for the office of collector in the Northern Neck. This was about the date when the measure was still under discussion. In his account of how he came to seek the position Lee wrote as follows: "I was informed by a gentleman of the intention of Parliament to lay a stamp duty in America, with a friendly proposition on his part to use his influence to procure for me the office of stamp collector. I call it friendly, because I believe the gentleman no more than myself, nor, perhaps, a single person in this country, had, at that time, reflected the least on the nature and tendency of such an act. Considering this only in the light of a beneficial employment, I agreed the gentleman should write and I wrote myself. It was but a few days after my letters were sent, that, reflecting on the nature of the application I had made, the impropriety of an American being engaged in such an office struck me so strongly that I determined to exert every faculty I possessed, both in public and in private life, to prevent the success of a measure which I now discovered to be, in the highest degree, pernicious to my country."

However shortsighted his application for the new office may have been before the scope of the proposed law was really understood by him, his whole course as soon as its true nature had become clear to him was entirely consistent with a genuine abhorrence of the principle which it embodied. Not long after the passage of the Declaratory Act, which first proclaimed Parliament's supposed abstract right to tax the colonies, he called the Assembly's attention to it at the earliest session of that body which followed. He was placed on the special committee which was appointed to draft an address to the King, a memorial to the House of Lords, and a remonstrance to the House of Commons. He was selected to write the text of two of these important documents. He was so keenly sensible of the injurious effect to be wrought by the policy authorized by the Declaratory Act, he continued to assert with emphasis again and again in public that it would throw the colonial people into a state of "Egyptian bondage" by depriving them of the protection of the British Constitution, which guaranteed their right as English subjects. When the passage of the Stamp Act actually occurred, he denounced it as a fatal blow to the liberties of America. Nor was he satisfied to confine his condemnation to words. He used his influence to form an association for the sole purpose of discouraging acceptance by any Northern Neck citizen of the office of stamp vender, as well as for awing into silence and inactivity all who were inclined to advocate the right of Parliament to tax the colonies.

One of the most significant clauses of the charter of this association was its declaration of the signers' sincere devotion to the King; but more in harmony with the resolute feeling of the hour was the statement that it was the "birthright privilege" of every Virginian as a British subject to be taxed only with the consent of a Parliament in which

PLATE XIX. *From a copy of the original by Peale made by his great great grand-daughter, Harriett Lee Montague. Photo Cook.*

RICHARD HENRY LEE

he was represented by persons who themselves were to come under any levy imposed upon the property-holders at large. "We are determined at every hazard, and paying no regard to danger or to death," the document proclaimed, "to exert every faculty to prevent the execution of the Stamp Act in every instance whatever within this Colony."

Methods closely resembling those of the modern Ku Klux Klan were soon adopted to put a stop to the collection of stamp duties. When it was learned that a certain citizen of the Northern Neck, appointed to undertake this function, was about to begin doing so, Lee called together the members of the local volunteer company of light-horse, in which he held the post of captain, and at their head marched to the home of the unpopular official. When the latter came to the door, he was ordered to show his commission; and when this had been done, he was commanded to deliver up all the stamps in his possession and to take an oath that he would not attempt to promote the sale or use of similar paper thereafter. When the collector refused to do this, after much hesitation of manner, a very stalwart trooper in the company advanced upon him suddenly and so frightened him by a loud order to swear, that the man yielded in a state of great trepidation. The stamps which were in his custody were quickly brought out of the house and burnt in a small bonfire in his yard. Lee justified this more or less violent act by publishing an address to the people of Virginia in which he warned them that "should the Stamp Act go down in the Colony, the people of England would go on to tax them every year, because the more they should tax them, the less necessity there would be to tax themselves."

However much the members of Parliament might increase this burden, there could be no remedy for the Virginians, since not being voters in the English elections, they would be unable to aid in expelling these men from their seats. Lee estimated that the Stamp Act would drain the colony of at least fifty thousand pounds sterling annually.

One of the first steps taken by the Rockingham administration, which succeeded the Grenville, was to repeal the Stamp Act; but unfortunately, the general right to tax the American colonies was still formally reserved as an abstract principle. Very correctly this reservation continued to be a cause of apprehension to farsighted men like Richard Henry Lee. So odious to him and his neighbors in Westmoreland County was the Stamp Act, even when revoked, that when a Tory who was opposed to the repeal recovered judgment for an assault made on him on that account by a headstrong patriot, these gentlemen came forward promptly and paid the imposed fine. In doing this, they declared in writing that they wished "to evince their attachment to the cause of liberty by supporting its generous asserters." Of the ten signatories of this spirited document, six bore the name of Lee, most of these, apparently, brothers of Richard Henry.

Not long after entering public life, Lee had been brought into close personal intercourse with Patrick Henry, a man whose ardent soul and bold temper he fully shared. It was a fortunate circumstance for the patriot cause that on the threshold of the movement two persons of such extraordinary eloquence, clear foresight, and resolute purpose should have been found in sympathetic coöperation. Said Henry, after the Revolution had ended in triumph, speaking to a son of Lee, "Your father and myself always agreed upon the great principle of freedom. We differed on some questions of internal policy, but liberty we alike fondly loved." There could not be a more impressive proof of the substantial identity of their political convictions than Lee's approval of Henry's famous resolutions submitted to the House of Burgesses in 1765. He had not reached Williamsburg when the vote was taken, but he pronounced emphatically in their favor when informed of their passage, thus, like Henry, planting himself firmly in opposition to the more conservative members of the House. In turn, Henry arrayed himself with Lee when the latter brought in a resolution calling for the separation of the offices of speaker and treasurer, both of which were at this time filled by John Robinson, one of the most powerful upholders of the reactionary sentiment prevailing in a portion of the Assembly. Lee's motion was sustained, and it was afterwards believed that its success was distinctly promotive of the patriotic cause.

In 1767, as Lee had anticipated, the attempt by the British Government to tax the colonists was renewed. One act of this body in the course of that year imposed a duty on all tea and other articles specifically named in its text which had been landed in the American ports. A second act required the colonists to support at their own exclusive charge a part of the British regular army stationed in their midst. The latter measure was the more reprehensible of the two, as its burden was unescapable. The weight of the tax on tea fell most sensibly on the large towns on the northern seaboard. Nevertheless, the Virginians recognized as clearly as the people of the northern colonies the pernicious significance of these two impositions by the mother country. Lee acted with characteristic promptness. He introduced in the House a petition to be submitted to the King, in which he firmly and boldly pointed out the unhappy consequences that had already sprung from the enforcement of the new military and revenue decrees. The British Government, for instance, had suspended the legislature of New York because that province had refused to shoulder the expense of quartering the local British troops. On the other hand, the importation of tea had already led to open violence elsewhere.

By 1768 the cause of disagreement between England and the colonies had become more acute, and the ultimate upshot was seen by Lee to be inevitably war. He became extremely solicitous that the bonds between the colonies should be drawn more tightly together as the best means of strengthening and directing their spirit of resistance. Apparently, even as early as this, he seems to have considered the true issue to be not redress of grievance, but complete independence. He warmly advocated the formation of committees of correspondence by means of which the people of all the colonies should be kept informed of the progress of events, especially of those in violation of their constitutional rights.

For this purpose the latest intelligence of the acts of the British Parliament or the proceedings of the British Government was to be obtained as being the most important in their political pertinency to America. Lee was appointed a member of the Virginia committee.

Some years before, he had endeavored to organize a private corresponding society. His object then was to induce a definite group of distinguished men residing in the different colonies to contribute to the newspapers articles that would enlighten the people at large on the subject of their rights and to raise in them a firm determination to oppose every encroachment on those rights by the British Government. He sought subsequently to carry out this purpose by maintaining alone an active correspondence with many persons of political influence scattered throughout the country. Among the most conspicuous of these was John Dickinson of Pennsylvania. In one of his letters to this patriot he accurately described his attitude in the existing crisis by saying that "he could not go along with those who derive the security of the Colonial people from their submission." But he was not satisfied to confine his political correspondence to prominent Americans. In 1769 he addressed a letter to Lord Shelbourne, in which he frankly gave his impression of the wrongs that England at this time was committing by the measures aimed at the colonies. He was kept well informed of the public opinion on colonal subjects prevailing in the mother country through his repeated exchange of letters with his brother, Arthur Lee, now a resident of London, and in constant friendly intercourse with the foremost men of the Kingdom.

When in 1770 Lord Botetourt dissolved the House of Burgesses because under the influence of Lee and his associates it had passed resolutions condemning the infringement of the inherited rights of the American people under the English Constitution, a private conference of the members was quickly held, the result of which was that they agreed to bind themselves to discourage the importation and the use of British merchandise by every means in their

240

power; and they formally urged that every other citizen should imitate their example. The association formed by the burgesses was soon duplicated in other parts of the colony. No one was more zealous than Lee in upholding the principle so boldly announced. He was not content simply to enforce it in his own family, but was also solicitous to prevent its disregard in the community at large. The colonists were clearly aware of the British tradesmen's sensitiveness to any interference with the freedom of their business, and the effect of this new plan proved again the correctness of their impression. A vigorous and even clamorous opposition was now raised by the British merchants to the policy of their government; and there was substantial reason for their adopting this attitude of hostility, for many wealthy Virginians now undertook to supply their households with the goods previously bought in London and other English towns, by manufacturing them under their own roofs from raw materials produced on their own plantations. Thus we find Lee, in 1769, not only weaving cloth on his own looms, but also sending to England wine which had been expressed from his own grapes.

Whilst resisting the arbitrary duties which had been imposed by the British Parliament, the Virginian patriots were equally bold and resolute in opposing the establishment of courts with admiralty jurisdiction and powers. Their reason for objecting so firmly to these courts lay in the fact that the judges were to be appointed by the Crown and that no juries were to be impaneled to serve in any case before them. This would leave the decisions to the discretion of men naturally leaning to the side of the King who had elevated them to office. The evil to flow from this condition was, as soon as it was threatened, regarded with acute apprehension by Lee, who was always particularly alive to the violation of the colonists' constitutional rights, especially those involving questions of property. He took advantage of his membership in the House of Burgesses to introduce a resolution praying the King to anticipate and prevent the injustice which was certain to be done by this new court through its discard of American juries. He was correct in thinking that only such juries could be relied upon to safeguard every form of American property from English encroachment. How far the British Government was ready to go to evade the feeling of local patriotism was indicated by an order from that Government that all those persons implicated in the burning of the *Gaspee* should be transported to London to be tried by an English jury.

No sooner had Lee received information that an admiralty court was to sit in Providence, than he opened up an anxious and indignant correspondence with John Adams and John Dickinson. He also enclosed the recent resolution of the House of Burgesses which he had drafted. His purpose was to strengthen the rising spirit of opposition by further stimulating the leaders to resist. An additional step in the same direction was the appointment by the House of a committee of influential members to correspond with similar committees in the other colonies. Lee was one of the most zealous participants in the course pursued by this committee. When news arrived that the port of Boston was to be closed by order of the British Government, he prepared a series of resolutions emphatically condemning so arbitrary a step; but he was prevented from submitting them by the dissolution of the House at the Governor's command. At a private conference of that body which immediately followed, the summoning of a continental congress was urgently recommended by Lee, but this proposal turned out to be premature at that hour. The General Assembly met at Williamsburg August 1, 1774, and it was not until then that it was decided that all the colonies should be requested to send delegates to a general congress to be held in Philadelphia.

This Congress came together in September, and one of the seven members from Virginia was Richard Henry Lee. His associates were drawn from the rank of the ablest and most distinguished men in Virginia. They were George Washington, Peyton Randolph, Patrick Henry, Edmund Pendleton, Richard Bland, and Benjamin Harrison. After the Congress opened, Patrick Henry was the first to take the floor. He was followed by Lee, whose chaste and classical style of speaking was in strong contrast with the more passionate style of his great rival in oratory. Lee was one of the two members named to represent Virginia on the committee which was quickly selected to "state the rights of the Colonies in general; the several instances in which those rights had been violated, or infringed; and the means most proper to be pursued to obtain a restoration of them." This language, doubtless, had its origin with him alone. He was very earnest and persistent in advocating a policy towards Great Britain which would not only shut out all the merchandise that the English should send to American ports in the future, but also put a stop to further exportation of colonial products to the mother country. By this means he was hopeful that the most influential section of the British people, the merchants, could be made to perceive that the course pursued by the ministry was in direct antagonism to their special interests. Lee foresaw what was equally obvious to all his political associates, that if this policy of non-exportation and non-importation—in other words, general non-intercourse—should fail to arouse this class in England to the justice of the American grievances, then the ultimate upshot of the existing friction could only be war. But he was ready to take this chance rather than give up the only policy that was at all likely to allay the bitterness of the present controversy.

A conspicuous proof of Lee's sincere desire for absolute fairness in the colonies' relations with England was revealed in his resolution frankly acknowledging that it was unreasonable to expect the mother country to support standing armies in America for the defense of its people. Therefore, in his opinion, it was the duty of all the colonies—and Congress so urged—to raise, equip, and discipline an efficient militia which could be depended upon to give protection in case of an attack by a foreign enemy. It was with undisguised disappointment that he found most of his colleagues unready to take so bold a stand as this, although

243

willing to sustain his views in a modified degree.

Lee met with still firmer opposition when he offered a resolution advising the people of Boston to abandon that town in a body, rather than to remain submissively there whilst General Gage was throwing up earthworks that would virtually imprison its citizens and thus enable him to hold them as hostages in all his future dealings with the colonists at large. The majority of the members of Congress preferred to adopt a conciliatory attitude. Lee, on the other hand, was convinced that the encroachments of the British were largely due to their strong impression that the Americans could not be provoked to make any serious resistance to the most arbitrary measures. For that reason he was confident that the bolder and more resolute the colonists' opposition to these measures, the more probable it was that they would be dropped.

Doubtless he discovered a keen satisfaction in his appointment as one of a committee of three to draft an address to the people of the colonies with the object of impressing upon them the wisdom of strictly carrying out all the recommendations of Congress as the only means of preserving their rights and liberties under the English Constitution. This document was drawn by Lee, and it is one of the great state papers of the Anglo-Saxon race, bold yet conservative, firm yet conciliatory, emphatic yet without violence, inviting peace, yet ready to fight should such an issue be raised. This was one of the utterances of that great Assembly which excited the profound admiration of Chatham and prompted him to exclaim, "In solidity of reasoning, force of sagacity, and wisdom of conclusion, under such a complication of circumstances, no nation or body or men can stand in preference to the General Congress at Philadelphia."

In March, 1775, there came together in Richmond a second convention of popular delegates, who met for the purpose of putting the community in a condition of defense by arming the militia. Henry took the lead in submitting the measures looking to this end, and his efforts were vigorously seconded by Lee. But a strong opposition had to be overcome before this could be effected. Previous to adjourning, the Convention appointed Lee a representative in the Congress which was to assemble in Philadelphia in May. On his way to that city to attend, he had an opportunity at Fredericksburg to commend the determination of the large body of soldiers who crossed his path there on their march to Williamsburg to resent Dunmore's removal of arms and other military stores from the magazine situated at that place. After the Convention met, Lee was appointed a member of several important committees. The first of these was designed to provide the means of establishing posts for the conveyance of intelligence from colony to colony. Another had been chosen to inform the Convention then sitting in Massachusetts as to the proper manner of "taking up and exercising the powers of civil government." A third was to draft an address to the English people; and a fourth to secure the ways and means of introducing the manufacture of saltpeter.

The breadth of Lee's services was clearly illustrated in the highly varied nature of the purposes which these committees were expected to subserve. He was also a member of the committee appointed to draw up the commission and formulate the instructions to be delivered to General Washington for his guidance in the command of the American armies, which he was so soon to assume.

Lee had been the chairman of the committee named to write an address to the English people, as previously mentioned. This address was produced by his pen and was worthy of the reputation which he enjoyed as a writer and a patriot. It began with an invocation to "Friends, Countrymen, and Brethren," but it stated with perfect firmness and in the most candid language the wrongs which had been inflicted on the American people by the curtailment of their constitutional rights: the deprivation of their property by illegal taxation; the practical annulment of their charters; the establishment of arbitrary courts; and, finally, the destruction of American lives by deadly weapons in the hands of English soldiery. These were the main points of the indictment and made the strongest appeal.

"Our enemies charge us with sedition," exclaimed the writer. "In what does it consist? In our refusal to submit to unwarrantable acts of injustice and cruelty? We are accused of aiming at independence, but how is this accusation supported? By the allegations of your ministers, not by our actions. Abused, insulted, and condemned, what steps have we pursued to obtain redress? We have carried our dutiful petitions to the throne. We have applied to your justice for relief. We have retrenched our luxury, and held our trade. What has been the success of our endeavors? The clemency of our sovereign is, unhappily, diverted; our petitions are treated with indignity; our prayers answered by insult. Even under these circumstances, what measures have we taken that betray a desire for independence? Have we called on the aid of those Foreign Powers who are the rivals of your grandeur? When your troops were few and defenseless, did we take advantage of their distress, and expel them from our towns? Or have we permitted them to fortify, to receive new aid, or to to acquire additional strength? Your ministers, equal foes to British and American freedom, have added to their former oppressions an attempt to reduce us by the sword to a base and abject submission. On the sword, therefore, we are compelled to rely for protection. Of this at least we are assured: that our struggle will be glorious, our success certain, since even in death we shall find that freedom, which, in life, you forbid us to enjoy."

Lee was a member of the Congress which met in Philadelphia in 1775. War had now broken out, and there had already sprung up a considerable sentiment in favor of a formal declaration of independence from the mother country. The principal question now was: What was the best manner of defending the colonies, and how were the means to be procured to meet the expense of the defenders? Lee was appointed on several committees selected to weigh the various propositions advanced to obtain success in both directions; and in addition he was delegated with two other representatives to visit the camp at Cambridge in order to consult Washington on the proper method of "continuing, supporting, and regulating a continental army." The governors of Connecticut, Rhode Island, Massachusetts, and New Hampshire were also to be consulted during this visit to New England. At a later date, Lee, in association with several other congressmen, was selected to confer with General Schuyler for the same special purpose. About the same time he was chosen chairman of a committee that had been named to issue a reply to a proclamation, drafted by the British Government, which threatened extreme punishment to all assisting in the execution of the various measures adopted by Congress for the prosecution of the war.

Lee also represented Virginia on a general committee which was instructed to devise ways and means for furnishing the colonies with a navy. This was the first step towards the establishment of a national naval force. It reveals Lee's reputation for practical business talent that he should have been appointed to membership in every committee organized for the military defense of the colonies, both by land and by sea.

The year 1776, which had now arrived, was to prove the turning point in the great conflict of interests that had arisen between the colonies and the mother country. Should the American communities declare their independence or should they continue the fiction of political identification with the British? The general sentiment prevailing among them would apparently have been content with a redress of grievances even this late in the controversy, but there was a rapidly growing impression that all hope of a return to the old happy relations between the two peoples was now passing and that the only means of preserving the liberties of the colonies lay in a total separation from the kingdom oversea. This had been the conviction of Richard Henry Lee during at least two years before the differences between Great Britain and the colonies had reached an acute stage. There is reason to think that he was one of those who used their influence to persuade the Virginia Convention to propose to Congress the adoption of a resolution which would proclaim the independence of America. This resolution was actually submitted in Congress by Lee. The words employed were as follows: "that these united Colonies are and of right ought to be free and independent States; that they are absolved from all allegiance to the British Crown; and that all political connection between them and the State of Great Britain is and ought to be totally dissolved."

During several days there was a searching debate in which various objections were urged against the step proposed: the want of money, ammunition, and armies to sustain the contest certain to be precipitated; the absence of unanimity as to the wisdom of assuming so extreme an attitude towards the mother country; doubtfulness as to the course of foreign nations now in friendly relation with the English; and finally, the vast superiority of the British people in military power.

Lee firmly combatted these adverse views. In the end a resolution was adopted, under the authority of which a committee to draft a declaration of independence was named. Undoubtedly, he would have been chosen as its chairman had he not been abruptly summoned to Virginia by the alarming sickness of his wife. The Declaration was drafted before his return, but it fully reflected the opinions which he had long entertained. As soon as he resumed his seat in Congress, he was appointed a member of the committee to which was referred the negotiation of treaties of alliance with several of the most powerful nations in Europe. This was the first exercise of the right to play an international part on a footing of equal dignity with other countries. He was also chairman of a committee authorized to confer extraordinary powers on General Washington as commander in chief. No man was more opposed to dictatorships than Lee, but so profound was his confidence in Washington and so unpromising was the military outlook at this hour that he considered the measure entirely justifiable.

So active was his participation in the business of the Congress that his health became infirm, and from time to time, in consequence, he was compelled to seek rest at his home in Virginia. While there, during one of these intervals of recuperation, he unintentionally aroused a strong suspicion against himself by permitting his tenants to pay their rent in produce instead of in the paper money issued by the state. The market for crops was very restricted at this period of the war, and his aim was to make the rental settlements as easy as possible for them. Unfortunately, another interpretation was given to his act. It was whispered about that his real object was to depreciate in this indirect way the value of the state currency, in order to increase the difficulties of the political and military situation for the Americans. So successful was this slander that Lee was not reëlected to the ensuing Congress. He promptly demanded of the State Senate an inquiry into the accusations which had been launched openly against him, and by that body he was not only acquitted of these baseless charges but was thanked warmly for his public services.

In 1778 Lee was again an occupant of his former seat in Congress, and although his health remained seriously impaired, he displayed his previous energy in promoting the business of that body, especially as it related to the vigorous prosecution of the war. Not an important committee was appointed in which he was not included. One of the most delicate subjects with which he dealt in this capacity was the proposed increase in the number of articles embraced in the Constitution of the Confederation. Any addition to the powers of the Central Government was regarded with jealousy and suspicion. But his attention was not restricted to the business coming before Congress. We find him at one time engaged in the preparation of a plan of defense for the coasts of Virginia, and he also personally urged the governor of that state as well as the governor of Maryland to put a stop to the trade which the people of these two communities were carrying on with British ships of war then cruising in Chesapeake Bay.

On Lee's return to Congress in 1778 he was appointed the chairman of the committee to which had been referred the treaty of alliance with France. That document had recently arrived from Paris and was now to be adopted in a formal way. This act was announced to the people of the United States in an eloquent address which bears all the earmarks of Mr. Lee's finest composition. He was also the chairman of the committee which drafted the formal ratification of the consent of all the states to the amended Articles of Confederation.

The extent of Lee's usefulness was again exhibited in the succeeding Congress by the variety of the subjects with which the committee under his chairmanship were directly concerned. These were too numerous to be mentioned here, but in dealing with them all he revealed the same depth of knowledge, the same assiduity and industry, and the same unselfish patriotism which he had previously always shown; and this, too, in spite of his rapidly increasing physical infirmities, which made the volume of his mental labors appear almost incredible. "His mind," said Dr. Rush, "was like a sword which was too large for its scabbard." One of his last services was the use of his influence in securing for his country the free and entire navigation of the Mississippi River; and he was also equally solicitous that the states should retain the right to fish along the coasts, in the bays, and on the banks of Nova Scotia, on the banks of Newfoundland, in the Gulf of St. Lawrence, and off the shores of Labrador.

Subsequently Lee served in the Virginia legislature, which was engaged at this time in the settlement of numerous matters of extraordinary local interest. Elected again to Congress in 1784, he was chosen the presiding officer of that body. At the end of a single session he resumed his seat in the General Assembly of his own state. He was not a member of the Convention of 1787; but it was generally known that he was opposed to the ratification of the national Constitution in its original form because he considered it to be destructive of the independence of the individual state. The last office which he filled was that of a national senator. This he occupied during two terms; but in the end he was forced to give up his seat, owing to his feeble health. He survived until 1794, a model of what a patriotic citizen should be.

Chapter XVI

GENERAL GEORGE WASHINGTON

THE SECOND General Congress assembled in Philadelphia in May, 1775. The principal work before it was to establish a confederacy, in which Congress itself was to exercise certain powers for the security and prosperity of the Union as a whole, but in which each of the states was to regulate its own local affairs without federal intermeddling. The executive functions of the Central Government were to be lodged in a committee of twelve to be appointed by Congress. Congress now adopted numerous military measures for the prosecution of the war and the defense of the colonies. These had for the most part been suggested by Washington, a member of the body, as the fruit of his military experience.

After these measures had been passed, Washington's name was proposed for the post of commander in chief of the Continental armies. He was chosen unanimously, and no weight was accorded to his modest disclaimer of fitness for the responsible office. In accepting, he assured Congress that he would decline all offer of pecuniary reward for his services beyond what was necessary for his unavoidable expenses, an exact account of which he would keep; and to this resolution he remained faithful until the end of the war. "There is something charming to me in Washington's conduct," wrote John Adams at the time. "A gentleman of one of the first fortunes on the Continent leaving his delicious retirement, his family, and his friends, sacrificing his ease, and hazarding all in the cause of his country. His views are noble and disinterested." Washington at this hour was in the prime of life. Before setting out for the army, he held a review of numerous troops that had been assembled in Philadelphia. The imposing height of his figure and the firmness and dignity of his bearing as in full uniform, and mounted on a spirited horse, he rode up and down the ranks, made a profound impression on the multitude of spectators.

Boston, where a large body of British soldiers had been concentrated, was now in a state of siege. The American troops belonged to different provinces and were under no common leadership. Nor had they been subjected to any severe discipline. They were armed only with their own rifles and fowling pieces, and most of them wore homespun clothes.

The Battle of Bunker Hill had been fought before Washington's arrival in Cambridge. On the road thither a message announcing that event was brought to him by a courier.

"How did the militia act?" he anxiously inquired.

"Bravely," was the reply.

"Then," he exclaimed, "the liberties of the country are safe."

On reaching Cambridge he was lodged in the house which in after times won additional fame as the residence of the poet, Longfellow. On the following day he formally assumed command under a tall elm which stood on the common. This tree survived down to recent years. On going to inspect the different bodies of his troops he found them posted in a semicircle of hills that looked down on Boston, now occupied at every strategic point by the enemy under the command of three distinguished officers, Howe, Clinton, and Burgoyne. The compactness of their position contrasted favorably with the more or less scattered positions held by the Americans.

Washington's first action was to enlarge the forts and to strengthen the weak parts of his line. He was soon joined by numerous highly practised rifle companies, a part of which was led by the Virginian, General Morgan.

As the days went by, the situation of the British became

precarious, since they were now cut off from all supplies of food from the land side. Washington was hopeful that the enemy would be compelled either to advance upon the American entrenchments or to abandon the town altogether; but as they did neither, he sent a large force of troops after nightfall to take possession of a vacant hill commanding the British encampment on Charlestown Neck, an eminence which these troops continued to hold until the end of the siege. In December a long train of wagons arrived at the American headquarters, which were found to be full of ordnance and military stores. "At the sight," an officer present has recorded, "such universal joy ran through the camp, as if each one grasped a victory in his own hands." This collection of weapons and munitions embraced one thousand stands of arms, one hundred thousand flints, thirty thousand round of shot, and thirty-two tons of musket balls.

But the better protection which these military supplies afforded did not influence the soldiers whose terms had expired to reënlist or even to remain until militia substitutes had arrived. "They seem to be so sick of the way of life, and so homesick," said General Nathanael Greene at the time, "that I fear the greater part of the best troops from our Colonies will soon go home." Such was one of the serious conditions confronting Washington which so severely harassed him. His army continued to fall off in number until it had sunk to ten thousand men only, dressed in all sorts of unmilitary garments. "The reflection on my situation, and that of this army," he wrote to a friend, "produces many an unhappy hour when all around me are wrapped in sleep. I have often thought how much happier I should have been, if, instead of accepting the command under such circumstances, I had taken my musket on my shoulder and entered the ranks."

While depressed by these recurring reflections, news of the American defeat before Quebec arrived to discourage him further; and there was also danger of an attack in the rear of his own position by Tories from the Mohawk Valley.

But the condition of the British troops in Boston, already bad before winter began, grew steadily worse. Fuel, flour, and vegetables were all lacking, and smallpox had become epidemic. The situation of the American forces had in the meanwhile been improved by the arrival of Colonel Knox's sledges conveying over the snow from a great distance a large supply of ordnance and a still larger quantity of munitions. Ten regiments of militia were also added to the army.

Washington now decided to occupy Dorchester Heights. This was done under the cover of darkness, and the position was quickly fortified in spite of the hard frozen ground. When Howe, the next morning, observed the redoubts just completed, he exclaimed, "The rebels have done more work in one night than my whole army would have done in one month." An attack upon the American breastworks on the Heights was frustrated by a succession of storms. In the meanwhile, the American forces had made the town untenable. The British now came to the conclusion that they must withdraw, and this decision was confirmed by the Americans' capture of Boston Neck. There was no attempt to obstruct their departure, as their threat to burn the town, should their fleet be bombarded, had been designedly spread abroad. The vessels, loaded down with American loyalists as well as with British soldiers, sailed away towards Canada.

The troops which thus evacuated Boston were to return from Halifax and attack their opponents at another place. On June 29, 1776, an imposing fleet loomed up off the mouth of New York harbor and in a short time dropped anchor opposite Staten Island. The object of the British forces was to seize possession of New York City and the line of Hudson River, by which means the whole of New England would be cut off from the rest of the rebellious colonies, and a road also would be thrown open for the passage of British troops from Canada overland.

In anticipation of such action on the enemy's part, Washington had concentrated his forces in striking distance of the city, and with some anxiety he had been following the progress of events. At this hour, just before the outburst of battle, his spirit was cheered by the adoption of the Declaration of Independence, and in order to inflame his soldiers' ardor, he directed the great document to be read at the head of each brigade of his troops. New York City was infested with scheming Tories, and Washington urged the municipal authorities to drive them out. This was acutely desirable now, in the light of the inducements which Lord Howe, in command of the British fleet, was holding out to the people of the town and its vicinage to return to their allegiance to the King. An attempt was made by him to begin negotiations even with Washington, but as the latter's official character and military rank were not recognized, he refused to join in them. The only favor promised by Howe, in case of peace, was that the American rebels would be pardoned.

While these events were taking place, a band of one thousand Hessians arrived; the high ground on Staten Island was fortified; and Haverstraw Bay was occupied by two men-of-war. The force on the Island was rapidly increased by other soldiers landed from later fleets, until the British army numbered about thirty thousand men, whom the Americans at first could only confront with seventeen thousand. The earliest movement of the British commander was to transfer a force of nine thousand from Staten Island to Long Island, which compelled the American troops to fall back to the Heights of Flatbush. The enemy's aim was to capture the Heights of Brooklyn, as this would at once put New York at their feet. Washington, alarmed by the disorder prevailing among the American soldiers holding the ground just opposite the British front, appointed Putnam to their immediate command and rapidly strengthened his lines.

It was now near the close of August. On the twenty-fifth a powerful British movement began, which culminated on the night of the twenty-sixth in a rapid advance. Washington, who had remained in New York City up to this time, in apprehension of an attack on the town by the British fleet, crossed over the East River to Brooklyn Heights. The battle had now opened at all points, and the Americans in the end, outflanked and assailed with superior numbers, found themselves thrown into confusion, but they nevertheless continued to fight with courage and firmness. Especially was this so with the troops of Stirling and Smallwood. The American loss was estimated at two thousand killed, wounded, or captured. The adverse upshot of the battle was due partly to the necessity imposed on Washington to reserve a large force in New York City, and partly to the wide distribution of the American troops on the Brooklyn side of the river. The failure to post a strong force in the passes of the hills had allowed General Clinton to march behind the American army and assault it in the rear.

On the morning of the twenty-ninth a thick mist blanketed Long Island, and when it partially lifted, Washington and his officers could see that some unusual movement was under way on the part of the British fleet lying off Staten Island. Fearful that its real purpose was the capture of New York City and the virtual investment of the American army on Long Island, a council of war decided that the American troops should be withdrawn under the cover of the ensuing night. This was done in secrecy with perfect success, as the darkness of the hour was increased by the return of the fog. Washington himself went over in the last boat.

On September 7, as the city was exposed to bombardment and encirclement by the British ships, he concluded to abandon it; and this seemed all the more advisable as so large a number of its people had become disloyal. By September 23 he was encamped at White Plains, north of the town, in a position which he had strongly fortified. Early in the following month the British troops came up in force to make an assault, but soon deserted their trenches and marched to the Hudson to destroy the American forts along its banks. Fort Washington was surrounded and captured while Washington and his officers, unable to assist the garrison, looked on across the river. The fall of this stronghold threw open the navigation of that great waterway to the British, and

Washington was constrained to retreat into the Jerseys.

His army, at this hour, was deeply disheartened by its repeated disasters. By the time it reached New Brunswick it had dwindled to four thousand men. On December 2, it was encamped at Trenton. The country traversed in this retreat was in a state of disaffection to the cause, owing chiefly to Howe's proclamation offering to pardon all who should return to their British allegiance. Washington himself was discouraged and actually thought of retiring to the mountainous region of Augusta County in Virginia and even of taking refuge beyond the Alleghenies. The British commander, who had been pursuing, was brought to a halt at the Delaware River, as the boats had been removed by the Americans to the right bank of that stream. He stationed his German troops directly on the left bank, while his main force was encamped in the country further behind.

Charles Lee, an English adventurer, who was at the head of that part of the American army which was supposed to be advancing in the rear, under the influence of traitorous motives not revealed until long afterwards, had not moved forward from the Hudson further than Morristown, although sternly ordered by Washington to follow him rapidly. At this place he was captured by connivance with the enemy.

A turn in the ebbing tide of the American fortunes was now at hand. Washington had been informed by his spies of the lack of vigilance which prevailed in the cantonments of the Hessian contingent at Trenton. He had now about six thousand men fit for service, and with a part of them he determined to attack these hireling troops. Boats were quickly assembled. On Christmas night the passage was undertaken. The weather was very cold and the river full of running ice which threatened to crush the boats to pieces, but before dawn arrived, the army with its artillery had landed on the other bank, and the march on Trenton had begun. The blanket of snow on the ground muffled the sound of tramping feet and rolling wheels. The outposts were driven in, and all opposition to the American rush, after some fighting in the streets, ceased. About one thousand prisoners were taken. With large bodies of British troops stationed not far away, Washington considered it to be prudent to recross the Delaware.

Within a short time eight thousand British soldiers had been assembled at Princeton under Cornwallis' leadership and were feverishly preparing to march against Washington's army. By the second day of December they were advancing towards Trenton in force. The American troops, increased by several thousand recruits, were stationed on the Assumpink. When Cornwallis came up with them, he encamped for the night before attacking, and Washington took advantage of this delay and the darkness to march around the British position and assail a British force which had been left at Princeton. By sunrise he had arrived within a short distance of that town, and there he came face to face with a detachment of the enemy that had set out to join Cornwallis. A section of the American troops was thrown into confusion and General Mercer was killed. Dashing forward on his white horse, Washington rallied his panic-stricken soldiers. In the end the British were defeated, and nearly the whole of one regiment was captured. The rest retreated in disorder to Brunswick. Washington at the head of his army followed in their rear, but soon halted and then returned at leisure to Morristown, a position of strategic importance.

In the meanwhile, Cornwallis in keen chagrin had by rapid marches arrived at Brunswick, anxious to protect his stores. The complexion of the campaign had by this hour been entirely altered. Washington, instead of being pursued, had become the pursuer; and from this time he enjoyed the unreserved confidence of the American people. He was soon known as the American Fabius. The British had now learned, as was said at the time, that merely to run through a province did not necessarily mean its conquest.

In May, 1777, Washington withdrew from Morristown to Middlebrook, which was nearer to Brunswick. His army at this place alone did not exceed seven thousand men in all. The British army, reinforced by German mercenaries, was

PLATE XX. *From the painting by Faed. Photo Gramstorff.*
GENERAL GEORGE WASHINGTON AT TRENTON

now stationed at Brunswick, with Sir William Howe at its head and protected by strong fortifications. Various maneuvers by the enemy now began for the purpose of drawing the principal American force from its intrenchments, but Washington contented himself with sending out light troops to hang on the British flank. This policy of prudence in the end so discouraged the British commander that he withdrew his whole body of men to Staten Island. His action was to some extent perhaps suggested by the advance of Burgoyne's army from Canada—one part of it by way of Champlain, the other part down the Mohawk Valley—with the object of forming a junction with Howe on the line of the lower Hudson. Anticipating this purpose, Washington dispatched troops to Peekskill and sent word for the militia of eastern New York and Connecticut to be called out for immediate service. General Sullivan was ordered to march with his division towards the Pompton Lakes so as to be in striking distance of the Hudson Valley, while Washington himself retired to Morristown.

Burgoyne was in command of nearly eight thousand men, fully equipped and carefully trained. His main force advanced up Champlain in two divisions, one on the west side of the lake, the other on the east. By July 1, 1777, he had arrived within a few miles of Ticonderoga. By taking possession of an unguarded hill standing between Lake Champlain and Lake George, which commanded both of the American forts, the British compelled the American garrisons to evacuate their posts. Although this was done under cover of night, the American troops were pursued, and one-half of their number captured or killed.

Schuyler was in command of all the American soldiers in this quarter. Washington, who was in close touch with him, warned him not to concentrate his men too much; and he also wrote to the brigadier generals in the western parts of Massachusetts and Connecticut to march to Saratoga, while he saw that other troops were sent to Vermont to harass Burgoyne's flank. In the meanwhile, a large British fleet was transporting the greater part of the British forces in New

York to the Capes of the Delaware. Precarious as the situation was in his own theater of operations, he dispatched Colonel Morgan and his riflemen to Schuyler's assistance. There were at this time two threatening opponents in different quarters for him to consider—Burgoyne, in the valley of the Hudson, and Howe, off the coast of Jersey and Delaware and likely at any time to disembark.

Washington was now so fortunate as to receive as volunteers Lafayette, De Kalb, and other French, German, and Polish officers. Especially valuable was to prove the gallant Lafayette, a young French nobleman who had in a spirit of great enthusiasm and without permission left his native country to join the Americans. He was appointed soon after his arrival to the rank of major general and, being quickly attached to Washington's immediate command, became one of his most reliable subordinates and devoted friends.

Within a few weeks the American army, after an imposing parade through Philadelphia, took position near the Brandywine, in the path of the British, who had landed below the Head of Elk after a voyage up the Chesapeake. Washington had determined to strike a blow in battle before he would make up his mind to abandon Philadelphia to the enemy. He therefore quietly awaited attack, with his forces formidably distributed along the stream. A series of skirmishes opened the fight. Finally, the British drove the Americans, under Maxwell, back across the river. It was soon reported that Howe, unable to capture the lower ford, had dispatched troops to seize the upper ones, in order to break in behind the American army. To do this, a circuit of seventeen miles had to be traversed. With the view of rendering this movement abortive, Sullivan, on the right, was directed to assault the advancing foe at once, while Wayne and Greene diverted the attention of the British troops still striving to cross below.

But the defense on the right proved to be ineffective. The American divisions were compelled to retreat to the protection of a neighboring wood, where the pursuing British soon became deeply entangled. In the course of this operation Lafayette was severely wounded. Greene was now summoned to the support of the disorganized right wing and succeeded in rescuing it by a firm resistance to the overconfident advance of the British. Finally, he drew off in safety, and this movement was quickly imitated by Wayne at the lower ford. The British by this time were too fatigued to continue the attack. In his subsequent advance on Philadelphia, after a diversion towards Reading, General Howe halted a part of his troops at Germantown, while he sent Cornwallis forward to take possession of the city.

These unfortunate events in Pennsylvania and Delaware were counterbalanced by Burgoyne's capture at Saratoga. That officer had been weakened by the desertion of his Indian allies and the incessant assaults on his flanks and rear. His unconditional surrender was quickly followed by the British evacuation of Forts Ticonderoga and Independence.

In September, 1777, the American army resumed active operations. Howe having detached a part of his main force for an assault on the American fortresses situated on the Delaware, Washington thought the hour full of promise for an attack on the remaining British troops, now posted at Germantown. He arranged his own in such manner that two-thirds of them could be directed against the British right wing, since its defeat might compel the surrender of the British left also. As fifteen miles had to be traversed before the blow could be struck, it was close to dawn (October 14) when Germantown was reached. There was at that hour a thick fog hanging over every object. The first rush of the Americans was successful. In pressing forward, they passed the Chew house, a conspicuous local landmark. Unfortunately, it remained in the occupation of a British detachment, which was able by a steady fusillade to halt the American rear as it came up and to cut it off from the van. A delay of half an hour resulted, which crippled the effectiveness of the troops ahead. These, however, were making a rapid advance, when a panic seized them in consequence of one division's mistaking another for the enemy, which aroused among them a fear that they were surrounded. As they fell

261

back, the British recovered their coolness and, aided by reinforcements from Philadelphia, pressed closely on the retreating Americans, who continued to give ground until twenty miles had been traversed.

Washington, who during the battle had exposed himself to the hottest fire, was very much mortified by the result. "Every account," he wrote to the president of Congress, "confirms the opinion I at first entertained, that our troops retreated at that instant when victory was declaring herself in our favor. The tumult, disorder, and even despair, which, it seems, had taken place in the British army, were scarcely to be paralleled; and it is said so strongly did the idea of retreat prevail that Chester was fixed on for their rendezvous." "Though we gave away a complete victory," wrote an officer who was present, "we have learned this valuable truth, that we are able to beat them by a vigorous exertion; and that we are far superior in point of swiftness."

Having been reinforced, Washington took position at a place situated within fourteen miles of Philadelphia, where he could cut off all supplies intended for the enemy coming to them from the north and west. The main purpose of the British at this hour was to destroy the forts standing along the Delaware, and in this endeavor at first they obtained but small success. In the meanwhile, a cabal had been formed which, using Gates's triumph at Saratoga, sought to undermine Washington's popularity and to take the command away from him. To this conspiracy Gates eagerly lent his influence, even declining to send the troops which Washington needed for his own reinforcement. But the latter refused to give way to passion and resentment, though fully aware that he was the object of attack. A board of war was now named, of which Gates was a member and which he dominated to the disadvantage of the commander in chief.

Before the hostile plans of this board could be consummated, winter (December, 1777) set in, and Washington withdrew his forces into cantonments at Valley Forge, where he was not too far from Philadelphia to be able to observe the movements of the British. His soldiers were soon housed in rude huts built by themselves, while the officers were similarly sheltered. All were wretchedly clothed; there were no blankets; and the food was short in quantity and poor in quality.

This winter was the darkest interval in the history of the Revolution. But though oppressed with anxiety for his men and country, and also fully informed about the plottings of the Gates-Conway cabal for his removal, Washington not for one moment lost his courage or slackened his faith in his cause. Never to be forgotten was his act of retiring alone to the woods, under the darkness of night, with the snow on the ground, to appeal to Providence for help in that terrible crisis. His first relief came in the public announcement of the treaty with France. A banquet held at Valley Forge in May, 1778, to celebrate this event revealed the depth of the soldiers' affection for their commander. Expecting now a war with France, and considering Philadelphia for this reason an unsafe place, the British decided to evacuate that city. They were able to do this before the French fleet had dropped anchor in the mouth of the Delaware. Had this latter event only occurred earlier, the subsequent victory at Yorktown might have been anticipated. Clinton, after beating off Washington at Monmouth, found refuge in New York City, where it was not possible for the American forces to attack him. Washington now posted his army again at Morristown.

In April, 1780, General Benedict Arnold was brought to trial for irregularities in connection with his military government of Philadelphia in 1778. He had fallen notoriously in debt while in command there and had also made himself offensive to the president and executive council of Pennsylvania. During this time he had been very conspicuous in his attentions to Miss Shippen, a member of a prominent family that was strongly suspected of disloyalty; and his other social affiliations in the city seem to have been chiefly with persons under the same cloud. Charges against him were first submitted to Congress, but a special committee of that body exculpated him in a careful report. Congress then re-

WASHINGTON, REVOLUTIONARY GENERAL

ferred the same charges to a second committee, who recommended that he should be summoned before a court-martial appointed by the commander in chief. Arnold resented this on the ground that he had already been acquitted by the act of the first committee. The court-martial, like this committee also, acquitted him of criminality but advised that he should be reprimanded by Washington. The soreness aroused by this rebuke was to lead to his subsequent treason, but he managed to conceal his traitorous purposes until he obtained the command of West Point. The possession of this place was supposed to carry with it the ultimate success or failure of the American cause.

Arnold fixed his headquarters at Beverley House on the east side of the Hudson River; and here he began a secret correspondence with the British commander in New York, looking to the betrayal of his post. Before his appointment a French fleet had appeared off the coast with five thousand well-disciplined troops on board. These had been promised by France under the influence of Lafayette's solicitation in person. The officer in charge was Count de Rochambeau, but his instructions required him to obey the general orders of Washington. The original plan was for a combined attack on New York City by the French fleet from the sea and by Washington from the land; but this was frustrated for the moment by the arrival of a British naval force.

By this time Arnold had obtained command of the post which he so evilly coveted, and he thought that the hour was close at hand for the consummation of his treachery. It was now arranged that Admiral Rodney should ascend the Hudson to the Highlands, while Arnold was to give up to the British fleet the fort at West Point, under the pretense that he did not have sufficient troops to hold it. It was expected that the surrender would halt any further attempt by the French and American forces to capture New York City, and would permanently separate New England from the rest of the communities in rebellion.

The chief agent for carrying out Arnold's design was Major André, a young and accomplished British officer. It was planned that a meeting between him and Arnold should take place on neutral ground near Dobbs Ferry, but this was prevented. The British sloop of war, *Vulture*, was sent up the river to facilitate the negotiations. On board was André, who went on shore below Stoney Point and there in a thicket conversed long with Arnold. He lingered on throughout the second night. In the meanwhile, the *Vulture* was compelled by American cannon to drop further down the river. In the end, André, being unable to embark, was forced to set out for New York by land and was captured on the way. Arnold was informed of this fact in time to escape to the *Vulture*. Ultimately, the unhappy André was tried and hanged as a spy. Arnold was rewarded for his treason with the rank of major general in the British army and subsequently was appointed to the command of a large force which invaded Virginia. He spent his last years in England, held in little honor, while his name became in America the synonym for a traitor who was as black as Judas himself.

While these events were taking place, Gates had been defeated at Camden in South Carolina, and General Greene had been appointed to succeed him in command of the American troops fighting in that quarter. Soon Cornwallis was advancing from the south, with Greene in retreat; and in time the former was successful in reaching a point as far north as Charlotte. At this crisis Washington was posted with about four thousand effective men just above the Highlands on the Hudson, and with these he gradually drove the British back to New York City. He then threw up breastworks along the line of Harlem River, where he was joined by four thousand French troops. With these eight thousand men he determined to march to Virginia, in the hope that with the aid of a French fleet in the Chesapeake he would be able to capture Cornwallis' army. The soldiers were not aware of their destination.

By August 30, 1781, he had reached Philadelphia. Here he learned through dispatches from Lafayette that Cornwallis had decided to establish his camp at Yorktown and that, in order to shut him in on the landside, the American troops then in Virginia were concentrating at Williamsburg. Near Chester in Maryland Washington received an express informing him that Count de Grasse, with twenty-eight ships, had anchored in the Chesapeake. The investment of the enemy needed only Washington's troops to be complete.

On September 9 Washington crossed the threshold of his own home at Mount Vernon for the first time in the course of six years, and on the twelfth, ahead of his army, he joined Lafayette at Williamsburg. Cornwallis, deeply alarmed by the arrival of De Grasse in the Bay and by the reinforcements which were sent to Lafayette from the French fleet, decided to retreat into the Carolinas, but the moment for safe withdrawal had passed. Recognizing this, he began fortifying his position.

By the twenty-fifth all the American and French troops from the north had arrived at Williamsburg, where they formed a junction with Lafayette. The enemy, protected by a strong line of redoubts and field works around Yorktown, awaited there the expected assault. A few days later Cornwallis drew all his men back into that town, leaving the outworks to be seized by detachments of the American and French soldiers. The two allied armies numbered about twelve thousand men, without counting the Virginia militia under General Nelson's command. By October 1 they had taken position about two miles from the enemy, in the form of a semicircle, which touched the river on either side of the town. De Grasse, in the meanwhile, was anchored in Lynnhaven Bay, in order to guard the entrance between the Capes. The land on the Gloucester side of York River was also closed to the British by a strong French force. During the first American fire on the town Nelson ordered the cannonading to be directed against his own house.

The policy of the Americans was to draw nearer and nearer to Yorktown by successive parallels, a fierce fire being kept up all the time, which was returned by the enemy. Two British redoubts were especially galling to the Continentals. One of these was assaulted on the fourteenth by a French force; the other, by an American, under command of Colonel Hamilton, who led his men in person. Both were captured and afterwards formed a part of the second parallel. To diminish the effect of the batteries in this parallel, Cornwallis took steps to silence two of them by assault. The movement at first was successful, but in the end the enemy were compelled to abandon what they had won. Despairing of drawing off the opposing army, Cornwallis endeavored to escape to the north side of the river; but the boats, after the first division had crossed, were scattered by a great storm and could not be got together in time for the second division to follow.

On the morning of the seventeenth Cornwallis opened negotiations for the cessation of hostilities for twenty-four hours, but Washington was willing to grant only two, as he feared the arrival of British reinforcements by sea. Cornwallis' proposals were rejected, and the American commander substituted such as he would consent to allow. On the nineteenth Yorktown and Gloucester were surrendered, and the British troops became prisoners of war. Two lines, one of the Americans, the other of the French, were formed, each about a mile in length. Washington held one and Rochambeau the other, with their respective staffs. At two o'clock the British army passed between the two lines. General O'Hara offered his sword, with an apology for Cornwallis' absence, but Washington simply pointed to General Lincoln as the officer to receive it. The British soldiers were led into a field, where they grounded their arms, some with such violence as to break the muskets.

A few days after the surrender, Sir Henry Clinton appeared off the Capes, with a large fleet and seven thousand men; but he was too late to reverse the situation, and he returned to New York.

Such was the concluding military stroke of the Revolution. On November 25, 1783, Washington took possession of New York City, which had up to this time remained in the hands of the British. Nine days afterwards, before starting for Annapolis to resign his commission, he bade farewell to his principal officers at Fraunce's Tavern. "On entering the room, and finding himself surrounded by his old companions in arms, who had shared with him so many scenes of hardship, difficulty, and danger, his agitated feelings overcame his usual self-command. Filling a glass of wine, and turning upon them his benignant but saddened countenance: 'With a heart full of love and gratitude,' said he, 'I now take leave of you, most devoutly wishing that your latter days may be as prosperous and happy as your former ones have been glorious and honorable. I can not come to each of you, but shall be obliged if each of you will come and take me by the hand.' General Knox was the first to advance. Washington, affected even to tears, grasped his hand and gave him a brother's embrace. In the same affectionate manner he took leave severally of the rest. Not a word was spoken. Silent and solemn, they followed their loved commander as he left the house, passed through a body of light infantry, and proceeded on foot to Whitehall Ferry. Having entered the barge, he turned to them, took off his hat, and waved a silent adieu."

Chapter XVII

GENERAL GEORGE ROGERS CLARK

ONLY TWO facts about George Rogers Clark's ancestry seem to be indisputable: (1) the name of the emigrant was John Clark; and (2) the color of his wife's hair was red. One of their descendants is reported to have been blessed with thirty-one children, of whom twenty-nine were sons. The house in which George Rogers Clark in 1752 first saw the light was situated on the hill that slopes down from Pantops in Albemarle County to the east bank of the Rivanna River. No vestige of this house remains. It stood in sight of Monticello, the home of Jefferson, and of Edge Hill, the home of Governor Randolph; and it looked out upon one of the noblest mountain landscapes in the world.

In these pre-Revolutionary days the rush for new lands not only encouraged enterprising young men to adopt surveying as a profession, but also turned their eyes westward as offering a more profitable field in which to pursue this calling than the older communities of the East did during that period. When nineteen years of age, Clark joined a large surveying and exploring party which was about to set out for the regions lying far beyond the rugged crest of the Alleghenies, but it was not his intention at this time to leave Virginia permanently. Much of the journey beyond the mountains was made in a canoe and through a land occupied only by Indian tribes, always ready without provocation to rob and to murder.

The region between the Monongahela and the Ohio soon began to fill up with settlers, and Clark decided to return to it after a visit to his home in Virginia. He obtained a patent to land situated south of the modern city of Wheeling, and building here a cabin for his own shelter, he combined the pursuit of agriculture with the pursuit of surveying. The two afforded him a steadily increasing income. This mode of life was an excellent preparation for the strenuous and exposed military campaign which he was so soon to undertake north of the Ohio River, in a country of a very similar character. At this period he was not satisfied to remain all his time under his own roof. In 1773 he locked his door and joined a party of Virginians who were passing on their way to Kentucky; in the following year he was a member of a military expedition which crossed the Ohio River and put to the torch numerous Indian villages; and afterwards he took part in the excursions that culminated in the Battle of Point Pleasant. This victory widened the region already safe for white settlement and stimulated the rush of eastern adventurers to take up the lands in that quarter.

Kentucky seemed to offer a new earthly paradise to these bold and enterprising men, and Clark, being of the like temper, could not resist the urge of the southwestward tide that was flowing in such enthusiastic volume by his cabin. He is known to have visited that region in the spring of 1775. But this was for the purpose of carrying out an agreement to make surveys for the Ohio Company, and he also obtained patents to lands for his own benefit, a privilege which had been granted to him by that Company. Finally, he was led to acquire title to soil on the Kentucky River by the expectation of spending there much of his time. Describing the spot as the richest and most beautiful in America, he persuaded his parents to remove thither from the East and seat themselves permanently there.

Owing to a conflict of claims between Virginia and the Henderson Company, which had founded the Transylvania settlements, there was doubt among the people of Kentucky as to which of the two authorities was entitled to their allegiance. A public meeting was held at Harrodsburg in June, 1776, to find out the best means of removing the causes of the perplexity. Should they establish a new government or should they attach themselves openly to the government of Virginia? Clark was chosen one of two delegates to represent Kentucky in the Virginia legislature. It was necessary for him and his companions to traverse over seven hundred miles before they could reach Williamsburg; and much of this distance had to be covered on foot over the roughest frontier roads.

The General Assembly had adjourned before Clark arrived at that place, but he determined to have an interview with Governor Henry before returning to the West. He was specially anxious to obtain a supply of powder for the Kentucky settlements as a means of protection against Indian invasion. Henry was found to be in keen sympathy with his visitor's purposes, but he was powerless, as only the executive council had the authority to deliver the powder; and this at first they were unwilling to do, without imposing such conditions as Clark could not safely accept. Adroitly pointing out that Virginia could retain Kentucky only by removing all temptation from its people to apply to some other community for its defense, he ultimately succeeded in altering their resolution so far that they agreed not only to supply the powder, but also to transport it to Pittsburgh, to be there held subject to his written or verbal order.

It was a source of satisfaction to Clark that the Virginia government by this appropriation tacitly acknowledged the region beyond the Cumberland Mountains as a part of the state, although the General Assembly refused to admit him and his fellow-delegate to seats at the next session. Still, the power of his influence as an adviser during that session was shown by Kentucky's elevation to the status of a county, fulfilling all the administrative purposes which the creation of Transylvania had had in view. Clark was thus virtually the father of the state of Kentucky, since the boundaries of the state followed exactly those of this original county.

After his arrival at Harrodsburg on his return, he perceived that the only prospect of putting an end to the Indian incursions, which had thrown that whole region into confusion by jeopardizing the life of every citizen, was to send out an expedition against the Indian tribes roaming north of the Ohio. It was known to all that the constant massacres of the whites were really instigated by the British military officers in command at Detroit, Vincennes, Kaskaskia, and Cahokia. No doubt Clark understood clearly that the suppression of the Indian marauders on their own ground would signify in reality the destruction of the British power throughout the Northwest. He had by this time acquired extraordinary popularity and was acknowledged by all to be the leader of the community. But he was without authority to undertake a campaign against the Indians and British in the Illinois without the permission of the government at Williamsburg; and to that government he must also look for the necessary military supplies.

He started for the capital on October 1, 1777. The surrender of Burgoyne had just taken place, and the feeling on all sides was in consequence favorable to a more active military policy. Clark quietly submitted his scheme to Governor Henry, who, approving it himself, called into consultation Thomas Jefferson, George Wythe, and George Mason. They, too, accepted it without any reserve; and this was also the Council's attitude on receiving the details from the governor. The General Assembly in turn followed the example set by the Council. This favorable action was taken on the second day of January, 1778. To hasten recruiting, three hundred acres of public land were promised to each soldier participating in the campaign, in case it proved to be successful.

When the troops for the invasion of the Illinois country had assembled, it was found that most of them were Virginians. Clark and all four of his captains were from that ancient state; and this was exactly what was to be expected, since the proposed expedition had been authorized and paid for by the representatives of its people. There was no ground for the assertion by the historian Bancroft that the commander relied solely on volunteers from among the Pennsylvania, Tennessee, and Kentucky backwoodsmen. Virginia alone had any real claim to dominion over the Illinois country by royal charter right; and this claim was to be fully confirmed by the conquest so soon to take place by her own independent troops. It was with less than five hundred men that Clark planned to seize the whole of this vast empire, already occupied by hostile British soldiers and their Indian allies posted at strategic points. In the beginning he was able to muster only one hundred and fifty men; and with these he fell down the Ohio on the twelfth of May, 1778. His first landing was made at the mouth of the Kentucky River; thence the voyage was continued to the falls of the Ohio; and here his little army, somewhat swelled by additional recruits, was organized for the expedition against the British forts. During some time the troops were encamped on an island in the river, at that period covered with buffalo cane. Cabins, storehouses, and fortifications were soon built, and rules of strict discipline adopted.

Up to this hour it was not known to the soldiers that Clark had decided upon so dangerous a purpose as a march to the Northwest to capture the British garrisons. When this fact was revealed, some of the troops deserted, but because of constant supervision of the water passage to the bank of the river, the slinking away failed to become serious.

The advance began in boats down the river, as it was designed to capture Kaskaskia first. The rank and file numbered about one hundred and seventy-five men. It was a critical moment, for had this small army halted or turned back, it is quite possible that the Northwest would never have been conquered, and as a result, the boundaries of the United States, when peace was signed, would have stopped on the west at the banks of the Ohio River. "I knew my case was desperate," said Clark long afterwards, "but the more I reflected on my weakness, the more I was pleased with the enterprise," an expression fully in accord with the spirit of one of the bravest and most fruitful campaigns in all history. The soldiers in his train were worthy of such an intrepid leader. Hardened by continuous exposure to weather, accustomed to the privations of the wilderness, prepared to face with coolness the attacks of Indian and wild beast alike, these sturdy men, skillful with the rifle and profoundly versed in woodcraft, did not shrink from the unknown scenes into which they were about to plunge, although their departure was made more solemn by an eclipse of the sun.

The boats at first were never tied up to the bank night or day. After passing the mouth of the Tennessee, Clark decided to disembark his troops and make the rest of the journey overland. There were no wagons, pack horses, or other means of transportation for the baggage and munitions. These impediments had to be shouldered by the men. About one hundred and twenty miles had to be traversed, the first part of which was expected to be through a difficult country of swamps and woods. At the end of fifty miles the open prairie was reached. On the evening of July 4, the town was sighted in the distance, and having in the meanwhile broken up his troops into two divisions, Clark crossed the Kaskaskia River under darkness and by dawn had taken possession of the streets and captured the governor. Not a gun had been fired, so ignorant had the inhabitants been of the presence of an enemy. It reveals the chivalry of the man and the time that, although it was suspected that the governor's wife had concealed important papers in her trunk, Clark at first refused to permit it to be rifled. But less consideration was shown her at a later hour, for all the property of the governor was seized and sold for the soldiers' benefit, and his instructions from his superior officers were carried off to Williamsburg.

The scene which arose before Clark's gaze as he entered the fort alone has been often described, although the accuracy of the incident has been questioned. "The officers had given a ball," says Roosevelt in his *Winning of the West*, "and the mirth-loving creoles, young men and girls, were dancing and reveling within, while the sentinels had left their posts. Advancing to the great hall where the revel was held, Clark leaned silently, with folded arms, against the door-post looking at the dancers. An Indian, lying on the floor of the entry, gazed intently on the stranger's face as

PLATE XXI. *From a painting by an unknown artist in the Virginia State Library, Richmond, Virginia. Used by courtesy of the Governor of Virginia. Photo Cook.*

GENERAL GEORGE ROGERS CLARK

the light from the torches within flickered across it, and suddenly sprang to his feet uttering the unearthly war whoop. Instantly the dancing ceased; the women screamed, while the men ran towards the door. But Clark, standing unmoved, and with unchanged countenance, grimly bade them continue their dancing, but to remember that they now danced under Virginia's and not Great Britain's flag. At the same time, his men, who had been standing round about the entrance, burst into the fort and seized the officers."

The first step which Clark took after reconciling the people of Kaskaskia to American rule (which he was soon able to do with the aid of Father Gibault, a French priest who had become his ardent partisan and coadjutor) was to send a part of his small army to get possession of Cahokia and other French villages on the banks of the Mississippi. Cahokia was situated nearly opposite the modern city of St. Louis. The soldiers, perceiving the need of quickness, vigilance, and secrecy in this expedition, gave up all thought of rest during three nights. Through Father Gibault's influence, Vincennes yielded without a blow when the people, who were of French origin, were informed that the French nation had recently arrayed itself on the side of the Americans against the British. Clark now adopted plans for the permanent retention of the invaded country, and this he was assisted in accomplishing by the readiness with which the whole of the French inhabitants changed their allegiance. The large population of Indians was also conciliated. These tribes had with few exceptions been allies of the English.

Clark was on one occasion in imminent personal danger while holding a conference with a group of Indian representatives. A band broke into his lodging and was prevented from carrying him off only by the prompt intervention of a sergeant. The Indians exhibited a more friendly temper when they found that the French were on the side of the intruders. Clark understood the Indian character thoroughly, and his success in mollifying the Indians was largely due to this fact.

While engaged with so much shrewdness in pacifying the

country which he had conquered, he was informed by means of an intercepted letter that Governor Hamilton, stationed at Detroit, was collecting a large force for his expulsion from the Illinois. In reality this force was already in possession of Vincennes, and a small detachment had for some time been hovering about Kaskaskia itself. Clark, unaware of danger, started with the escort of a few men for Vincennes, and on the road, while attending a ball at Prairie du Rocher, he heard that the British were marching in strength against Kaskaskia, which he had so recently left. The alarm proved to be false, but it caused him, after his rapid return to that town, to put it in a condition of defense. He was soon reinforced there by one of his lieutenants, who was in command of two companies.

Hamilton at Detroit was now engaged in furnishing arms and ammunition to the Indians and in encouraging them by every means in his power to harry the frontiers. After each expedition they would return to the British Government and present the bloody trophies of their victims' scalps. In one instance one hundred and twenty-nine of these hideous prizes were brought in by these inhuman creatures as a gift to the governor. Clark refused to employ Indians in actual warfare against the British. "We never wished them to fight for us," he said. "All we wished for them to do was for them to sit still and look on."

When Hamilton descended from Detroit to recapture the forts now in Clark's possession, he was in command of an army of six hundred men. His first objective was Vincennes, which was then defended by a garrison of twenty-one soldiers. When the enemy drew near, the officer in charge, Captain Helm, had a cannon rolled to the entrance of the fort and declined to surrender unless he should receive the honors of war, which the British granted under the impression that the fort was held by a large number of soldiers. No further attempt was made by the enemy to dispossess the Americans until the following spring.

In August, 1778, Rochblaue, the captured governor of Kaskaskia, was sent under a strong bodyguard to Virginia, and it was this party that carried thither the news of the exploits of Clark and his men. Popular excitement arose in consequence, and Governor Henry at once suggested to the General Assembly that Clark should be reinforced sufficiently to enable him to capture the British post at Detroit. The country so recently overrun was organized by that body into the county of Illinois, with the proper officers to administer its affairs. It was anticipated that this step would have the effect of curbing the Indians and bringing them finally into such a state of subjection that their marauding incursions would cease. Clark was retained in his rank as commander of all the troops already stationed in the posts north of the Ohio River.

Before the letters which Henry wrote Clark in order to convey all this information could reach him, Hamilton had taken possession of Vincennes and was developing his plans for the complete expulsion of the Americans from the Illinois. Clark determined to anticipate the next movement, which would be against Kaskaskia, by striking immediately at his enemy, in the hope of conquering him in a single battle. "We must either quit this country," he said, "or attack Mr. Hamilton. No time is to be lost. Were I sure of reinforcement, I should not attempt it. Who knows what fortune will do for us? Great things have been effected by a few men well-conducted. Perhaps, we might be fortunate. We have this consolation, that our cause is just, and that our country will be grateful, and not condemn our conduct in case we fall through." At this time the force under Clark embraced only about one hundred American soldiers, while his French contingent hardly rose to as many. The Indians had returned to their British allegiance. As for supplies of all sorts, he was too far away from Virginia to expect any from that quarter, and there was no other to which he could look. He afterwards accurately described his position when he said: "My number of men was too small to stand a siege, and my situation too remote to call for assistance." His condition was made more desperate by the failure of the Virginian reinforcement to appear. But he refused to yield to discouragements. In the spirit of true military genius he determined not to wait for Hamilton to attack in the spring, but himself to attack Hamilton so soon as Vincennes could be reached by an overland march. He was led to this decision by information brought to him by Colonel Francis Vigo, who had recently left that town. Vigo reported that the attitude of its French people was favorable to the American cause and that Hamilton's army was now steadily dwindling.

There were four companies reserved for the land campaign, while forty-six men were assigned to a bateau which was to carry down the Kaskaskia and Mississippi rivers and up the Ohio and Wabash the two cannons and four swivels, and the ammunition, provisions, and other military supplies which were to be used in the actual assault on the town after the land force had reached the valley of the Wabash. This river expedition turned out to be abortive, as it failed to arrive in time to take part in the capture.

The march began in February, in the midst of a harsh spell of weather. There were no tents. The distance to Vincennes was, as the crow flies, about one hundred and seventy-five miles, but somewhat greater by the trail which Clark traversed. By the eighth of the month the little army had entered the prairie region, which in consequence of the protracted rains was to some degree under water. The streams were crossed by felling the timber growing on their banks. When the Little Wabash was reached, a canoe was built, in which a few men were sent ahead to explore what was known as the Drowned Lands in the valley on the other side. After receiving their report, Clark ordered the main stream to be followed by the troops, who, entering the Drowned Lands, floundered through the water until a hillock standing above its surface was arrived at, where they encamped. In spite of the hardships and dangers just passed through, the troops stacked their arms in fine spirits. Much amusement had been caused among them by the sight of a little drummer boy making the voyage on the top of his drum.

PLUNGE THROUGH THE WATERS

But the worst was still to come, for the Big Wabash had yet to be crossed. The French troops here began to show signs of rebellion and were disposed to return on their tracks, although the morning and evening guns at Vincennes were plainly audible. The sea of water seemed to be endless, and there was now at every step the peril of being submerged. A dry hillock was picked up only at long intervals. In the meanwhile there were no provisions to allay the soldiers' hunger. Clark had resort to various amusing devices to raise their spirits by diverting their thoughts from their situation, now made more painful and difficult by masses of ice floating in the water. There was a very tall sergeant in the ranks, and the little drummer was ordered to mount his shoulders and beat his drum in its most stirring tones. Clark himself walked immediately behind them, waving his sword, and giving the command to all to follow in his footsteps. But more effective still was his quiet order to a lieutenant in the rear to shoot down any soldier who refused to advance any further.

On February 23 the troops arrived at a place known as Horseshoe Plain, which was four miles in length and covered with water breast-high. Clark led the way, after seeing that the few boats in his possession were reserved for the sick and disabled. A second reach of submerged lands was next crossed, and soon the walls of Fort Sackville situated in the outskirts of Vincennes, which looked to it for defense, came into full view. The plunging through the waters had taken ten days to complete. It was probably the most singular military advance in all history and was made successful by the very fact of its difficulties. What foe, however foolhardy, would venture to seek a path, even in boats, through those now deep, now shallow floods?

Clark and his troops were quickly in clear sight of the enemy whom he was seeking to subdue, and by the stratagem of disappearing behind a hillock and frequently repeating their reappearance, left the impression upon their opponents that they were more numerous than they were in reality. After the fall of night, when land had been made, the march was directed towards the rear of the group of houses. No evidence of resistance was yet to be detected, and Clark ordered one of his captains to deploy his men and fire upon the fort, while the bulk of his army was taking possession of the main part of the town.

When the bombardment of the fort began, some of the British officers were diverting themselves with a game of cards, and the playing was enlivened with the drinking of many whiskey toddies. It happened that among the prisoners was Captain Leonard Helm, one of Clark's most trusted aides, and it was he who mixed the beverages. When the first volley against the stronghold went off, the balls struck the chimney of the room occupied by the officers while playing, and a large quantity of dirt fell into the vessel in which the liquor was brewing. "Gentlemen," exclaimed Helm, "that is Clark's soldiers, and they will take your fort, but they ought not to have spoiled this apple toddy."

Soon detecting the embrasures in the forts, and their guns having got an accurate bearing on them, the American riflemen compelled the British cannoneers to retire further within their wooden walls, after closing their ports. So soon as one of these was opened, a fusillade was directed straight at it, with the result that many of the British gunners were killed. A mine was begun for the purpose of blowing up the magazine, and breastworks were also thrown across the street. In the meanwhile, the vessel from Kaskaskia which had started down the Mississippi before the main army set out overland had not yet turned up, and it was feared that a shortage in munitions would occur if its arrival was delayed much longer. There was danger, too, that the Indian tribes in this vicinity would rise and attack. This combination of circumstances caused Clark to decide to make an assault on the fort in the hope of carrying it with a rush and capturing all the troops concentrated there. After the first firing had continued for some time, Clark sent under a flag of truce a letter to Governor Hamilton, who was in personal command of the fort, calling upon him peremptorily to surrender himself, his garrison, and his stores. "If I am obliged to storm," he concluded, "you may depend on such treatment as is justly due to a murderer." Hamilton replied with dignity to this rough demand, "Lieutenant Governor Hamilton begs leave to acquaint Colonel Clark that he and his garrison are not disposed to be awed into any action unworthy of British subjects."

The firing then recommenced with increased sharpness. But before any real execution could be done, Hamilton became aware of the uselessness of further resistance and dispatched an overture for a three days' truce. Clark positively declined to agree to this, but sent word that he was willing "to hold a conference with the British commander in St. Xavier's church." Hamilton accepted and at the meeting submitted the terms on which he was ready to give up. Clark rejected these and demanded an unconditional surrender. Hamilton shrank from yielding so absolutely. "What are your reasons," he asked Colonel Clark, "for insisting on such harsh terms?" Clark replied that he was fully aware that the greater part of the principal "Indian partisans of Detroit" (British officers) were in the fort and that he wished to get possession of their persons so as to punish them for having instigated so many Indian massacres.

Major Hay, one of these officers, had accompanied Hamilton to the conference. "Pray, Sir," said he to Clark, "who is it that you call 'Indian partisans'?" "Sir," replied Clark, "I take Major Hay to be one of the principal." The American commander, in relating the story of the conference long afterwards, recorded that he "had never seen a man, in the moment of execution, so struck as Hay appeared to be, pale and trembling, scarcely able to stand. Hamilton blushed, and was much affected at his behavior."

Clark warned the governor that in case of the fort's capture by storm it would be impossible to restrain his soldiers from a general massacre, as they were greatly incensed by the story of the outrages which had been committed by the Indian allies of the British, under British stimulation; and he frankly stated that among those who would be shown no mercy at all were officers like Colonel Hay. All such were certain to perish in any event, unless the attack could be beaten off, which seemed improbable. After a short silence, Clark decided, without, however, revealing his purpose at the moment, to modify his terms of unconditional surrender, but in order first to consider the matter more carefully, he directed the adjournment of the conference. All fighting was to cease. He informed Hamilton that should he in the end be willing to give easier conditions than those which he had first offered, he would raise his flag; but if he should prefer to storm the fort, the roll of his drums would indicate his intention. He finally granted lenient terms, and the fort was surrendered.

Thus was extinguished forever the dominion of the British in the country of the Illinois.

Clark decided that he would not advance against Detroit at that time, as he thought that his present body of troops should be reinforced from Virginia and Kentucky before so serious an expedition should be undertaken. Several other reasons also influenced him in putting off the proposed march overland. In the first place, the soldiers had been deeply fatigued by the tramp from Kaskaskia and the sharp fighting which had followed; and in the second, they were suffering from an epidemic of sickness, which was aggravated by the trying weather. Moreover, the number of British captives was so large as to cause apprehension. Could they be safely left behind by the American army when it should set out for Detroit? To remove this danger, Clark released very many of the prisoners on parole. Those who had been conspicuous in encouraging the Indians to commit all sorts of barbarities were threatened with chains, but apparently not even they were severely punished.

In March the more prominent officers like Hamilton, Hay, Lamothe, and Masonville were sent off to Kentucky; eighteen British privates accompanied them as fellow-prisoners; and all were under the guard of two American officers and a squad of twenty-five soldiers. After the party arrived at the falls of the Ohio, an order came to dispatch them to Williamsburg; and thither they were escorted by a detachment of Kentucky militia. At this time the American people were keenly aroused by the treatment which their unfortunate countrymen were receiving in the British prison ships and by the open aid which the British military authorities were giving to the Indians in all their bloody incursions along the western frontiers. Jefferson, now Governor of Virginia, thought it only just that Hamilton and his fellow-officers should be made to suffer severely, not only personally for their own inhuman acts, but also vicariously for the ruthless spirit which their Government had shown everywhere in carrying on the war against its former American subjects.

At Chesterfield, near the modern Richmond, Hamilton was put in handcuffs, and so were Captain Lamothe and Captain de Jan; and in this plight they traversed about sixty miles, part of the way on foot. At Williamsburg fetters were substituted for handcuffs, and the unlucky foreigners were then thrown into jail. Only these three seemed to have been exposed to such an indignity, and this was because they had been peculiarly guilty in their military relations with the Americans. Subsequently this harshness was relaxed on Washington's advice, and Lamothe and De Jan were sent to Hanover Courthouse and there permitted to go much at large on their parole. Hamilton and Hay rejected the privilege and remained in confinement at Williamsburg. The authorities of Virginia refused to exchange Hamilton for fear that, after returning to the Illinois country, he would be able to jeopardize the permanence of the American dominion there. He was finally released on parole and granted the right to join the British in New York, with the understanding that his movements there were to be restricted within certain limits. It was not until March, 1781, that he was exchanged.

In the meanwhile, various obstacles had again arisen to prevent Clark from starting upon the expedition which he had long projected against Detroit. June, 1779, had been selected by him as the month for the beginning of the march. Provisions in large quantities for the soldiers had been collected in anticipation of the movement, but when the hour arrived, the expected reinforcement had not deployed on the ground. Through its county lieutenant, Colonel John Bowman, Kentucky had promised a band of three hundred men, but only thirty turned up at the rendezvous. The Virginia contingent also dwindled to one hundred and fifty. The value of paper money, too, had declined so much that it could be no longer used in the purchase of supplies; and there was no other means by which they could be obtained. Clark was led by these adverse conditions to abandon his proposed campaign for the present.

He now keenly regretted that the march had not begun immediately after the fall of Vincennes. At that hour Detroit was protected only by a dilapidated fort, and the inhabitants were so much in sympathy with the American cause that they celebrated the capture of the former town with feasts and dances through three days. Later the British rebuilt the fort at Detroit and strengthened the other defenses of the place. In the end Clark decided that the only step which he could take with safety was to hold the ground that he had already won, and he therefore for garrison purposes divided his troops among Vincennes, Kaskaskia, Cahokia, and the falls of the Ohio. He had not abandoned all hope of capturing Detroit, but he perceived that this could be accomplished by him only with the assistance of the Virginians; and this assistance could be assured only by personal interviews with the Virginian authorities. In 1780 he visited Williamsburg with that object in view, and while there he had a share in repelling Arnold after the British advance to Richmond. Jefferson gave his plans hearty support, and to prevent his being outranked by any Continental officer who might happen to be stationed in the Illinois country, commissioned him brigadier general of all the forces that should take part in the proposed expedition.

Washington also expressed his emphatic approval of General Clark's projected campaign. But the practical difficulties that would accompany it were brought at once to light when a draft was issued for two thousand recruits. The ardor for the war had died out among the people at large, and few persons were willing to join in an excursion attended with so many dangers at every stage and certain to draw the participants far from home. The few volunteers who came forward could not be supplied with the right equipment, owing to the condition of the Virginian finances at this hour. A regiment under Colonel Gibson, who had been assigned as Clark's first subordinate, was diverted to another duty, considered more urgent at the moment. Clark was therefore left dependent on raw militia. He had planned to depart from Pittsburgh by June 15, 1781, with a force of two thousand men, but the number that really accompanied him two months afterwards did not exceed four hundred. "If I find a prospect of completing my army in any other country, I shall do it," he wrote to the governor of Virginia at this time, "and make my strikes according to circumstances. I feel for the dreadful consequences that will ensue throughout the frontier, if nothing is done."

There was an understanding between Clark and Colonel Lochry of Westmoreland County, Pennsylvania, that the latter would set out for Wheeling with a formidable band of riflemen and rangers and with a company of horse. But when this force began the march, it contained barely one hundred and seven men. Clark waited for it to come up as long as he thought it safe to do so, for his troops, now grown very restless, were disposed to desert. Colonel Lochry, missing him at Wheeling, followed him down the river, but finding it impossible to catch up with him, sent a small band of soldiers ahead to overtake him. This band carried a letter disclosing the weak condition of the Pennsylvania contingent. As these men paddled down stream, they were halted and seized by the Indians. The letter revealed to the British officers the perfect safety with which Lochry's main force could be attacked. In an ambuscade laid for their approach near the mouth of the Miami River the Pennsylvanians were suddenly assaulted, and all who were not killed were captured. Thus vanished the last hope which Clark entertained of completing the conquest of the Northwest.

But the American grip on the Illinois region was so strong

that in the treaty of peace between Great Britain and the United States the vast territory from the Ohio to the Lakes was conceded to the latter as the actual possessor. It was due primarily to the courage, perseverance, and resourcefulness of General Clark that this empire now constitutes one of the great divisions of our country. His subsequent career was full of adventure, but it contained no episode equal in importance or romance to the campaigns against Kaskaskia and Vincennes or the attempted expedition against Detroit.

At the end of the Revolutionary War, being on the Virginia military establishment, he lost his commission when the state's military forces were contracted in number in order to ensure economy. It was not until his old age, when he was a cripple from paralysis, that he was awarded a niggard pension of four hundred dollars. Erysipelas had set in in one of his legs, and in consequence it had to be amputated. Before the operation began—it was before the day of anesthetics—the old hero ordered a namesake to have drums and fifes beaten and blown while the operation was in progress, and with his fingers he kept time to the music as it rose. Finally, the music stopped. "Is it off?" he calmly asked. He was shown the severed limb. With this characteristic scene, we drop the curtain on the life of this primitive hero.

Chapter XVIII

GENERAL DANIEL MORGAN

THE MILITARY career of General Morgan, coupled with the similar careers of Washington and George Rogers Clark, reveals the vast extent of the field which the officers and private soldiers of Virginia tramped over and fought over in the course of the Revolutionary War. Washington, as we have seen, had as a simple colonel a conspicuous share in driving the French from the West; and as commander in chief in the War of Independence, he conducted the far-reaching operations which ended in the complete victory at Yorktown. Clark, on the other hand, organized the campaigns that made the country north of the Ohio a permanent part of the United States.

Morgan filled no such position of supreme importance in the Revolution as either of these contemporaries, but as an officer of high rank in the expedition against Canada, as a decisive factor at the Battle of Saratoga, and as Greene's indomitable lieutenant in the desperate conflicts on the soil of the Carolinas, he carried the flag of his commonwealth into the only regions which had not been traversed by Washington and Clark and their gallant troops. Like the military careers of those two great leaders, his own career is an integral part of the history of Virginia because it was an integral part of her share in the military history of the Revolution; and as a man of vigorous personal qualities, as a soldier of genius, and as an unselfish servant of his country, he was worthy of having his name associated forever with the names of the two illustrious commanders to whom the

United States is most indebted for the possession of the ground which forms the greater part of the present national domain.

Morgan was not a Virginian by birth, but from the age of seventeen his life, independently of his campaigns, was identified with its soil. In his boyhood he must have enjoyed hardly one intellectual advantage, for he seemed to possess a very small portion of the simplest rudiments of an education. Indeed, he found it difficult to write his own name or to read the plainest sentences, or to add or subtract or divide in dealing with figures. His person, when a young man, gave evidence that he had as a farmer's boy been roughened by the labor of mauling rails, digging ditches, and driving the plough. In manners, in these early years, he was wholly devoid of polish, but the impression of this defect was softened by his native shrewdness, by his perfect candor of spirit, and by a coolness of nerve that no peril could shake.

From the very start he was accepted as a leader by his associates and looked upon with equal admiration and affection. This standing with his companions was confirmed by his possession of athletic powers notable even in the frontier community of the lower Shenandoah Valley, where he made his home after his arrival from New Jersey. The refinements of civilization had not yet fully penetrated this beautiful region. The life which the people led there was one of more or less hardship and privation and always beset with danger from the inroads of the Indians who roamed west of the Alleghenies. It encouraged a spirit of self-reliance, of indifference to personal perils, and of an ardent love of freedom. All this was congenial to the rough breast but manly soul of Daniel Morgan.

When war began in fierce earnestness with the French in the valley of the Ohio, Morgan, who seems at this time to have been engaged in farming, volunteered to offer his wagon and horses and his own services as driver to General Braddock, to aid in the transportation of baggage and provisions for the troops on their march to Fort Duquesne. He did not take part in that shambles of a battle, owing to the fact that his vehicle was attached to the contingent in the rear, which was slowly bringing up the principal part of the artillery, munitions, and provisions. In consequence of the heaviness of these loads, as well as of the primitive rudeness of the highway, this section of the British forces was quickly left far behind. The first knowledge which the men had of the disaster to Braddock was the arrival of a stream of fugitives, panic-stricken by their recollection of the massacre from which they had barely escaped with their lives only two days before. Many of the soldiers of the rear contingent at once joined in the flight for the settlements, and their example was followed by most of the wagoners, who cut their traces and rode away at top speed. Morgan refused to take part in this disgraceful stampede. He remained, with others equally brave, to convey the wounded to Fort Cumberland. His wagon was one of those which passed over the spot in the road where Braddock's body had been buried, in the expectation that the wheels would obliterate all traces of the grave and thus save it from the desecration of savage hands. Morgan was rewarded for his fidelity in that terrible campaign by his assignment, with his wagon and team, to the quartermaster's department.

It was while he was in this service that he became involved in an altercation with a British officer who in a moment of ungovernable fury struck the gigantic wagoner with the flat of his sword. Morgan resented the indignity by at once knocking the offender down. For this act of insubordination he was tried by court-martial and condemned to the lash. The whip was laid on so unmercifully that the flesh is said to have hung in strips from his back. Only a man of an iron constitution could have survived. Certainly only a man of a magnanimous soul could have forgiven such an indelible disgrace. This Morgan did when a contrite public apology was made to him by the officer, who acknowledged himself in the wrong so soon as a cooler mood had returned.

It was in defense of Fort Edward, situated northwest of Winchester, that Morgan first appeared in an active military capacity. Nearly the whole of its garrison had been slaughtered (1759) by a marauding company of French and Indians; and the militia, in which Morgan was now enrolled, was called out to reoccupy the captured stronghold, still of importance, because standing on the western frontier. Hardly had possession of it been resumed when the French and Indians again attacked it in force. Morgan struck down four savages with his own hand, and as the enemy retreated, in consequence of the resolute defense, he called out to his fellow-soldiers, "Let us follow the red devils," and led the way. The foe were quickly overtaken, and all who were not captured or killed were driven into a headlong flight.

So deep was the impression which Morgan's courage made on this occasion that he was recommended to a captaincy in the impending campaign against Fort Duquesne which General Forbes had organized. Governor Dinwiddie, however, in a spirit of ungenerous perversity, was willing to confer on him only the commission of an ensign, although it was known to all that Morgan's higher promotion, owing to his personal popularity, would have drawn many recruits to the ranks.

It was while he was stationed at one of the forts near Winchester that he was sent with a small escort to carry important dispatches to the commander at Winchester. On the road, while he and his companions were threading their way through a dark defile in the mountains, they were fired on from an Indian ambush. Every man of the escort was killed on the spot, and Morgan received a shot that struck him on the back of the neck and, passing through to the left of the neckbone into the mouth, ploughed an outlet thence through the left cheek. Retaining his consciousness after this fearful blow, he leaned forward, and grasping his spirited horse's mane, urged her to the height of her speed back towards the fort from which he had so recently departed. In spite of the strenuous exertions of one of the Indians to overtake the fugitive at the start, he succeeded in escaping. Morgan declared in after years that he would always remember the expression of the Indian's face as he ran, with open mouth and tomahawk in hand, by the side of the mare, expecting every moment to see his victim fall. When the panting savage found that the horse was rapidly leaving him behind, he threw his tomahawk without effect at the wounded rider and abandoned the pursuit with a yell of disappointment. It was six months before Morgan recovered from the lacerations of the terrible wound.

At that time he had not long passed his majority, and from this hour until his twenty-seventh year was reached his life became irregular and dissipated. He was addicted to gambling, was often deep in his cups, and was repeatedly involved in brawls. One place constantly visited by him and his boon companions was a neighboring tavern, known as Battletown on account of the number of fist fights and still more bloody encounters which so frequently disgraced the spot. Morgan became the champion of the large band of roughnecks who haunted this threshold night and day; and it began to look as if he would sink irretrievably into a slough of vice and lawlessness.

From this pit he was saved by a passion which he came to feel for a very lovely woman who now entered his life and whom he soon married. They established their home at a place to which he gave the name of Soldier's Rest, and here they were residing when peace was signed by the French and English. But this event was quickly followed by Pontiac's War, which lit the torch of destruction and death all along the frontier from Detroit to the Carolinas. One thousand militia were summoned to arms in order to complement the regular forces, and to a lieutenancy in this regiment Morgan was at once appointed in recognition of his reputation as an Indian fighter. Owing to the decisive victory won by Colonel Bonquet in the course of the first campaign, the western Indians withdrew precipitately to their towns in the valley of the Ohio and sued for peace.

During the ensuing nine years Morgan was chiefly interested in the cultivation of his farm and in the ejoyment of the happiness of his own abundant fireside. He had by his industry, economy, and foresight, become a man of considerable wealth. He spent many hours also in lessening the shortcomings of his early limited education by reading. From the beginning of the controversies with Great Britain he allowed no opportunity, public or private, to pass without advocating the justness of the American claims and contentions. He had not lost his military tastes, and it was with keen gratification that he received a commission to serve as captain of the militia of Frederick County. When Lord Dunmore's war in defense of the frontiers broke out, Captain Morgan and his troops were promptly called into service. They first took part in the invasion of the Indian towns in Ohio by Major McDonald and participated in the sanguinary retreat from the Muskingum. Morgan and his company next joined Dunmore in the expedition to the valley of the Scioto; but General Lewis' victory at Point Pleasant made the Indians disposed to drop hostilities, and as Dunmore, anticipating trouble with the colonists, now wished to cultivate the good will of the tribes, peace was soon negotiated, to the regret of the officers of the American troops, who were eager to retaliate for the outrages which had been committed along the frontiers.

When Morgan reached the white settlements on his return towards home, he was startled by the news that the port of Boston had been closed by act of Parliament, and that a continental congress had been summoned to meet in Philadelphia. "Upon learning these things," he afterwards recorded, "we, as an army victorious, formed ourselves into a society pledging our words of honor to each other to assist our brethren of Boston in case hostilities should commence." Events now advanced with sensational rapidity; but that which came closest to the life of Morgan, the soldier, was the call of Congress for the services of ten companies of riflemen, two of which were to be enlisted in Virginia. Morgan was soon chosen as the captain of one of the latter companies, which he himself had recruited from among the young men of the Valley. Its members were expert marksmen noted for their gallantry and for their ability to endure every form of physical hardship. By the end of twenty-one days, Morgan and his company had arrived in the

PLATE XXII. *From an engraving by Chappell. Photo Cook.*

GENERAL DANIEL MORGAN

neighborhood of Boston, after traversing six hundred miles on foot, without the loss of a man by sickness or desertion. In the month of June, 1775, an expedition against Canada was organized, with General Montgomery at its head. Montreal was ultimately captured. Under orders to coöperate with this army, Arnold was dispatched by Washington with a large force to invade the lower valley of the St. Lawrence by way of the Kennebec River. The goal was to be the city of Quebec. Among the companies attached to this force was Morgan with his Virginians. They started September 13, 1775, by sea and soon made the mouth of the Kennebec. There Arnold arranged his troops in four divisions, one of which, composed partly of the Virginians, was placed under Morgan's command. Each of his men carried a rifle, a tomahawk, and a long knife, and was dressed in a flannel garment, with rough buckskin breeches and buckskin leggins and moccasins. The upper part of the body was also covered by a hunting shirt. Each cap was inscribed with the words "Liberty or Death." Morgan's division served in the role of an advance guard.

The first stage of the journey was made in bateaux headed up stream, and the men were often waist deep in water. During the second stage they were frequently compelled to carry their boats over portages through a region of thick woods and deep ravines. The difficulties and obstacles increased with each mile in succession. Morgan especially distinguished himself in these trying situations, rendered more exasperating to him by the fact that the greater part of his command was composed of companies with which he had not been associated until the expedition started. The members of his original company of Virginians obeyed his orders implicitly, but the other companies, for different reasons, were jealous of his control and disinclined to submit to his strict regulations. The food began to run short, which further deepened the discontent; and sickness grew epidemic among the soldiers.

The army was in this crippled and disheartened state when it arrived at the portage which separated the Kennebec and Chaudiere rivers. The latter stream flowed north-ward and could be used as a highway by the troops in their further advance. Morgan carried over the divide all the bateaux that belonged to his company, thus showing a degree of foresight not exhibited by the other commanders. There were still sixty miles to be traversed before any set-tlement towards the north could be reached, where sup-plies could be obtained. The food was now nearly exhausted, and the men were also sinking under fatigue. At this critical moment word was received from Arnold, who had pushed on ahead, which brought new courage to the soldiers' breasts. In the descent of the Chaudiere all of Morgan's boats and their contents were dashed on the rocks, and the men barely escaped with their lives. All the provisions and the extra clothing were lost. The soldiers were compelled to boil their buckskin moccasins, breeches, and cartouche boxes to serve for food. Indeed, the entire force was saved from starvation only by the arrival of several head of cattle sent back by Arnold.

On November 9 the troops, refreshed by supplies, en-camped within four leagues of the St. Lawrence River. By this date they had traversed a space of about six hundred miles, which was apparently made far longer than it was in reality by the roughness of the country. After debouching from this tangled wilderness, the little army was received with effusive kindness by the simple-minded people of the country, most of whom were hostile to the British. As soon, however, as its presence became known to the Canadian authorities, reinforcements were hastened to Quebec, and the town was put in a state of defense, which was further strengthened by a concentration of warships in the river. When the appointed hour for crossing the stream to attack the city arrived, Morgan, at the head of his riflemen, was the first to embark under cover of darkness, and on reaching the north shore, he sent out scouting parties to reconnoiter the plain near the town. When most of the troops had crossed for his support, he urged Arnold to make an immediate as-sault on the enemy, but this bold advice unfortunately was rejected. Had it been adopted, Quebec would have quickly fallen, since the gates had not yet been shut. When the advance did begin, the British were on their guard, and at once a sharp fire was opened by their batteries placed on the ramparts, which in the end caused the Americans to withdraw to their quarters.

Having captured Montreal, Montgomery set his face, with three hundred men, towards Quebec, and on joining Arnold at Point aux Trembles, gave orders for an advance on that city. Morgan and his riflemen led the van and halted only when almost under the walls. He was followed by the rest of the American army, about one thousand strong, who undertook at once to invest the town. Breastworks having been constructed of the snow, firing began, but it proved so ineffective that a council of war was held to consult whether an assault would not be more successful. Morgan strongly favored the change, and his advice was followed. The attack was to be launched at night, on the occurrence of the next snowstorm.

When the storm arose, the divisions advanced according to the plan previously agreed upon, under the provisions of which the onset was to be made at different points. While leading one of the divisions, Arnold was struck down by a ball that shattered his leg, and Morgan at once took command in that quarter. At the head of his men, he mounted the wall in front of him, and as the upper part of his body appeared above it, a platoon of musketry was fired at him by the enemy at such close quarters that his hair was singed and grains of powder were imbedded in his skin. But unhurt, he leaped down to the ground on the further side, and with his men close behind him pursued the retreating foe into the neighboring houses. Had the main American army followed up this success immediately, the whole of the lower town would soon have been captured. His own force was too small to effect this alone, and he was ordered to wait until General Montgomery should come up. He received this instruction with keen chagrin and always asserted that the city would have been taken but for his inopportune detention.

Montgomery, approaching in another direction, had been checked, a fact which gave the enemy time to re-man the defense of the walls that stood in front of Morgan, who, owing to the increasing confusion, now decided to advance on his own motion, although invaluable time had been lost in consequence of the previous order.

The British now fell back behind the barrier, and a rapid exchange of shots began. The Americans were huddled up in the street exposed to the fusillade from the windows beyond this rampart. Morgan and his band of riflemen placed scaling ladders against its massive walls and were successful in mounting it, but the defense was too firm and vigorous to be overcome. Many of the American soldiers were killed, and the rest were compelled to throw themselves into the neighboring houses for safety. Morgan and a few of his officers refused to follow this example, but no gain resulted. The Americans were now surrounded and, despairing of reinforcements, were compelled to surrender. Morgan is said to have wept like a child at this upshot and for a time declined to give up his sword. In the meanwhile, Montgomery, who had advanced against the town along the margin of the river, had been killed in front of a blockhouse, and his troops had been forced to retreat. The combination of disasters brought the attack on the city to an end and, as time was to prove, secured for Great Britain the indefinite possession of Canada.

The British commander put forth the most extraordinary exertions to alienate the American officers and privates from their allegiance. Morgan was a conspicuous object of this dishonorable solicitude. "I hope, sir," he said when importuned to join the British army, "that you will never again insult me in my present distressed and unfortunate situation by making me offers which plainly imply that you think me a scoundrel." The prisoners were in the end released and permitted to return to their homes. When Morgan again touched American soil, he threw himself on the ground, as if to embrace it, and cried out with moving fervor, "Oh, my Country!" As soon as his parole expired, he reënlisted for active service and with one hundred and eighty recruits joined the American army, then stationed at Morristown. Washington received him with marked satisfaction, as he was fully aware of Morgan's military value and that of his band of seasoned sharpshooters.

After taking a conspicuous part in the campaign in the Jerseys, Morgan, in anticipation of Burgoyne's descent from Lake Champlain down the valley of the Hudson, was ordered to unite his riflemen with the force posted at Peekskill, which was expected to hold this movement in check. The British commander was accompanied by many Indians, who had already aroused terror among the country people in the path of the British army, and it was thought that this feeling would be removed by the arrival of such skillful Indian fighters as Morgan's soldiers. By August his troops had reached Albany, where they were received by General Gates, who had succeeded Schuyler as the general in chief of the American forces collected in that region.

The first duty of Morgan's command was to serve as a vanguard to observe the enemy's movements; the second, to attack, should the opportunity appear to be favorable. Morgan first sighted the British army at Behmus Heights, where it had gone into camp. By this time he had been reinforced. When the British started forward, they soon came into contact with his troops, which were now advancing in two lines. The first assault made by the enemy Morgan's men were successful in repelling, but the second threw them into disorder. They were, however, quickly brought together by their commander's sounding a loud call on a bone which was used in Virginia in decoying wild turkeys; and resuming the attack, they drove back the enemy to a place known as Freeman's Field. Here the British made a stand, and Morgan, in turn, was compelled to retire behind the screen of a wood. Again rallying his six hundred riflemen, he gradually forced the enemy to withdraw, but in the end he was himself driven back a second time to the protection of the wood. The battle continued thus to sway to and fro until nightfall.

GENERAL DANIEL MORGAN

The brunt of the fighting on the American side so far had been borne by Morgan's corps. It was the first to enter the field and the last to leave it. Gates himself, not a generous commander, in a letter which he wrote to Washington after this event, protested against the proposed return of Morgan's force to the Jerseys, on the ground that it was the one "the army of General Burgoyne was most afraid of."

During the interval of quiet that followed, Burgoyne looked for reinforcements from New York City under Sir Henry Clinton. He was in a precarious situation. His own army was dwindling in size and on the edge of starvation, while the Americans not only were rapidly increasing in number, but also possessed ample supplies. Retreat to Canada, he knew, would be a fatal step. He soon decided, therefore, to push boldly forward. General Frazer, with a body of Tories and Indians, was ordered to advance, in the hope of getting to the American rear on the left, while the main body of the British army should follow ready for battle. So soon as information of this maneuver was sent in by the scouts, Morgan and his corps moved forward and at his own suggestion to Gates took position under cover of the woods growing on a hill situated on the enemy's right flank. From this point of advantage his men could begin a sharp fire on this right flank, so soon as the battle between the two armies should start.

The opening shot in the frontal attack was the signal for a rush of Morgan's soldiers against the British right flank, with an outburst of their guns directed straight at the mass of the passing ranks. Under this double assault the whole right wing of the British troops wavered and temporarily gave way, but they were finally rallied by their officers to the renewal of the conflict, only to fall back again in hopeless disorder. General Frazer had been strongly reinforced by Burgoyne in order to defend this wing in case of need, and he now hurried forward to stop its flight, but in the end he and his men became involved in the confusion and turned their backs like the fugitives. Morgan had observed an officer mounted on a black charger riding up and down

298

the hesitating ranks and endeavoring to restore confidence. He thought that if this officer could be killed, the last prospect of rallying the retreating troops would be removed. Calling to his side twelve of his most skillful marksmen, he instructed them to fire upon the gallant Englishman so soon as he should come in reach of their guns, "He is a brave man," Morgan said, "but he must die." In a few minutes the officer, who was General Frazer himself, was fully exposed to their aim. A simultaneous explosion from the twelve guns brought him dead to the ground.

Morgan pursued the right wing to their camp, and the left wing as well as the center of the British army took refuge there also. The fight was renewed behind the breast-works. After a furious musketry fusillade between the two armies, Morgan and his rifle corps charged the intrench-ments, and passing them, began a hand-to-hand combat with the enemy, but he was compelled to withdraw before a bayo-net charge delivered by a strong British force. Night closed the struggle.

"Morgan," exclaimed Gates to him on his return to head-quarters, "you have immortalized yourself, and honored your country. If you are not promoted immediately, I will not serve another day."

"For God's sake, General," replied Morgan, "forbear this stuff, and give me something to eat and drink, for I am ready to die with hunger, fatigue, and exhaustion."

Burgoyne retreated to Saratoga, followed all the way by Morgan and his rifle corps. Within a short time he was compelled to surrender his army. When introduced to Colonel Morgan, he said, "Sir, you command the finest regiment in the world."

Elated by the triumph of the campaign, Gates nursed the hope that he would soon be promoted to Washington's place as the head of all the American armies, for which consum-mation intrigue had already been at work. He hinted this ambition to Morgan, pointing out the purely presumptive fact that the troops were dissatisfied with the present man-ner of carrying on the war and that unless the present commander in chief were superseded, many of the officers would resign. "I have one favor to ask of you," replied Morgan bluntly and sternly, "which is, never to mention that detestable subject to me again, for under no other man as commander in chief would I ever serve." In his resentment Gates held back in his dispatches descriptive of the campaign all substantial recognition of the vital part which Morgan and his riflemen had played in winning the triumph over Burgoyne and his army, an act of meanness plainly showing the character of that weak and misguided soldier of fortune.

Another act of the like malignant spirit is recorded by Morgan's biographer. "This officer," says Mr. Graham, "had occasion, during one evening, to seek an interview with General Gates on business connected with his command. He was ushered into the dining-room, and having arranged the matter in hand, was permitted by the General to withdraw without even the empty ceremony of an introduction to the British officers present. A number of the latter, struck by the commanding figure and the noble mien of the Colonel, and noticing that he was a field officer, inquired his name as soon as he retired. On learning that it was Colonel Morgan, they instantly rose to a man from the table, overtook him on the road, and severally taking him by the hand, made themselves known to him, frankly declaring, at the same time, that they had felt him severely in the field."

After the close of the Hudson River campaign with the surrender of Burgoyne, Morgan was transferred to New Jersey and there, under Washington's eye, participated in all the military movements of importance which took place on the soil of that state in the course of 1778, including the Battle of Monmouth. It was while so engaged that he was appointed to the command of Woodford's brigade, which was the signal for the termination of his connection with his famous corps of riflemen. In March, 1779, he was commissioned colonel of the Seventh Virginia Regiment, but he was now strongly of the impression that his services entitled him to a higher rank still, and he was also mortified

300

PLATE XXIII. *From an old engraving. Fridenberg Galleries.*
GENERAL DANIEL MORGAN

by seeing men of a rank below his own promoted over his head. In the summer of 1779 he resigned his post in the army, in opposition to General Washington's remonstrances, and withdrew to his home in Virginia. Here he remained until the unhappy result of the Battle of Camden roused him to offer his sword to his discomfited old commander, General Gates, now stationed at Hillsboro, in North Carolina. Congress promptly promoted him to the rank of brigadier general. After he and his troops reached the field, they possessed neither tents nor wagons and were forced to rely upon their own excursions for provisions.

In November General Greene superseded General Gates in the command of the southern army. The condition of military affairs at this hour was well calculated to excite a spirit of despondency. Both South Carolina and Georgia were in the enemy's hands, and North Carolina was torn between embittered Whig and revengeful Tory. Greene decided to divide his troops into two bodies. Of one he retained the command himself, while Morgan was put in command of the other. Greene's principal object now was to divert Cornwallis from the invasion of North Carolina and Virginia, which that British officer had under advisement, and the only way in which this could be accomplished was by harassing the British flanks. Morgan was ordered to take position for this purpose in the region of the Broad and Pacolet rivers, where he was reinforced by a band of two hundred and sixty mounted Carolinians; but his army was still not strong enough to undertake military operations on an imposing scale. He had to content himself with annoying the enemy, collecting provisions and forage, and establishing storehouses for their preservation. He also took advantage of every opportunity to disperse the Tory marauders.

In January, 1781, Morgan determined to strike a bolder blow, and he set out with his army to attack and capture Ninety-Six, now a British post of great importance. Cornwallis, very much alarmed, dispatched Tarleton in pursuit with a formidable force. Morgan had soon reached the banks of the Pacolet, but he thought it wisest to retreat towards the upper fords of the Broad. In retiring, he came to a place known as the Cowpens, where he ordered a halt to be sounded for the purpose of waiting for the enemy to arrive and give him battle.

He was joined at this critical moment by a large body of militia under Colonel Pickens. But he had more reliable troops than these to support him. There was the gallant brigade of Colonel John Eager Howard, the veteran corps of cavalry under Colonel William Washington, and a considerable body of Virginians, practised in the use of the rifle and skillful in woodland warfare. The little army, now in high feather, did not doubt its ability to contend successfully with the enemy, although Tarleton's superiority in number of infantry, cavalry, and artillery combined was known to all. Morgan trusted to the markmanship of his riflemen and the advantages of his defensive position. A cavalry corps was at once formed of volunteers, and patrols were sent out to observe the enemy's movements. "The evening previous to the battle," says an officer who was present, "General Morgan went among the volunteers, helped them to fix their swords, joked with them about their sweethearts, and told them to keep in good spirits, and the day would be ours. He told them that the old wagoner would crack his whip over Ben [Tarleton] in the morning as sure as he lived. 'Just hold up your heads, boys. Three fires and you are free, and then when you return to your homes, how the old folks will bless you, and the girls kiss you, for your gallant conduct.' "

The next morning Tarleton advanced against the American position, which extended from front to rear, about five hundred yards and which was crossed by two moderate ridges. There was a growth of small pines spread over a part of the surface of the ground.

Morgan had now in battle array about eight hundred troops fully prepared to receive the approaching British. The most seasoned of the regulars were placed on the crest of the first eminence; the next in experience were disposed in their immediate rear. Howard's battalion of light infantry occupied the center. On the second eminence Colonel William Washington was posted with his cavalry. The militia were stationed in front of the line of regular troops drawn up on the first eminence, and ahead of them was a small body of riflemen, who, after firing, were expected to retire. The main body of the militia behind them were to imitate their example after delivering two rounds.

Morgan passed from rank to rank, exhorting all to show their courage by resisting and defeating the enemy. Word was sent by him to Colonel Washington, who held the second eminence, to keep himself in readiness to protect the retreating militia in front and to charge the foe at a moment's notice.

Under cover of a heavy artillery bombardment, Tarleton's right wing advanced to the attack, and in a short time this action was imitated by his left wing and center. The American militia stationed in the van met the onset at first with such a deadly rain of bullets that the enemy halted in confusion, but recovering, again returned to the assault, driving the militia before them. So soon as the latter had passed to the rear, the American main line opened fire, under the terrible effect of which the advancing British troops halted and would have turned tail but for the arrival of their reserve infantry and the sweep of their cavalry to the left, in order to overwhelm the American right flank. To the defense of that flank the now rallied American militia came up, supported by Washington and his horsemen, who charged the British cavalry then galloping forward to attack the American right flank. At Colonel Howard's command, one of the companies on this right flank turned to assist the militia and Colonel Washington in warding off the assault of the British cavalry, and the whole of his line, under a misapprehension of the order, followed this company's example, which signified a general retrogressive movement. Colonel Washington, in the meanwhile, led an onset on the British cavalrymen, which so dispersed them that few of them had any further share in the battle.

The British army as a whole was now in a state of confusion and bewilderment. Washington, during his first charge, had observed this fact, and he therefore sent to Morgan for permission to throw himself on it with his whole force. By this time that part of the American line which under a false impression, in imitation of one company, had retired from the first eminence, was on the point of ascending the second, not far behind the first, when the order ran down the ranks to halt and face the enemy. "Give them one good fire," exclaimed Morgan, galloping up and down before his troops, "and the victory is ours." The British main force, now within forty yards' distance, received all along their front the full discharge of the American muskets, and before they could recover from the shock, Howard gave the command to his men to advance at quick step. As the enemy's cavalry had been dispersed, their infantry were now without support and were exposed besides to the charges of Washington's cavalry in their rear. Most of the British soon dropped their weapons and ran. One British battalion, posted on the American right, was forced by the militia to surrender. Another, under Tarleton's personal orders, was closely followed by Washington. There was a hand-to-hand combat between him and Tarleton, but before there could be a fatal issue, American troops came up and the British dragoon and his supporters turned and fled at the top of their horses' speed. The pursuit was continued for a distance of twenty miles. Previous to its close, Morgan, knowing that the British army was only thirty miles away, decided to retreat northward; and eager as Cornwallis was to catch up with him and bring him to battle again, he was successful in eluding the British grasp.

Before Morgan could be drawn into another important campaign, his health, which for some time had been greatly enfeebled, became so much further impaired that he was compelled to withdraw temporarily from his command and seek recuperation at his home in Virginia. He never again appeared in arms during the Revolutionary War except for a short time under Lafayette near Williamsburg, just previous to the siege of Yorktown. Here he was again forced to give up his command by the return of his former malady. In later life he took an important part in suppressing the Whiskey Insurrection, and this service terminated his military career.

For a time Morgan was a member of Congress, but this office he was also constrained to resign on the recurrence of severe ill health. It was even reported at this time that he had died, and the denial of this rumor called forth the following letter from Washington, which reflects the esteem in which he was held by that great man. "It gave me not a little pleasure to find that the account of your death in the newspapers was not founded in fact; and I sincerely pray that many years may elapse before that event takes place; and that, in the meanwhile, you may be restored to the full enjoyment of your health and to your usefulness in society."

Confidence in General Morgan was again shown by Washington when, in 1799, a war with France being threatened, he requested Morgan to recommend such officers of the old Virginia line as he should think fit to fill certain military positions. He died in July, 1802, and in the funeral procession there was noted the presence of seven of his riflemen who had accompanied him in his march to Boston nearly thirty years earlier. They had their old rifles in their hands, and they fired over his grave their last military farewell.

Chapter XIX

JOHN SEVIER

VIRGINIA HAS been extolled, not only as the mother of statesmen, but also, with equal pertinency, as the mother of states. None of her sons was more justly entitled in a direct sense to the name of commonwealth-builder than John Sevier, the founder of the modern community of Tennessee. His eyes first opened on the world in 1745, and he was therefore mature in age when the conflict of the Revolution began. He had been a boy of ten when the French and Indian alliance carried the torch, scalping knife, and bloodcurdling war whoop from the meadows of the Monongahela to the wild forests of the upper James. All the region which lay west of the peaks of the Alleghenies was at that day a scene of ambuscade, sudden massacre, and prolonged battle in the woods, and only the line of forts erected at Washington's advice saved the open country east of that range from complete depopulation by affording some protection against the destructive incursions of the pitiless enemy.

It required but to go back three generations of the Seviers to arrive at a period that was almost as violent and lawless. The grandfather of John had been a citizen of France contemporaneously with the revocation of the Edict of Nantes, a measure that had renewed the harsh persecution of the Huguenots and so harried them in their native scenes that thousands had fled in despair to alien lands. Among these was a young man who shared the same blood and bore the same name as St. Francis Xavier. This youthful Frenchman took refuge in London, married an English woman, and became the father of Valentine Sevier. After his arrival there he had quickly adopted the Anglicized pronunciation of his patronymic. Valentine, the son, animated by the spirit which his father had shown in abandoning France, crossed the ocean in an obscure immigrant ship and settled in that part of the beautiful but then remote valley of Virginia which is now embraced in the fertile county of Rockingham. Here in the backwoods he indulged rather notoriously in the vices of gambling and drinking, but in his case at least these infirmities did not prove inconsistent with the possession of a spirit of independence, courage, and self-reliance.

His son, John Sevier, even in his susceptible youth seems to have escaped all forms of moral contamination, and as he advanced in years he only grew in sobriety and firmness of character. In a frontier region still haunted by game birds and animals in extraordinary abundance, it was natural enough that he should have disclosed at an early age a keen taste for their pursuit in field and forest. There were the squirrels, pheasants, and turkeys of the lowland woods, the fox and deer of the open plain, the wolf and bear of the mountain hollows, to follow up on foot or horseback; and his eye became alert and unerring, and his frame vigorous and sinewy in this manly recreation during his hours of leisure. Nor was he lacking in the means of obtaining at least a homely education. In the vicinity of his father's dwelling house and store there was situated one of those primitive schools which were known even in the Colonial period as the "old field" schools. Each of these plain edifices was built at some central spot considered the most convenient for the attendance of all the children of a neighborhood. The structure itself was not superior in aspect, roominess, or comfort, as a rule, to the large cabins of the slaves; and the schoolmaster was too often a man who had failed in another calling requiring more activity of mind and more energy of movement. A very common characteristic was an irrepressible disposition—under the influence, no doubt, of intellectual deficiencies—to use the switch upon the tenderest parts of the pupils' bodies.

It was under a pedagogue of this sort that John Sevier sat as a boy in order to acquire the rudiments of spelling, writing, arithmetic, and geography. After securing a fair amount of knowledge of these elementary subjects, he was transferred to an academy in Staunton, where he enjoyed much higher advantages, of which he seems to have availed himself with very respectable success. His father was fully able financially to bear the charges of his son's matriculation in the College of William and Mary, the most advanced institution of its kind then to be found in any of the colonies, but John Sevier, apparently, was satisfied with the degree of general information which he had by this time reaped in school and academy. In fact, his natural disposition tended to draw him at an early period of his life into some pursuit that would test his capacity for action. He had no desire to be a clergyman, teacher, lawyer, or physician. His preference was to become a soldier or to enter some branch of public life that would open up a field for the display of his restless physical and mental energies. Before he had reached his majority, and seemingly—in part at least—as early as the intervals of his attendance in the Staunton academy, he had taken an active direct share in the wars of the frontiersmen with the Indians and had participated in the adventures of those wild campaigns. Before he could find a pursuit that was precisely in harmony with his manly spirit, he filled a clerkship in his father's store and subsequently aided in ploughing the fields of his father's farm; but these prosaic if not laborious occupations he constantly varied by following the hounds in pursuit of foxes and deer.

Having married and become a parent, Sevier determined to strike out for himself and his small family. His next step reflected that constructive turn of his mind which was afterwards to reveal itself on a far greater scale in founding a commonwealth—he laid the first cornerstone of a town, which still retains the glamour, not only of its establishment by a future commonwealth-builder, but also of that romantic battle in the neighborhood which was carried to victory by the valor of the youthful cadets of the Virginia Military Institute. Here for a time he was satisfied to fill the combined parts of merchant, innkeeper, and farmer. As merchant he was often brought into commerce with Indians who visited his store to exchange their pelts for the various articles which they held in particular esteem. They had come from the wild and distant region which lay beyond the crest of the Alleghenies.

Convinced, after securing a pecuniary independence by his three callings, that he could win a larger degree of prosperity in the Southwest, he decided to abandon Virginia and settle in east Tennessee, which at this time offered a more promising opening for the improvement of his family's fortunes. It is true that it was still inhabited by several powerful tribes—the Creeks, Chickasaws, Shawnees, Cherokees, and Chickamaugas, among whom the last two were preëminent. These found in war their principal cause for satisfaction with life, and it followed that they were constantly engaged in it. This was especially the case with the Cherokees, who entered so deeply into the future career of Sevier. They were distinguished far and wide for their revengeful spirit and their powers of endurance; and at the same time, they were more intelligent than the average specimens of their race and in consequence associated with the whites on a more nearly equal personal footing.

The largest settlement at that date in the area of modern east Tennessee was founded on the Watauga River by William Bean, who was soon followed by many other Virginians, among them James Robertson, afterwards identified with the first colony to be established in western Tennessee. This was situated on the Cumberland River. Immigration in a short time began to pour in from North Carolina, with which addition to its people Watauga soon assumed the numerical proportions of an important community. Its growth was rivaled by that of the settlement on the banks of the Nolichucky River not far away. Gradually with the increasing population a demand arose for the inauguration of a more definite political system. The people were not for a long time aware whether their homes were situated in Virginia or in North Carolina. When it was decided that they were really seated within the boundaries of the latter colony, sharp discontent was aroused because it was considered impossible for any strong political authority to be wielded from so distant a quarter for the protection of the inhabitants west of the mountains. In 1772 the people in the valley of the Watauga agreed to unite and draft the articles of a general association, which, when written, were promptly signed by every adult male citizen in that region. Each man thus formally bound himself to obey the new constitution and to uphold the five commissioners who were chosen to transact the routine business of an ordinary court of law.

At this moment Sevier was visiting the Watauga group of settlements. Although he did not expect to remove his family from Virginia until the following year, he consented to be elected to one of the five commissionerships. It was hardly possible for him under these circumstances to have performed any of the duties of the office during the first year. Doubtless he had, in passing through the valley of the Watauga in 1772, expressed his intention of establishing his home there just so soon as he could wind up his affairs in New Market without any pecuniary loss. He was the more ready to do this as he had been very much pleased by all that he had seen in 1771 of the rich soil and the countless wild game. During his sojourn Sevier had won the good will of the people along the North Holston and Watauga rivers by his manly, winning bearing, and also their respect by his reputation as a fearless fighter of the Indians who had harried the Virginian frontiers. He seems to have been accompanied to the North Holston by his parents as well as by his wife and children; and he was also thrifty enough to carry along with his party the contents of his abandoned store in Virginia, which, now that the immigration into east Tennessee was rapidly increasing, soon doubled in value. In addition to using the opportunity opened to him in that prosperous region to augment his fortune, he early began

310

to nurse an aspiration for political office.

The new community which his family had now entered as permanent residents was more primitive than the one which they had left behind in the valley of Virginia, but in the respective characteristics and manner of living of the two peoples the difference was not important after all. The dwelling houses were made of rudely hewn logs; the windows were open squares in the wall, with movable shutters; and the chimneys, as a rule, were constructed of rocks and mud. The furniture was of domestic manufacture; so were the clothes in use in the household. The loom and the spinning wheel were to be found under every roof, and also the implements of the shoemaker. The moccasin, however, was a common covering for the feet. Equally remindful of the frontier were the leather leggins, the hunting shirt of deerskin, and the cap of raccoon or fox fur.

When the Dunmore War, stirred up by the mutual hatred of whites and Indians, broke out, Sevier, having enrolled many recruits and secured a large quantity of provisions and ammunition for the main army then concentrated on the Ohio and the Kanawha, remained at Watauga with a body of men sufficiently numerous to repel an Indian assault on the more or less scattered community; but he sent his son Valentine to New River to join the regiment stationed there under the command of Colonel Christian. Valentine was one of the first scouts to detect the furtive approach of the chief Cornstalk with a thousand warriors through the underbrush, to attack the unsuspecting army of General Lewis at Point Pleasant. A battle began at dawn in the surrounding forest; it continued to rage behind the trunks of trees until nightfall; but in the end the Indians gave ground and after darkness retired across the Ohio River. It was a Watauga scout who had first seen the enemy; and it was a Watauga officer who had turned their flank and forced them to take refuge in retreat.

When a constitutional convention was summoned by North Carolina to meet in November, 1776, the Wataugans sent to it a petition for the conversion of their district into

311

a county, with the right to be represented in the approaching assembly. This petition was ultimately granted, and Sevier was chosen as one of the three delegates of the new local division. His expectation of the final establishment of an independent state west of the mountains was indicated by his advocacy of a resolution—afterwards inserted in the Declaration of Rights—refusing to prohibit the creation of more than one commonwealth in that quarter.

A few months before the members of the Convention came together, a battle had been fought with the Indians near Fort Watauga, which was now occupied by a garrison of forty men under the command of Captain James Robertson and Lieutenant John Sevier. In a hand-to-hand combat, before the assault on the fort began, the principal Indian chief had been killed by the blow of a tomahawk. The assault was carried out with the usual Indian furtiveness, and in consequence it took place at a moment when many of the women were engaged in milking the cows beyond the line of the palisade. With fierce yells the savage warriors rushed towards these workers but were unable to cut them off, with the exception of a young girl, who, finding herself shut outside the closed gates, endeavored to climb up the panels of the great fence. Sevier, hearing her screams, leaped to the top of the palisade, killed the nearest pursuer, and dragged the fainting girl over the tall barrier before the baffled Indians could injure either her or him.

During the following month he was employed in serving at the head of a company of scouts, in which he gained distinction for his bravery against the enemy as well as for his skill as a woodsman. After the retreat of the principal bodies of the neighboring Indians to their fastnesses in the Allegheny spurs, the white men organized numerous vigilance committees, which night and day explored every part of the Watauga region that was likely to give shelter to obtruding marauders. In Robertson's absence Sevier took the lead of these frontiersmen, and it was due to his alertness that the slinking bands from the hills were prevented from renewing their murderous assaults on the outlying farms. The most resolute of the Indian tribes were the Chickamaugas, who had established themselves permanently far down the valley of the Tennessee River in what were known as the Five Lower Towns, from which they stole out to harass the white settlements in their vicinity. An expedition under Colonel Shelby, in the hope of putting an end to the repeated depredations, invaded these towns, destroyed the wigwams with the torch, drove the inhabitants into the forests, and carried off their corn and livestock.

Many immigrants were now encouraged to come into the region of the Watauga and Holston. A new county was soon formed, and Sevier was chosen to be its military governor. The Tories, who were partisans of England in the war now in progress (1778-79), were by this time causing as much anxiety to the patriotic citizens as the Indians had been doing. Their lawlessness, indeed, was often carried so far that Sevier felt constrained in some cases to hang the culprits to the nearest tree. In the meanwhile, he made his home on a very fertile farm situated in the Nolichucky River. This he stocked with horses, cattle, and Negro slaves; and here he lived with his family in the full enjoyment of the country pursuits which had always afforded him so much happiness. But these occupations did not prevent him from performing with ardent fidelity the public duties which he had undertaken as the military protector and political servant of the community at large. It was during his residence on this plantation that he won the sobriquet of "Nolichucky Jack" for his success in holding in check the local incursions of the prowling Indian bands. When his wife passed away he consoled himself with marrying the young woman whom he had rescued so bravely during the attack on Fort Watauga four years before.

In 1779 the British captured the city of Savannah, and the people of the South found themselves confronted by war at their very doors. The next town to fall was Charleston, from which expeditions were soon dispatched in several directions to spread a net over all the small local seats of population. These separate armies were ultimately organized

313

to subdue the mass of the inhabitants dispersed over the face of the surrounding country. These bodies of troops were largely recruited from the extensive circle of persons known as Tories, who were savagely disaffected to the American cause and who were disposed to reveal their venom by acts of inhuman ruthlessness. The enrollment of these men in the British ranks further inflamed the bitterness of the redcoats against the Carolinians and Georgians as rebels; and this feeling was returned by the patriots with all the greater keenness because of the presence of these traitors among the enemy. Small American detachments under resolute and courageous officers moved backwards and forwards, striking the British at every available opportunity and skillfully evading them when the preponderance of numerical strength was adverse to the American side. One object that especially fixed the attention of these detachments was the army which Cornwallis was slowly leading northward, with the intention of embracing the conquest of North Carolina in the scope of its operations.

One of his most energetic lieutenants was Colonel Ferguson, who was sent off to the eastern slopes of the mountains in order to gather up additional recruits among the Tories in that remote corner. At this time Colonel Charles McDowell was, with his small force of seasoned troopers, lurking on Broad Creek, and noticing Ferguson's movement westward, and surmising its design, he hurried away a messenger to warn Shelby and Sevier beyond the Alleghenies of the British approach to the eastern spurs of that great barrier. The Indians were now menacing the Watauga region with an incursion under British instigation, and Sevier thought it would be dangerous to leave those communities stripped of defenders, but he soon collected a band of three hundred expert mounted riflemen and dispatched them in haste to join McDowell in South Carolina. Another band of the like intrepid and trained backwoodsmen was subsequently sent forward to strengthen that officer further. In the onsets of these men they used both the muzzles of their rifles and the butts; and besides this action they brought their knives

314

and swords into mercilessly slashing play. Their fights were almost always hand-to-hand, and quarter was neither asked nor given.

At Musgrove Mill, a son of Sevier belonging to the corps of riflemen recruited from the Watauga settlements was hotly engaged, along with his comrades, in repelling the fierce British assault delivered there, only to be thrown back by the unflinching resistance which met its impact all down the American line. The defeat of Gates at Camden occurred almost simultaneously, and so soon as Shelby, in command of the troops at Musgrove Mill, heard of this disaster, he retreated to the mountains, pursued for a long way by the British cavalry. McDowell, too, was compelled to retire to a similar place of safety. Ultimately, the same asylum was found for a time by both officers in the distant region of the Watauga.

Making faces at them from the other side of the great range of mountains, Ferguson was compelled for the moment to restrict his efforts at actual capture to insolent messages conveyed through prisoners. Urged on afterwards, however, by Tory recruits familiar with the passes, he decided that he would renew the march in pursuit. When Shelby, now resting at Watauga, heard of the enemy's intention, he set out to consult with Sevier at Nolichucky. The two men promptly agreed that the riflemen of the surrounding country should be summoned at once to begin an early excursion across the mountains to attack Ferguson in his camp. The twenty-fifth of September was selected as the date and Sycamore Falls as the place for the rendezvous. Shelby returned to Watauga to call together his riflemen, soon to be increased by a large body of militia from Virginia; and Sevier, with equal resolution, assembled his riflemen and added to their ranks the soldiers who had followed McDowell in his retreat across the Alleghenies. Colonel William Campbell brought down from the upper Holston four hundred experienced Virginian frontier fighters.

Even with the forces of Shelby, Sevier, Campbell, and McDowell all combined, the number of men at their back did not exceed, possibly did not equal, a thousand; but their hearts were filled with that determined ardour which only unselfish patriotism can inspire; and they were eager to defy every hardship and every peril in order to strike an effective blow in the defense of their pioneer homes, their wives, and their children. The men were dressed in hunting shirts and were armed with rifles, tomahawks, and butcher knives. There were few among them who had not engaged in hand-to-hand fights with Indian warriors, and some had met the trained English troopers of Tarleton in the country towards the sea without the slightest flinching. It was long remembered that when the march of the sturdy line of mountain riflemen began, Sevier was one of those who led the van, while close at his side rode his son of fifteen, in the full primitive uniform of a frontier soldier. Nor was it forgotten that during the battle, fought a few days later on the other side of the great hills, this boy proved himself by his courage worthy to be the comrade of those heroes of the frontier. The revered clergyman of the Watauga district, Mr. Dook, implored the blessing of Heaven on the expedition as it was starting and begged every soldier present to "smite the enemy with the sword of the Lord and Gideon." The outfit of each man was a shot pouch, a tomahawk, a knife, a knapsack, and a blanket. He slept at night on the ground where he bivouacked, and much of his food was procured by his own rifle. Most of the mountain paths traversed had not been trodden before except by the feet of wild beasts.

The little army crossed the mighty ridge by a rugged gap and then descended into the region of the waters of the upper Catawba River. Here a considerable body of militia, under the command of Colonels Cleveland and Winston, joined their ranks. The frontiersmen were now moving too rapidly to halt even to select a supreme leader. On arriving at the place where they had expected to find the hostile troops, the site of the latter's camp was discovered to be abandoned; the approach of the Watauga soldiers had, in fact, been announced by deserters; and Ferguson promptly decided that he lacked the strength needed to resist such a force. He therefore fell back in the direction of Cornwallis, having first sent him word to hasten forward reinforcements. It now became the aim of the mountain leaders to overtake Ferguson before he could find protection with the British commander in chief or receive assistance as he retreated. Nearly a thousand carefully selected riflemen were ordered to mount their horses, refreshed for the advance, and set out in pursuit.

By October 6 Ferguson was encamped on a rough spur of King's Mountain. Indifferent to heavy rain and muddy roads, the riflemen pressed on, swerving neither to the right nor to the left of the way. At last they came in sight of the mountain. A plan of action was quickly adopted—a cordon was to be drawn around the foothill on which the British troops were posted, and then the ascent was to be begun from every quarter simultaneously. A stealthy approach was made to the base of this outlying hill. It was now about three o'clock in the afternoon, and the sentinels of the enemy had not yet detected the nearness of the frontiersmen. The latter, on arriving within a short distance of the bottom of the hill, dismounted under the cover of the forest and tethered their horses to the trees. The British force which they were advancing to assault, now perched in a camp on the hilltop, was made up of a mixed collection of troops, in which Northern and Southern loyalists formed an important part. They had, however, been well drilled, especially in the use of the bayonet, an object of keen aversion to the colonials, who were successful in combatting that weapon only by their marvelous aptitude with the rifle.

The first act of the American officers was to encircle the hill with the soldiers of their little army. This was carried out with some difficulty, as the surface of the ground was covered with a growth of trees and underbrush up to the site of the British encampment itself. This condition screened for a time the engirdling maneuver, but a few moments' exposure of a small section of the line not far from the summit raised the alarm among the hitherto unsuspicious

British sentinels. The drums were quickly beaten; the commander blew his silver whistle and mounted his white horse; and there was an immediate rush to arms. The British firing began at once. At first there was no response to this fusillade by the American riflemen, who continued all around the hill to move steadily upward to the particular height previously selected by their colonels as the line at which their guns were to be first employed in the attack. When this point was reached, a mighty shout was raised at command by the whole force, and their rifles began to play with destructive effect upon the ranks of the redcoated soldiers, who were now descending the rough and precipitous sides of the hill above. A fringe of fire was now running all around the hill, and the air was shaken by the continuous explosions. The rush of battle swayed irregularly backwards and forwards and upward and downward. Several times the riflemen were pressed back to the bottom of the declivity by the thrusts of the British bayonets, and then, recovering, they poured such a rain of homemade bullets into the breasts of their pursuers that the latter wavered and broke and retreated up the height, followed closely by the frontiersmen.

At one ciisis in the fighting, the largest section of the British troops was concentrated against Sevier's division, only in the end to shrink back slowly towards their camp at the top. To this point they were followed, and the soldiers from Watauga and Nolichucky were the first to leap into that enclosure. In the meanwhile, the rest of the Americans had been making their way steadily upward, until what remained of the hostile army was hopelessly surrounded. Ferguson, with a few desperate companions, endeavored to cut his way through, but quickly fell before a shower of bullets. In a short time his successor in the command raised a white flag, and the surviving British soldiers surrendered. The next day the body of the brave but unfortunate Ferguson was consigned to the earth in the hide of an ox, while his noble white horse, which had been a conspicuous object in the battle, was assigned to the senior American officer. The British tents and baggage wagons were burnt; a few

318

Tories were hanged; the prisoners were strung together in a long line; and the little American army began its march towards the region beyond the mountains. They moved forward at double step, as it was rumored that Tarleton was in pursuit. Another reason for speed was the danger of Indian attack, which now hung like a black cloud over the settlements situated in the valley of the streams west of the Alleghenies.

When Sevier arrived at home, he found that the people had fled from their outlying farms to the shelter of the forts. Fatigued as he was by the long journey which had just ended, he took but a brief period for rest. At the head of two hundred riflemen, he set out against a large body of Indians who were known to be lurking near the French Broad River. In a sharp battle at Boyd's Creek he permanently checked the Indian advance and afterwards, in coöperation with Colonel Campbell, carried the torch into the numerous villages that stood on the streams flowing into the upper Tennessee. The feeling against the savages was made all the more bitter by the discovery of written proof of their collusion with the British officers operating in the Carolinas across the barrier of the mountains. Notwithstanding this fact, Sevier and Cleveland endeavored by numerous overtures to persuade the various tribes to put down their arms and enter into advantageous treaties with the whites, but there was no response within the time allowed for an answer. Suspecting that the Cherokees, who were seated on the Alleghenies' western slopes, were one cause of this silence, Sevier determined to lead an expedition against them for their complete suppression. He was successful in destroying their principal towns, in killing many of their bravest warriors, and in carrying off into captivity a large number of their women and children. These, however, were in most instances subsequently exchanged. When the Cherokees began to commit depredations again in 1781, he was equally triumphant in the second campaign which he launched against them.

That Sevier was not indifferent to the condition of the

319

American cause in the closing struggle with the British in the South was shown by the promptness with which he responded to the summons of General Greene to hasten across the mountains to aid in intercepting Cornwallis, should that general turn back at any time in his northward march to repost his army near Charleston. When Sevier arrived with two hundred mounted riflemen at Charlotte, he was told that the British had surrendered at Yorktown. It was only the delay in receiving Greene's dispatch many weeks after it was written which prevented him and his men from sharing the glory of the enemy's defeat in Virginia. As it was, they now joined the troops of the gallant Marion, who was engaged in driving out of the Carolinas the remaining forces of the British. Before this could be fully accomplished, Sevier and his soldiers were recalled to the Watauga to resume the warfare with the Indians for the defense of their homes.

The tribes west of the mountains, naturally exasperated by the intrusions on their lands of new white settlers, had again snatched up their weapons and were now ferociously busy committing many murders. This was especially the case with the Chickamaugas. Sevier assumed the command of a large force sent against the towns of the latter and was successful in inflicting so much damage that peace was soon sued for by that entire nation. A new era had now dawned. The War of the Revolution had virtually closed with the surrender of Cornwallis. There was afterwards no real cause for disturbance to be anticipated from that source, while the Indian warriors in the upper Tennessee and Holston valleys had been so frequently beaten, and their property and people so steadily depleted, that the white communities in that quarter had no further occasion to look forward to a repetition of the destruction which had through them so often previously taken place there. Hitherto the career of Sevier had been that of a pioneer, an Indian fighter, and an officer in the Revolutionary armies. In each capacity he had performed with eminent success the part of a brave, determined, capable, and patriotic citizen, and

320

had obtained, as the reward which he valued most for his services, the respect and confidence of his people. Now that peace had returned to the beautiful transmontane land in which he had cast his lot, a new chapter began in his life that was to bring far-reaching fame to crown his previous achievements as a military defender of his local community and his country.

In 1784—the year following the adoption of the treaty between Great Britain and the United States—the area of the modern state of Tennessee was ceded to Congress by North Carolina in settlement of its share of the debt incurred in the triumphant prosecution of the Revolutionary War. The several counties embraced in that area at this time consented to the transfer, should Congress by the end of two years decide to accept it. In the meanwhile, the people residing there undertook to form a government of their own. Sevier was elected to the office of president of the convention which was summoned to draft a permanent framework of administration. Before this was submitted, a resolution was passed declaring the combined counties represented in the convention to be an independent state. A second convention was next called to meet during the ensuing autumn, but before it could assemble, a division of sentiment arose. One faction was in favor of founding the projected commonwealth at once; the other counseled delay until public opinion should agree with practical unanimity upon the proper course to pursue. Sevier approved the latter attitude.

As soon as news of the first convention was brought to the members of North Carolina's General Assembly, that body promptly repealed the act of cession which had conveyed the western territory to Congress. It next laid off that territory as a judicial and military district and appointed Sevier to the office of brigadier general of the local militia. The contingency of armed opposition to the establishment of the new state which he had anticipated was now imminent, and he urged the people to accept the provisions which the parent legislature had announced for their government. But they were in no mood to give up their original intention. A convention was summoned to meet in December, in which all the transmontane country was to be represented. When this occasion arrived, a constitution was submitted and adopted; and another convention, to meet in November, 1785, was ordered to be called to ratify it. In the meanwhile, a day was named on which all the officers to carry on the local administration were to be nominated. An assembly was chosen on that day, and its first act was to elect Sevier governor of the infant commonwealth, a remarkable evidence of the popular confidence in his talents, experience, and integrity, as he had not at first been in favor of the policy approved by the convention of the previous December.

Among the other acts of this first legislature was the appointment of a supreme court, the addition of several counties to the original group, and the incorporation of an academy. Skins were authorized to be received as legal tender, and so far was this form of currency used that Sevier himself was paid with this commodity.

When Governor Sevier informed the North Carolina governor of the erection of the new state, the former was told that unless his people should return at once to their original allegiance, troops would be sent across the mountains to put an end to the new local government by force of arms. Congress positively refused to assent to the change when a petition for approval was submitted to that body, then in session at Philadelphia.

When the date previously chosen for the ratification of the constitution arrived, namely, November, 1785, a divergence of opinion as to its acceptability arose. Two of its provisions caused a warm debate. No one, it affirmed, should be empowered to hold office if he disbelieved in the Bible, the Trinity, and Heaven and Hell; nor should a clergyman, lawyer, or physician be permitted to be elected to such a post. In the end, this instrument as at first framed was rejected; and at Sevier's suggestion, the constitution of North Carolina was in large part substituted. The name adopted for the new state was Franklin.

Before the close of the first year the partisans of the discarded constitution had established throughout the new commonwealth both general and local courts that acknowledged allegiance to North Carolina alone. An extraordinary condition of confusion followed, which the parent state endeavored—without success at first—to allay by promising the people of Franklin ultimate independence, if all would only give up their new commonwealth for a time. Gradually, conciliatory acts and words effected this purpose. With the expiration of Sevier's term of office, the state of Franklin lost its independent existence. The end came in March, 1788. At once there broke out a bloody local conflict with Sevier and his allies on one side, and the partisans of North Carolina, in the old controversy, on the other; hand against hand, as it were; and it was quieted only by Sevier's withdrawal from the scene in order to protect the western frontier from an Indian incursion. After passing through an interval of violent rows with personal enemies who had him arrested on a trumped-up charge of treason and subjected him to other undeserved indignities, General Sevier entered public life again as a member of the State Senate. This was followed by his election to Congress so soon as the National Constitution was ratified. He was the first member of that body to represent the vast territory lying west of the lofty range of the Carolina mountains as far as the banks of the Mississippi River. There could not have been found another man whose life had reflected more fully and more faithfully the whole course of this region's history since it was first opened up to settlement by the hardy pioneers from the East.

The work which Sevier was now called upon to do at home was almost as important as his work there had been at an earlier date. One reason why the people of the defunct commonwealth of Franklin had been so anxious to establish an independent political community was that it would give them a more unobstructed hand in settling the numerous controversies arising with the Indians along their borders. With North Carolina again in control of their local government, they were compelled to reckon with her disapproval, if not with her direct interference, when they came to allay these antagonisms in the manner that should appear to them to be best promotive of their own safety. By the advice of Sevier, the inhabitants who were most exposed to the savages formed themselves into an association, not only for protection against these marauders, but also for punishment of white outlaws; and these articles of agreement remained in force until 1790, when North Carolina again ceded to the United States all her territory situated west of the Alleghenies. No objection was now offered to acceptance by Congress.

The transmontane region, formerly known as the state of Franklin, was soon merged, by an act of the national legislature, with all the rest of the country lying in that general quarter, under the name of the Territory Southwest of the River Ohio. William Blount, a man of superior talents and unusual social refinement, was appointed by President Washington to the office of governor of this imperial domain, which was destined in time to form several populous commonwealths. John Sevier and James Robertson were put in command of the militia, each with the rank of brigadier general. The eastern district was assigned to Sevier; the western to Robertson. The Territory was to be admitted to the Union as a state so soon as the number of its inhabitants should have increased to sixty thousand.

The Cherokees were invited to participate in a conference which was called to meet at White's Fort, the modern Knoxville, for the purpose of securing from that tribe a permanent title to all the lands situated south of the Holston and French Broad. The Indians hesitated to attend until Robertson visited their capital at Echota and assured them of a safe passage. Governor Blount appeared upon the council ground at the date selected, dressed in a brilliant uniform, with a three-cornered hat on his head and a gold mounted sword at his side, and accompanied by a staff in uniforms equally as showy and imposing. Among the members of this staff was John Sevier, who was scrutinized with keen interest by the group of Indian chiefs whom he had so often defeated in the forest battles. A treaty of peace was signed, by the terms of which the Cherokees abandoned the wide area of country on which so many white settlements had already been planted; and they also consented to the free navigation of the Tennessee River and to the building of a road for wagon and horse, which was to extend as far as the banks of the Cumberland. In return they received a large quantity of merchandise of many sorts and were promised an annual subsidy from the American Government. Such an impulse was given by this treaty to the growth of the settlement at White's Fort that it was not long afterwards named in honor of General Knox, Secretary of War under Washington, and was adopted as the capital of the Territory.

Owing to constant encroachments by the increasing white population and to the intrigues of Spanish agents and traders in the Indian villages along the southern frontier, the tribes seated there became once more restless and menacing. Sevier, as the commander of the militia in the eastern area of the Territory, was eager to repeat the aggressive tactics of his former campaigns, but it was considered wisest at first to stand upon the defensive. He therefore contented himself for the time being with building a line of blockhouses to serve as a barrier against the Indian incursions, and all settlers were warned to erect palisades about their cabins as a means of affording protection in case of assault. Bodies of rangers were kept patrolling the most exposed areas in forest, and subsequently expeditions were sent out to burn the villages and destroy the corn of all those savages on the borders who persisted in their depredations.

In the long run, however, not even these more resolute steps were effective in checking permanently the violations of the treaty by the tribes. The rumor spread that the latter proposed to combine and deliver a concerted blow all along the line of frontier, with the design of opening a road into the very heart of the Territory, even as far as the capital itself. This report proved to be well-grounded in fact. A band of a thousand warriors was successful in pushing its way to the vicinity of Knoxville and was halted there only by the sound of the morning gun, which was mistaken for a sign that the approach had been discovered and that a vigorous preparation had been made to meet an assault. In retiring upon their tracks, the warriors murdered the dispersed settlers to the right and left of their path. The people were now so madly aroused that instructions were given by the governor to Sevier to press rapidly in pursuit and in doing so to employ the most ruthless means of scattering the pitiless enemy, even to burning every vestige of their homes. At Etowah he struck a crushing blow in a pitched encounter. This was the last Indian combat in which he was ever engaged, for from this time, the Creeks and Cherokees in the eastern part of the Territory, whom he had been fighting during so many years, remained at peace. It is said that Sevier in the wars with these tribes had taken part in thirty-five battles as the leader of the whites, and that he had in all these fierce conflicts lost only fifty-six of his soldiers.

Not long after the victory of Etowah, the extreme western part of the Territory was compelled to take up arms to repress the Indians inhabiting that remote division of the country. This campaign terminated the conflicts there which had so often in the past brought on such terrible scenes of bloodshed. From this time all the white settlements of the mountains entered upon an uninterrupted course of expansion. The several communities, recruited by thousands of immigrants from the eastern side of the Alleghenies, both in Virginia and in the Carolinas, rapidly acquired the solid proportions of a prosperous state. Large and comfortable houses were built both in the towns and in the farming districts, church edifices were erected, roads opened up, postoffices established, and newspapers founded. The corner stones of many new schools were laid. Sevier was keenly interested in advancing the cause of education, and it was largely through his direct assistance that Washington College and Blount College, the latter the future University of Tennessee, were incorporated. The social life of the people improved in ease and refinement at the very time that the old amusements were faithfully retained, such as quilting bees, corn huskings, hunting trips, shooting matches, and horse races. In each neighborhood the spirit of hospitality was common to every family whether poor or well-to-do.

So happy was the condition of the different communities during the existence of the Territory that when its area had come to be occupied by the number of inhabitants which entitled it to statehood, there was a strong minority sentiment in opposition to making any change in the prevailing political status. But this finally yielded to the wish of the majority of the people, who were anxious to enjoy the privilege of voting in the presidential elections. When the Constitutional Convention assembled in 1796, it was Andrew Jackson who suggested that the name Tennessee should be given to the new commonwealth, in honor of the great river that swept so majestically across the face of the beautiful Territory.

The first legislature to meet under the new order assembled in March, 1796. One of its earliest duties was to count the popular vote which had been cast for the candidates for the governorship. It was revealed that John Sevier had been chosen to that office without opposition; and after the intermission of the fourth term, as required by the new state constitution, he continued to occupy that office during another period of three terms. Four times was he elected to a seat in Congress. During the War of 1812-15, he was offered by President Madison a generalship in the army, but deeming himself too far advanced in age for the performance of such strenuous duties, he declined the honor. He was now in his seventy-fifth year, with a frame perceptibly weakened by the rough campaigns in which he had again and again participated in the past. He found his principal pleasure near the end of his life in the quiet supervision of his plantation, the society of his large family circle, and the exercise of a lavish hospitality. He died while performing the part of a national commissioner in running the boundary lines of the lands acquired under the treaty with the Creeks. Practically from boyhood his life had been given up, in a military and civic way alike, to the promotion of the general welfare of his people.

He was buried with all the honors of war, and subsequently a lofty marble monument was erected in Knoxville to his memory. On the face of that monument these words, which summed up the spirit of his nobly patriotic career, were carved: "John Sevier, pioneer, soldier, statesman, and one of the founders of the Republic; Governor of the State of Franklin; six times Governor of Tennessee; four times elected to Congress; the typical pioneer, who conquered the wilderness, and fashioned the State; a projector and hero of King's Mountain; fought thirty-five battles, won thirty-five victories; [his Indian war cry] "Here they are! Come on boys!"